"Renaissance" Talk

Medieval and Renaissance Literary Studies

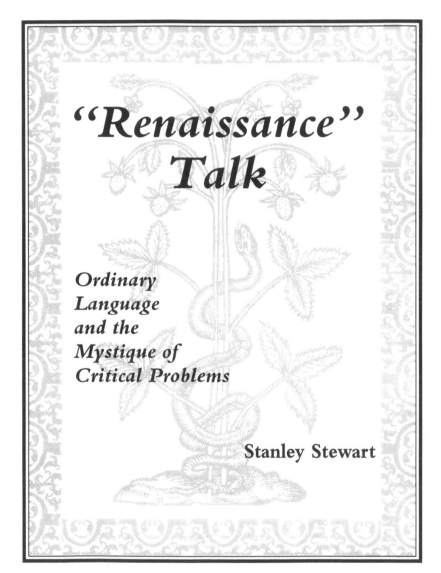

"Renaissance" Talk

Ordinary Language and the Mystique of Critical Problems

Stanley Stewart

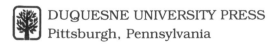

DUQUESNE UNIVERSITY PRESS
Pittsburgh, Pennsylvania

Published by

DUQUESNE UNIVERSITY PRESS
600 Forbes Avenue
Pittsburgh, PA 15282–0101

Library of Congress Cataloging-in-Publication Data

Stewart, Stanley 1931–
    Renaissance talk: ordinary language and the mystique of critical
problems / by Stanley Stewart
        p.   cm. — (Medieval and Renaissance literary studies)
    Includes bibliographical references and index.
    ISBN 0-8207-0273-0 (cloth: alk. paper). — ISBN 0-8207-0274-9
(paper: alk. paper)
    1. English literature—Early modern, 1500–1700—History and
criticism—Theory, etc.   2. Renaissance—England.   3. Criticism—
England.   4. Language and languages—Philosophy.   I. Title.
II. Series.
PR421.S67   1997
820.9'003—dc21   97-4871
                                                        CIP

For
Heather, Michelle, Ryan and Stephen

It is not our aim to refine or
complete the system of rules for the use of
our words in unheard-of ways.

For the clarity that we are aiming
at is indeed *complete* clarity.
But this simply means that the philosophical
problems should *completely* disappear.

— Ludwig Wittgenstein, *Philosophical Investigations*

Contents

ACKNOWLEDGMENTS

In two ways, this study is a product of collaboration. First and most obviously, I began writing on the problems addressed here while I and my coauthors, Bernd Magnus and Jean-Pierre Mileur, were working on *Nietzsche's Case: Philosophy as/and Literature* (Routledge, 1993), which questions the boundaries between philosophical and literary writing. While engaged with the Nietzsche project, I was also collaborating with James A. Riddell on *Jonson's Spenser: Evidence and Historical Criticism* (Duquesne University Press, 1995), which deals with the discovery of Ben Jonson's annotated copy of the 1617 Folio of Spenser's *Works*. Although these two books are very different, *"Renaissance" Talk* is largely an outgrowth of both, and a recantation of neither. I am indebted to my coauthors, Bernd Magnus, Jean-Pierre Mileur and James A. Riddell for their poise and confidence in articulating their perceived resolution of the problems we faced, which, I believe, were and are nothing short of those confronted by criticism at large. Although they might wish to distance themselves from the metacritical perspective elaborated in this book, they will no doubt find the argument familiar. Without these two collaborations, it is unlikely that the remarks in this book would have taken anything like their present form.

Less obviously, that form exhibits another way in which *"Renaissance" Talk* is a collaborative effort. Since probably

xi

some readers will not be comfortable with this form, explanation of this point might be helpful. My involvement with *Nietzsche's Case* and *Jonson's Spenser* altered my understanding of the collaborative aspect of what I had always thought of as "my own work." As a result, I wished to challenge the way certain critics proceed, but at the same time I wanted to indicate how my own suggestions are an outgrowth of the conversation of which these questionable proceedings are a part. Disagreement proceeds from agreement that disagreement leads somewhere. So as the dialogue form of chapter one suggests, I have learned from a variety of exchanges, including question and answer periods at many forums on many campuses and at many conferences. I have learned from students, friends and colleagues who have taken vigorous exception to arguments presented here. I hope that they will find that their objections led to some refinements, at least in my articulation of a point of view they do not always share. And perhaps they may, as I hope they will, recognize how much that articulation reflects their own thinking.

As the subtitle of this book indicates, I follow Wittgenstein's approach of "ordinary language analysis." In the process of writing this book, I have found that Wittgensteinians are generous people. Although I have thought of myself as a Wittgensteinian since my early days in graduate school, the endnotes and textual citations in this book cannot account for the shaping influence on every page of the last seven years that I have spent with the Wittgenstein Reading Group at the University of California, Riverside. As we read aloud and discussed Wittgenstein's major works (and several of the minor ones, too), the conversational strategy of this study emerged in my mind. I am deeply indebted to the Group's founder and discussion leader, Larry Wright, and to the "hard core" of that group: Brion Allen, Christopher Campolo, Kerrin McMahon, Sally Ness, Eric Reck, and Howard Wettstein. I owe much to Marjorie Perloff, whose wit, knowledge, and instinct for Wittgenstein and literary theory, provided an enormously valuable resource. Michael Nedo, Director of the Wittgenstein Institute in Cambridge, England graciously assisted my inquiry into Wittgenstein's interest in Sir Francis Galton's "composite portraiture" (see chapter 3). I am grateful, too, for the generous help of Mrs. Joan Bevan, who permitted me to examine Wittgenstein correspondence in her possession.

The good friends who read and criticized all or parts of this study in its various stages deserve special thanks. The detailed and, at times, exhaustive commentary of Thomas Clayton and E. W. Tayler, readers for Duquesne University Press, proved extremely helpful in preparing the final version of the manuscript. I am very grateful. Although in many ways my severest critics, Ralph Cohen, William Kerrigan and Albert C. Labriola were unflagging in their insightful attention to details of the argument presented here. Many other colleagues also offered criticism and encouragement: Arthur Kinney, Peter Medine, R. V. Young and Joseph A. Wittreich, Jr. I want to thank, too, all of my friends and colleagues in the Departments of English and Philosophy at the University of California, Riverside, for their unfailing encouragement of this project, in particular, Jean-Pierre Barricelli, Joseph Childers, Emory Elliott, Robert Essick, John Ganim, Ralph Hanna, Judy Kronenfeld, John B. Vickery and Zhang Longxi. I would be remiss if I did not express gratitude to the many friends and colleagues at the Henry E. Huntington Library and around the country who listened, in addition to those already mentioned, to my argument and offered helpful criticism and advice: Cyndia Clegg, David George, Robert F. Gleckner, Richard Harp, Grace Ioppolo, John King, Anthony Low, John Mulryan, Annabel Patterson, Martin Ridge, William Sessions, John Steadman and Paul Voss. I will not forget the patience and candor of this large contingent of faithful if informal collaborators. I consider all of them—I can think of no higher compliment—Wittgensteinians.

Sections of this book were presented to various forums at the University of Nevada, Las Vegas and at meetings, conferences or congresses of the International Shakespeare

Association, the Modern Language Association, the John Donne Society, Sixteenth Century Studies and the William Andrews Clark Memorial Library (UCLA). Versions or parts of chapters one, four, five and six have appeared in *New Literary History, Literature and History, Renascence* and *Soundings of Things Done,* edited by Peter Medine and Joseph A. Wittreich, Jr. (University of Delaware Press, 1996); I am grateful for their cooperation in permission to include that material in altered form.

As Wittgenstein discovered after giving away all of his great inherited wealth, thinking and writing require money as well as time. I owe much to many for both in abundance. The University of California may insist that faculty "publish or perish," but it provided me with an advantageous teaching schedule, a sabbatical leave, computers, office space and materials, support staff, and research money for travel and photocopying. Steven Axelrod, Chair of the Department of English Dean Carlos Vélez-Ibáñez and Associate Dean Carl Cranor, of the College of Humanities and Social Sciences at the University of California, Riverside, generously supported my work on Wittgenstein and Sir Francis Galton at the British Library and the Manuscript Room of University College, London. The staffs of the University of California, Riverside, the Henry E. Huntington and the British Libraries, especially Kelli Bronson, Alan Jutzi, Thomas Lange, Virginia Renner and Frances Rouse, were unfailingly helpful, as was my forbearing and resourceful editor, Susan Wadsworth-Booth.

Finally, I must thank the people closest to me—my wife, Barbara, my sons, Bradford and Duncan, and my daughter-in-law, Brenda—for their emotional support through the years. And I am more grateful than I can say for the time I have spent with my grandchildren, who have through these same years dispersed joy as effortlessly as Portia imagines the Deity imparting "the quality of mercy." I dedicate this book to them—to Heather, Michelle, Ryan and Stephen—for a debt that I can never repay.

Stanley Stewart

ABBREVIATIONS AND BIBLIOGRAPHICAL NOTE

Unless otherwise indicated, all citations from Spenser and Shakespeare in my text are from *The Works of Edmund Spenser: A Variorum Edition* (ed. by Edwin Greenlaw, et al., hereafter referred to as *Var*) and *The Riverside Shakespeare* (ed. by G. Blakemore Evans et al.). Throughout, I regularize i/j and u/v, expand contractions, and silently ignore obvious printers' errors, meaningless capitals, small capitals, italics and the like. Unless otherwise noted, books published before 1700 bear a London imprint. As is customary, references to the writings of Nietzsche and Wittgenstein will be to the abbreviated title, followed by the number of the part of the work, then the title (if any) of the section, followed by the number of the partition within that section. Where section numbers are not available or are inconvenient (as in part 2 of *Philosophical Investigations*), references will be to page numbers.

Abbreviations

BBB *Preliminary Studies for the "Philosophical Investigations": Generally known as The Blue and Brown Books*. Oxford: Basil Blackwell, 1958.

BJJ *The Ben Jonson Journal*

BWN   *Basic Writings of Nietzsche.* Trans. and ed. Walter Kaufmann. New York: Random House, 1968.

CV   *Culture and Value.* Ed. G. H. von Wright, in collab. with Heikki Nyman. Trans. Peter Winch. Chicago: U of Chicago P, 1984. 1st pub. 1977.

EH   *Ecce Homo (BWN)*

ELH   *English Literary History*

ELR   *English Literary Renaissance*

FQ   *The Faerie Queene (Var)*

GS   *The Gay Science: with a prelude in rhymes and an appendix of songs.* Trans. Walter Kaufmann. New York: Random House, 1974.

H&S   *Ben Jonson.* Ed. C. H. Herford and Percy and Evelyn Simpson. 11 vols. Oxford: Clarendon Press, 1928–52.

JDJ   *John Donne Journal*

LE   "Wittgenstein's Lecture on Ethics." Transcribed Friedrich Waismann. *Philosophical Review* 74 (Jan. 1965): 3–26.

NLH   *New Literary History*

OC   *On Certainty.* Ed. G. E. M. Anscombe and G. H. von Wright. Trans. Denis Paul and G. E. M. Anscombe. Oxford: Basil Blackwell, 1969.

PG   *Philosophical Grammar.* Ed. Rush Rhees. Trans. Anthony Kenny. Berkeley: U of California P, 1978. 1st pub. 1974.

PI   *Philosophical Investigations.* Trans. G. E. M. Anscombe. Oxford: Basil Blackwell, 1958.

RC   *Remarks on Colour.* Ed. G. E. M. Anscombe. Trans. Linda L. McAlister and Margaret Schättle. Berkeley: U of California P, 1977.

RFM   *Remarks on the Foundations of Mathematics.* Ed. G. H. von Wright, R. Rhees, G. E. M. Anscombe. Trans. G. E. M. Anscombe. Cambridge: MIT P, 1991. 1st pub. 1956.

RFGB   *Remarks on Frazer's* Golden Bough. Ed. Rush

	Rhees. Trans. A. C. Miles. Doncaster: Brynmill Press, 1979.
SEL	*Studies in English Literature*
SQ	*Shakespeare Quarterly*
TI	*Twilight of the Idols. The Portable Nietzsche.* Ed. and trans. Walter Kaufmann. New York: Viking, 1983.
TLP	*Tractatus Logico-Philosophicus.* Trans. D. F. Pears and B. F. McGuinness. Intro. Bertrand Russell. London: Routledge, 1988. 1st pub. 1961. 1st German ed. 1921.
UM	*Untimely Meditations.* Trans. R. J. Hollingdale. Intro. J. P. Stern. Cambridge: Cambridge UP, 1989. 1st pub. 1983
UV	*Ungathered Verse*, H&S, vol. 8.
Var	*The Works of Edmund Spenser: A Variorum Edition.* Ed. Edwin Greenlaw, et al. 8 vols. and index. Baltimore: Johns Hopkins UP, 1932–57
"WIASC"	"Why I am So Clever" (*EH*)
WP	*The Will to Power.* Trans. Walter Kaufmann and R. J. Hollingdale. New York: Random House, 1967.

Investigating Renaissance Criticism

Our investigation is
therefore a grammatical one. Such
an investigation sheds light on our problem by
clearing misunderstandings away. Misunderstandings
concerning the use of words, caused, among other things,
by certain analogies between the forms of expression in
different regions of language.—Some of them can be
removed by substituting one form of expression for
another; this may be called an "analysis" of our
forms of expression, for the process is
sometimes like one of taking
a thing apart.

— Wittgenstein, *Philosophical Investigations*

W hen Wittgenstein explains his use of the term that
would characterize his method after the *Tractatus*—"investigation"—he recalls Augustine's paradoxical

reflection: "'quid est ergo tempus? si nemo ex me quaerat scio; si quaerenti explicare velim, nescio'" (*PI* §89). (What is time then? If no one asks me, I know; if I should wish to explain it to someone asking, I don't know.) Wittgenstein was fascinated by an oddity, noted by Augustine, that a word or notion ("time") was clear as long as one took it unreflectively. But when one undertook to characterize "time"—"to explain it"—words seemed to fail. Wittgenstein finds Augustine's observation instructive: "Something that we know when no one asks us, but no longer know when we are supposed to give an account of it, is something that we need to remind ourselves of." Presumably, we can remind ourselves only of something we already know, so there can be no question in Augustine's example of a deep mystery, unless one thinks of forgetfulness as intrinsically mysterious. (Nietzsche did; Wittgenstein didn't.) Then why should the demand that one explain one's terms elicit puzzlement?

On reflection, perhaps one says that the substantive ("time") is unclear. Certainly in literary criticism we can imagine terms having the same effect. I ask a critic to clarify a remark made about *King Lear*, or to tender evidence to support it, and in response the critic declares that the instruction, "to clarify," is unclear, and moreover, with respect to "evidence," that arguments are won or lost before "evidence" has been either defined or adduced as a criterion of judgment. In effect, the critic declares the key terms in my request "unclear."

What would an appropriate response look like in this case? Given two such sweeping assertions, I might easily find myself in a quandary as to how I should proceed. It might make sense even to doubt that critical discussion *can* proceed, since by turning attention from Shakespeare's play to theoretical and philosophical issues, these assertions seem to undermine the conversation. For rather than discussing the play or its Renaissance setting, we must now address questions of epistemology and the philosophy of language. But suppose we were to concentrate instead on the original challenge to my request for clarification, and ask: Why should anyone think the imperative, "Clarify *P*," unclear? Isn't clarification an ordinary function of the way we talk? Don't we clarify expressions, oral and written, all the time—when we go to the market, for instance: "No, not that item, the one next to it"; and in our social life: "I meant that I would be there by seven o'clock *if* the meeting broke up in time, but not certainly." In everyday life we sort out misunderstandings with relative ease, as if the concept of "clarification" never entered our minds. "But how, without an understanding of 'clarification,'" one may ask, "can we clarify our expressions?" Well, isn't it enough that we do clarify them? Perhaps the question ("But how . . . can we . . .?") isn't helpful in this context. It might be more useful to distinguish two separate functions here: "explaining a categorical expression" and "doing something that someone might take as an ostensive definition of it." For instance, I can imagine having "clarification" satisfactorily defined and explained without dislodging my sense of puzzlement. For now, although presumably knowing what the concept means, I could still be puzzled by my interlocutor's claim that the order "to clarify" is unclear.

It might help to suppose that the communication is difficult here because of the way we talk when questions of this sort (of "clarity" or "evidence" and the like) arise in criticism. We seem to think of these words in their disciplinary context as like those familiar to us in our day-to-day activities, such as shopping in the market or conversing with friends. And yet, simultaneously, the temptation is to think of "clarification" as a process unique to the critical enterprise, as if the critical domain of experience required a renovated vocabulary. In critical theory, we imagine "clarity" as something extraordinary. Consequently, in "clarification" talk, "[w]e feel," as Wittgenstein puts it, "as if we had to *penetrate* phenomena" (*PI* §90). We think, if we get the expression of the subject just so, we can capture, if not "the thing itself," then its "essence" or "social significance" or "cultural representation." For the moment, forgetting that "[o]ur talk gets its meaning from the rest of our proceedings" (*OC* §229), we try ever harder to find the proper, rarefied expression. In the process, we look with disdain on "the rest of our proceedings" as if it were irrelevant to the daunting task of critical articulation. And here we make a mistake. For at the same time, since when pressed we admit that in everyday life we routinely clarify expressions, as if without thinking (although surely this is impossible), we must concede that the concept of "clarification" is not intrinsically murky. What we think of as a critical problem, then, must concern the difference between distinguishable uses of the term and the persistence, in one of them, of misunderstanding. In the one case, we proceed with no sense of impropriety or doubt; in the other we may not proceed at all.

For Wittgenstein, "investigation" refers to a process of inquiry into the structural differences in ways of talking, some of which produce, while others dissipate, misunderstanding:

> Such an investigation sheds light on our problem by clearing misunderstandings away. Misunderstandings concerning the use of words, caused, among other things, by certain analogies between the forms of expression in different regions of the language.—Some of them can be removed by substituting one form of expression for another; this may be called an "analysis" of our forms of expression, for the process is sometimes like one of taking a thing apart. (*PI* §90)

In practice, this analytical procedure—often referred to as "ordinary language analysis"—begins in misunderstanding. Misunderstanding presents both the need for and the occasion of correction. Since I am puzzled by the critic's rejoinder to my question, the first order of business would be to examine that critical utterance—to take the critic's assertion, stated or implied, "apart"—with the aim of clarifying it, of understanding where the problem lies. The assumption is that, by substituting problematic utterances with others in more familiar usage, we stand a better chance of erasing the sense of strangeness or oddity or puzzlement permitted or encouraged by the "problematic" utterance, and so of "going on together."

I do not mean to imply that this "going on together" is easy in criticism, or that it is easy to articulate in any circumstance. When do transactions end? "Well, that depends on the method of measurement one employs. Usually, we just 'know.'" We are talking now about what Wittgenstein characterizes as "a series"—he is thinking of a mathematical scheme (1, 2, 3, 4 . . .)—as "a visible section of rails invisibly laid to infinity" (*PI* §218). His point is that it is not a matter of choice: "When I obey a rule, I do not choose. I obey the rule *blindly*" (*PI* §219). We either put in the "5" "naturally," without effort or will, or we aren't following the rule of the system. A sociologist conducted the following experiment; anyone could do it. One pulls into a gas station (it would have to be "Full Service" for the experiment to work), and goes through the usual motions, expressing interest in having the tank filled, handing the attendant the credit card, and so on. But then the customer remains in the car, and doesn't leave. In this case, the attendant looks through the window, comes back out, nods with encouragement, wipes the windows clean, smiles and retreats to the kiosk, there to peep through the window again. The idea is that the driver remains expressionless, shows no irritation, but doesn't move. The attendant returns, now, not smiling, but still "cooperative," and carefully checks the air in the tires, filling one or two. The attendant then asks if the customer wants the oil checked. The driver shakes his head, "No," and the attendant returns to the kiosk, and, now with some apprehension, looks through the window again. Seeing that the car has not moved, he strides to the motorist, and says: "Okay, Mister, it's over!" Everyday life is rule-governed: Talk to a friend or colleague in the usual way, and then, without stopping, take a healthy stride of a yard or so closer without altering the volume of your voice, and continue as if no rule of social distance applied. "Going on together" is a result of countless instances of "blind" adherence to rules.

What happens when rules of interaction are "contested?" Then "going on together" or "going on," *simpliciter*, becomes a problem. There are no guarantees that our communication system works in every case. When a youngster is learning the arithmetic system, there are certain steps taken in teaching and learning:

> When in counting the pupil arrives at the numeral 20, one makes a gesture suggestive of "Go on," upon which the child says (in most cases at any rate) "21". Analogously, the children are made to count to 22 and to higher numbers, no particular number playing in these exercises the predominant role of a last one. The last stage of training is that the child is ordered to count a group of objects, well above 20, without the suggestive gesture being used to help the child over the numeral 20. If a child does not respond to the suggestive gesture, it is separated from the others and treated as a lunatic. (*BBB* 93)

Wittgenstein's point is that, when the learning process is successful, the child doesn't learn a discrete number of numerals, but a system of which the instruction "add '1'" is a part. This is what he means when he says that when one learns a language one comes to understand not merely *n* words in particular uses, but "a form of life." When one cannot "go on" with other members of "the tribe," it means much more than just that the child is not a responsive student of arithmetic. The child doesn't fit in in an *important* way: "It is separated from the others and treated as a lunatic."

"Ordinary language analysis seems, at least at first glance, gratuitously negative. Your example implies that, if people disagree with you, they are hopeless lunatics." Unfortunately, some critics will be offended by the metacritical strategy of "ordinary language analysis." After hearing my presentation of remarks on certain critics of

George Herbert (these remarks are expanded in chapter 5), a Renaissance scholar of good reputation inquired, "Why are you doing this?" Again, rules govern such interactions. But the very same question is posed by the department chair to the protagonist of Bernard Malamud's *A New Life*, who has, in his one year in the English Department, wreaked havoc with the curriculum, and slept with the chair's wife besides. In the Malamud novel, the protagonist manages, in the circumstances, an appropriately insolent reply. But in my very different situation, I muttered a suitably innocuous, academically vapid response. "Why do *that*?" Were my interlocutor's question about motives tendered and taken seriously as a comment on the investigative approach of "ordinary language analysis" taken in the talk—that is, the metacritical or metatheoretical approach—then a more appropriate response would have been in order: "Consider the alternative. Would it not be supererogatory to ask for clarification of critical statements that one perfectly well understands? When we are 'going on together,' what sense would it make to say, 'I don't get it?'" So, reasonably, the aim—to find a means by which the conversation can continue with misunderstanding dissipated—requires what only *looks* like a negative process, simply because it begins with a critique of critical vocabulary. After all, that is where puzzlement began—with the twin assertions that: A) the order, "Clarify *P*," is unclear; and B) the concept of "evidence" is critically irrelevant. Having established that it would be supererogatory to pass over problematic expressions to attend to others that seem transparent, we now see that such a choice would be obtuse as well. For by ignoring problematic locutions one would not be continuing the conversation at all, but merely changing the subject.

"So," the objection might be, "this study of Renaissance criticism purports to focus on critical problems that arise from critical talk about the Renaissance and Renaissance authors, including Spenser, Shakespeare, Donne, Herbert and others. What is new about that?" We know that critics talk in very different ways about "the same text," and that some of these ways seem odd—odd, I suspect, because we do not learn to talk "criticism" or "critical theory" or "philosophy" in the ordinary way. Literary and philosophical theories are more likely than not framed in specialized off-shoots of the language, which are often characterized by abstract vocabulary and technical jargon. There is nothing, *a priori*, wrong in this. I assume that our motives are benign. We try to fit our experiences with literature into specialized systems of critical talk, because we wish to draw fine distinctions about matters we think important. Or because we think that for our talk to acquire intellectual weight, it must sound like anthropology or sociology or psychoanalysis or political science—any discipline thought to claim a more "scientific" methodology (and prestige) than literary criticism. But since we are then talking in a way we do not ordinarily talk—since "the rest of our proceedings" has been set aside as unresponsive to our present needs—we often do so awkwardly. We know what we know, but, like Augustine when asked to say what "that" is, the more we try to say what we know, the further we get from a sensible reply. We are, as Larry Wright suggests, a little like the centipede, an acknowledged master in the art, who decides to give walking lessons: the more attention given to the verbal task of explaining the mechanism, the greater the risk of losing the natural skill.[1] Think of the proliferation of critical vocabulary in the last few decades. In Renaissance criticism alone, we have hundreds of books and articles every year representing a wide range of disciplines, interests, opinions and assumptions.[2] Given the American appetite for pluralism, we value them all, or at least pay lip service to valuing them all. Although we can hardly be faulted for this, the sense that we are obliged to do so, albeit for socially and politically expedient reasons, may not comport well with appropriate criteria of knowledge and judgment. When social values and critical faculties conflict, problems arise.

This does not mean, as some critics believe (their assumptions are the focus of chapter 1), that talk about the Renaissance is intrinsically "problematic." With "ordinary language" as a constant check on our proceedings, it should be no more "problematic" than any other talk about the past. Ordinarily, we talk about the past all the time without the slightest sense of theoretical or philosophical difficulty: "Ten years ago, before this tree grew to its present height of thirty feet, this side of the house was much warmer in the summer"; "The First Folio of Shakespeare's plays was published in London in 1623"; "George Bush defeated Michael Dukakis for President of the U.S. in 1988." We don't say that these assertions are "unclear" or "undecidable" or "problematic," but in criticism, sentences that appear grammatically very much the same in their assertive function lead to conflicting utterances. Critics may claim, implicitly or explicitly (some of these claims will be analyzed in chapters 2, 3 and 4), that one perspective in the plural system of valuation is superior to—more accurate, more relevant, more liberating, better than—the others. They attach themselves to labels, and attach labels to imagined allies and adversaries. It is either very good or very bad to hoist critical colors: New Historicist, Cultural Materialist, Feminist, Marxist, Marxist-Feminist, historical, radical, conservative, sociological, anthropological, psychological, functionalist, semiologist, structuralist, poststructuralist, postmodern, post-postmodern, deconstructionist, Freudian, Lacanian, Foucaultian.

Although it might not always appear so in the pages that follow, the investigative method employed here is, with respect to vocabulary, nonproscriptive. The assumptions about the contrastive features of the language working here militate against the ruling out, in advance, of any locution. We know, of course, that some critics cling to a particular diction as if their life (and not just the prospect for publication of their next book) depended on it. We should take that intensity of interest in particular locutions seriously enough to examine it. Does it make a significant difference if we say that a Donne elegy is "misogynist" rather than "misandrist" (a question addressed in chapter 4), or whether Herbert's poetry is "Calvinist" as distinct from "anti-Calvinist" (a problem of interest in chapter 5)? Wittgenstein addresses the grammar of such questions at a more general level than will be our focus here. For example, discussing an arrangement of nine squares variously colored red, green, white and black (let us say, a model of a given "text"), Wittgenstein suggests how a language might be made up of the corresponding words, "R," "G," "W," and "B." Then the question of "interpretation" arises: In an arrangement in which some of the squares are contiguous to others of the same color, do they comprise a sentence of four or of nine parts ("RRBGGGRWW")? Are the colored squares "simple" or "composite" (*PI* §48)?

We encounter arguments like this in Renaissance criticism often. The very "same" Spenser or Shakespeare or Donne or Herbert text provokes alternative, often mutually exclusive characterizations, and disagreements—even ideological differences—arise. So how would Wittgenstein resolve the problem? First, he engages his interlocutor, who is confused:

> But I do not know whether to say that the figure described by our sentence consists of four or of nine elements! Well, does the sentence consist of four letters or of nine?— And which are *its* elements, the types of letter, or the letters? Does it matter which we say, so long as we avoid misunderstandings in any particular case? (*PI* §48)

But as often in Renaissance criticism, so here, our interlocutor demands an answer to the question: Which is the proper way of characterizing the segmentation of the sentence ("RRBGGGRWW")? The interlocutor demands, four parts or nine? Wittgenstein neither answers nor evades the question, but responds to it by gently redirecting the interlocutor's attention to the purposive nature of language. How would a decision one way or the other make a difference to the communication? "Well," it could be said, "you claim Wittgenstein doesn't evade the question, but he answers the question with a question. So he *does* evade the question, which is about the number of parts of that sentence." Here, I would say, is our model of how to proceed. We might observe that a more charitable characterization would be to say that, rather than evade the question, Wittgenstein addresses a matter overlooked in its articulation. He asks, what difference would saying the one rather than the other make in our proceeding? His response, which takes the grammatical form of a question, redirects attention from the interlocutor's apparent assumption that something important hangs on the "meaning" of "simple" and "complex," namely, resolution of the question of the number of parts in the sentence. The interlocutor doesn't say how arriving at a resolution of that question would make a difference. If arriving at a decision about one or another designation makes no difference in our understanding of what the sentence *does*, then legislating one rather than another characterization looks like a pointless enterprise. The sense that a problem exists evaporates.

Wittgenstein's attitude toward language here—and it is an attitude as distinct from an insight into the phonemic structure of a particular language or dialect that interests me—bears on most of what follows in this book. I know no more succinct characterization of the purposive emphasis of Wittgenstein's thought than Heidegger's. The context of his remark involves, as it so often does in humanistic studies, interpretation. He has been discussing a particular expression in the *Fragments* with participants in the 1967 Heraclitus Seminar in Frieburg, one of whom is of the opinion that they were at the mercy of "the hermeneutic circle," trying to understand an expression that they must translate. To Heidegger's question, "Can we get out of this circle?" Eugen Fink replies that we must "rather enter into" it (Heidegger 16). Gently disagreeing, Heidegger invokes Wittgenstein:

> Wittgenstein says the following. The difficulty in which thinking stands compares with a man in a room, from

which he wants to get out. At first, he attempts to get out through the window, but it is too high for him. Then he attempts to get out through the chimney, which is too narrow for him. If he simply turned around, he would see that the door was open all along. (Heidegger 17)

Wittgenstein would first want to know what the problem is, and what opportunities are available for dealing with it. The fact that humans do not have eyes in the back of their head is not a biological bar to discovery of what lies behind them. The mistake interpreters make, Heidegger suggests, comes when they zero in on "the meaning" of a particular expression, as if it were an object apart from its linguistic surroundings. This is what Heidegger means when he says that they cannot solve the problem of the expression *panta* by taking into account all the uses of the term in all of the extant *Fragments* of Heraclitus: "everything we have of Heraclitus' fragments is not the whole, is not the whole Heraclitus" (17). It only *sounds* like a paradox to say that all of those uses do not comprise the "whole" of Heraclitus. When Heidegger says that such and such an expression "isn't Greek," and couldn't be what Heraclitus meant, he is talking about what Wittgenstein refers to as a "form of life," the human matrix in which the individual expression once made perfect sense, if, to a modern, little or no sense at all.

I would characterize Wittgenstein's attitude toward language as "modest" or "deflationary." It proceeds from the assumption that, although on many occasions our misuse of language can lead to a kind of "bewitchment," when patiently investigated for its purpose-driven functions, it is no more mysterious than most other human activities. Accordingly, our aim here is not to discover a proper mode of critical discussion, but, first, to look for accommodation between the language of the critic and a reasonable expectation of what a description of the object in question would, could and should look like. Although concern for the way critics talk is the practical essence of this study, this will not be the sole focus of the following investigation. The emphasis here will be metacritical, but not exclusively so. Elaborating on his remarks on clarification, Wittgenstein argues for the usefulness of methodological flexibility: "There is not *a* philosophical method, though there are indeed methods, like different therapies" (*PI* §133). Wittgenstein's term, "therapy," implies benign treatment of a disorder of some kind, which in medicine and related fields usually involves diagnosis of causes or so-called "contributing factors." Assuming that such pathologies, anomalies and problems occur in the critical literature, what causes them? Should we be looking for a methodology to deal with critical problems at large? Or would such a search only produce yet another set of symptoms? "A main cause of philosophical disease," Wittgenstein writes, is "—a one-sided diet: one nourishes one's thinking with only one kind of example" (*PI* §593). Perhaps we should not think of an "eclectic" or "unsystematic" approach as pernicious, much less otiose. It might be good to have a metacritical study dedicated to examples drawn exclusively from current Renaissance commentary, but this is not the kind that I have written. When assertions under consideration are about primary (i.e., historical) texts, I sometimes address "the text itself," but not as if that text were, like the sculptured heads on Mount Rushmore, physical monuments changeable only by eons of sun, wind and rain.

"Therapy" suggests treatment in the sense of intervention in a negative sequence of signs or symptoms of disorder. The medical overtones of the term imply—perhaps self-servingly—that ministration proceeds from diagnosis to procedure with benign intent. In accordance with the critical application of the Hippocratic oath, I have sought in what follows to "do no harm" to the integrity of Renaissance voices. The question that this remark entails— namely, that of whether any such thing as that integrity exists—is the overarching concern of the entire book and the central focus of chapters 2 and 5. Recognition of the difficulty and importance of this question should suggest that I do not think the metacritical approach through "ordinary language analysis" is without its inconveniences. Like physical therapy, the investigative approach in these pages involves repetition. Attention to certain locutions will recur in different parts of the discussion, sometimes with what might look like entirely different foci. I do not mean this remark as an apology for oversights as yet unrecognized on my part, but rather as a characterization of the investigative method employed. If I may move from my medical figure, suppose that the landscape of criticism can't be captured in a single, monochromatic photograph, or even in a wide-screen panorama. For a question about the flora of the various terrain, we might need many closeups of different sectors: pasture, meadow, forest, wetland; and as the seasons (critical epochs) change, we might need more examples, and these perhaps in color, so as better to allow for proper identification of the various plant species. If we plan to erect a permanent building or lay out plans for a bivouac, it might prove useful to have numerous aerial photographs (but, here, quite possibly monochromatic prints would suffice). My point is modest, but necessary: We want to know the use to which the pictures will be put—the critical claim that will be made—before saying how many pictures of what kind we will need.

Assuming that critical statements purport to establish contrasts, we will want to acquaint ourselves with the contrastive function, if any, of current usages. My assumption is, frankly, that unless that contrastive function is in place, the purposive direction of a line of thought is easily lost, and confusion sets in. For this reason, the focus on contrasts in this study is both a means and an end. In principle, this sounds easy, but in practice it turns out not to be so, because often critics will use a term that implies a categorical opposite without citing an alternative example. For instance, one critic, responding to other critics of George Herbert's lyrics, asserts that Herbert criticism is marked by failure:

> We do not know how to read his book [*The Temple*], for it does not secure words within the structures we recognize (beginning, middle, and end; sequence). Critics who despair of describing the elusive structure of the book settle for explications of individual . . . lyrics. These, too, cannot succeed. For there is no poem within *The Temple* that does not echo *against* [italics mine] other poems; no reading of an individual poem can account for all the echoes, nor would an attempt to construct a gloss to catch every echo produce the single poem. Echoes would multiply, refusing the coherence of critical designs. The totality of *The Temple* would remain as the critical question. (Goldberg *Echo* 109)

This is a puzzling line of thought. How is it that, without learning how to read *The Temple*, one comes to know that we don't know how to read it? Either the critic means something other than the ordinary notion of capability here, or the utterance is confused. Setting aside the question of whether the parts of *The Temple* are sequentially or randomly arranged (we return to this question in chapter 5, "Herbert and the Historicity of Critical Metaphor"), I want to suggest that analysis of this passage can helpfully proceed without appealing to the evidence of *The Temple*. Goldberg's claim rests on the assumption that, as long as elements of one text echo *"against"* those of other texts, no single account of any separate text can succeed. And, having established that no account of a lyric in the context of the larger, nonexistent sequence is possible, the critic in effect declares that, of necessity, all criticism of *The Temple* must fail. Even supposing that the statement that "no poem within *The Temple* does not echo *against* other poems" makes sense and merits assent, it would not follow that critical statements about individual lyrics must fail. For, given the stretch of the two major assumptions here, the critic erroneously assumes that any formulation that failed to take account of the imagined multiplicity of inaccessible echoings must fail. But if these echoes are supposedly unknowable, how on earth can we say that they bear on our judgment of earthly accounts?

Unhappily, there is an even more formidable inconvenience of this proposition of the necessity of failure of "explications of individual [Herbert] lyrics." In order for that proposition to hold, the critic must have access to the very information supposedly unavailable to Herbert critics; that is, to all of the echoes in every instance of every Herbert lyric, whether inside or outside of a nonexistent sequence called *The Temple*. I tell you that, of the many renditions of Bach's *Toccata and Fugue in C Major*, none has "succeeded." Moreover, I say that none will ever succeed for the simple reason that non *can* succeed. Well, does this mean that by some preternatural perception, akin to clairvoyance, I know all the extant and possible performances, and that these preclude any possible "going on together" in which individual or corporate satisfaction with the organ piece could occur? How do we know that these Herbert lyrics in fact echo against anything, except in such circumstances as one says, "See, there *A* echoes *'against' B*?" Why is it necessary to hear every echo in order to "go on together" as if "satisfaction" were at least possible? How can we be sure that "no reading of an individual poem" in *The Temple* can "succeed?" Without an ostensive definition of "success," how can all this talk about failure "succeed?"

Now discussion seems to founder on the aesthetic concept of "success." "After all, the critic is attempting to say something very subtle. Herbert's poetic expression is difficult and elusive." Wittgenstein writes:

> Here it is easy to get into that dead-end in philosophy, where one believes that the difficulty of the task consists in our having to describe phenomena that are hard to get hold of, the present experience that slips quickly by, or something of the kind. Where we find ordinary language too crude, and it looks as if we were having to do, not with the phenomena of every-day, but with ones that "easily elude us, and, in their coming to be and passing away, produce those others as an average effect". (*PI* §436)

When critical locutions lead into blind alleys, it is better to question the vocabulary than to proceed with credulity into further darkness, even if one calls that darkness light. It is true that the critic might justify departing from notions of "the book-within logocentric suppositions" on the grounds of "postmodernism,"[3] but this is only to nail to the mast the rule of "logocentrism's" logical opposite: illogic. Still addressing *The Temple*, the same critic asks if "the title page [is] a scene of masturbation?" (110) Well, suppose we answer "It is" or "It isn't" or "I don't know." What would agreement, disagreement, or a confession of ignorance amount to here? What are the alternatives to the critic's locution? A "scene," not "of masturbation," but of—well, what? How does the term "scene" function here? Is the item "masturbation" part of the English language in Herbert's time? "Well, the OED lists a reference to 'masturprator' in Burton's *Anatomy of Melancholy* in 1621. So whether pronounced with or without an 'r,' the word was in use in Herbert's time."

The issue of "usage" here is not simple. Wittgenstein writes that "it might be asked: Do I *understand* the word just b[y] describing its application? Do I understand its point? Haven't I deluded myself about something important?" (*PG* 65) Sometimes we mistake a lively question for an affirmative statement: "Is meaning then really only the use of a word?" But does showing that a term was in use in Herbert's time tell us when it was used properly? "Wouldn't it be possible for me to know the use of the word and yet follow it without understanding?" (65) For instance, I am at a ceremonial dinner of a group with which I am unfamiliar. Although I take care to speak with grammatical correctness, I use a certain word, and an awkward silence befalls the company at my table. I have the sense that I have made a mistake, and I understand what Wittgenstein was getting at when he said, "Isn't it [the significance of the word] the way this use meshes with our life?" (65) We want to know whether the term ("masturbation") fits in this particular literary "scene" (supposing, of course, that the concept of a literary "scene" is not it-self a historical solecism), whether it has purchase on Herbert's expression. If "its use" is "a part of" Caroline and Jacobean "life," then we must inquire "how *language* meshes with their [Caroline and Jacobean] life" (*PG* 65). Accordingly, in our metacritical inquiry into "Renais-sance" talk, we will want to know how such locutions "mesh" with the lives of poets and readers in Herbert's time. If the critic perceives "ejaculative traces" (Gold-berg 111) in Herbert's poetry, we must ask what other kinds of "traces" were possible in such contexts. In the unlikely event that the answer to our question is given, "*n*," we must say that then the critic owes participants in the discussion a selection of relevant Elizabethan, Jaco-bean and Caroline examples.

Questions about the success or failure of historical as-sertions are not easy to answer, but this doesn't mean that they are intractable. Sometimes dubious statements are made even more nettlesome by a failure on the part of critics to articulate the contrast that they are making, between success and failure, for instance; but there are many other pairs bedeviling current discussion: subject/object, subjective/objective, certain/uncertain, decidable/undecidable, undecisive/decisive, mediated/unmediated, deep/superficial, historical/unhistorical, gendered/ungen-dered, feminist/masculist, patriarchal/matriarchal, post-modern/post-postmodern, traditional/new, ideological/nonideological, constructed/unconstructed. And what about such terms as "gendered," "cultural," "ideological," "bias" and "constructed?" Do they invariably make con-trastive sense? If, as I believe, the contrastive elements are often vaguely implied or not spelled out at all, the effect can be confusing. Of course, critically astute readers can add to this list, which is not meant to be definitive. To it we should add all notions that, in and of themselves, are derived from the application of these or similarly vague categories.

This is not to say that such locutions are *intrinsically*

puzzling. I imagine that, with the proper background supplied, one could find any or all of them, even in the area
of critical theory, vehicles of significant communication.
There are many ways to make a point—a myriad of different expressions available. As we learned in discussion of
the block of squares, Wittgenstein modestly suggests that
it doesn't much matter what we say or how we say it. The
point is to make sense, so as to clear away misunderstanding. Fortunately, we have the investigative procedure available, because misunderstanding is not always avoidable. In
criticism, some statements and questions leave us unsure
of what to say. In these cases, even good intentions can
make matters worse: "A philosophical problem has the
form: 'I don't know my way about'" (*PI* §123). It is at just
such a juncture that ordinary language analysis can exercise its therapeutic function, what we might call a grammatical orientation, which elicits insight into the relations
of the parts that might otherwise have been overlooked:
"Such an investigation sheds light on our problem by clearing misunderstandings away" (*PI* §90). In these situations,
analysis and diagnosis of a critical problem are functionally
one and the same. If one takes a term from one discipline
or one context and employs it in another, inappropriate
associations often gravitate right along with it, and the
result is an unacknowledged equivocation. For instance, if
my interlocutor claims that "clarification isn't possible,"
I am at liberty to infer epistemological, sociological or
philosophical significance from the utterance. I could say
that the critic is addressing the age-old "problem of meaning." But suppose that critic meant only to warn me of the
difficulties often encountered in efforts to paraphrase. Then
my interpretive claims, and the objections concomitant to
them, would justifiably be regarded as off the mark.

It takes a huge reservoir of shared perceptions to make
disagreement even possible, much less useful. Obviously,
we cannot hope to agree with assertions we claim not to
understand, and our effort to refute them would, logically,
be pointless. We can, however, supposing only that we

understand our difference, "go on together" in disagreement. But if the conversation is—even theoretically—unintelligible, investment of time in "going on together"
must appear foolhardy. Since my aim is palliative, I would
argue at the outset, then, that when the critic asserts that
my instruction, "Clarify *P*," is unclear, I am free to infer
that this critic agrees with me on the importance of clarification. For by objecting to my lack of clarity, the critic
in effect declares that clarification is possible and valuable.
This concession, in turn, opens the door to discussion of
criteria for clarification. Thus, the corrective mode of clarification, even though it takes its rise from apparently negative assertion of a problem in critical articulation, may
require a charitable interpretive venture. I furrow my brow
and shrug my shoulders as if to say that I don't understand
in order to prompt my interlocutor's elucidation. But this
doesn't mean that I am guided by a single picture of clarification, or even that I have in mind beforehand what an
added clarification would look like. Even though we might
not be able to explain precisely what rule we follow in
arriving at such inferences, we recognize when we have
been insulted or paid a compliment. Understanding alters
behavior. The interlocutor continues or stops explaining;
I give further signs of questioning or desist.

We know that in criticism signs of quiescence may not
last long. As one matter is clarified, another becomes confused, or the original problem appears not really to have
gone away, or to have been only partially treated. Wittgenstein claims that "the clarity that we are aiming at is
indeed *complete* clarity" (*PI* §133). Who would argue
against *that*? No critic whose judgment we would trust
will hoist the flag for "partial clarification." And yet
Wittgenstein's point here is modest. He has been arguing
that we need not think of ordinary language analysis as an
attempt to renovate the way people talk or think. It is not
language, but the way we use it when we do things that
we are not used to doing, or are not very good at doing
(think of philosophy or critical theory here), that makes us

think we have encountered philosophical or critical problems. The aim is to dispel the notion that critical problems emanate from the nature of language or the nature of things in the world. Clarification is the constructive aim of such investigation: "But this simply means that the philosophical problems should *completely* disappear" (*PI* §133). With respect to our interest here, this means only that there are no critical problems—no insoluble riddles, no enigmas in the nature of things—unique to study of Renaissance literature or of statements made about it.

Moments ago, I chose to infer from my interlocutor's objection an assumed commitment to the shared value of "clarity." But in criticism how shall we recognize clarification? Surely "it" isn't a thing to be seen or clarified in itself; we recognize clarification as we do in ordinary situations— as in the market, for instance: by "going on together" with a sense of justified assurance. Now, some critics find the concept of "justified assurance" only code words for willful self-deception or worse. But, again, we depend on the sense of justified assurance all the time, and would probably find our existence in society intolerable without it. We pass hundreds of gas stations every week with justified assurance that, since the gauge doesn't read "Empty," we will not run out of gas; we leave home every day with justified assurance that we will find our way back. Of course, we could be, and occasionally are, mistaken. But this doesn't mean that our assurance wasn't or isn't justified. It serves its purpose. (Think of how inconvenient it would be to have the fuel and oil levels checked at every gas station we passed.) We behave with justified assurance that our interlocutors—loved ones, friends, or critics interested in the same subject—understand, because they give signs that satisfy rather than frustrate us. If, no matter what we said, they always scratched their heads and looked at us with amazement, it would mean that, in our case, the system of "ostensive teaching" hasn't worked: "If a child does not respond to the suggestive gesture, it is separated from the others and treated as a lunatic" (*BBB* 93).

We talk about the Renaissance, and we do so much as we talk about what we talk about most easily. We absorb and even advance knowledge. Difficulty arises, not from our capacity to understand artifacts written in the past (because those are the only kind of artifacts we have to apprehend in the present), but when, with the tools we have been handed, we question our capacity. (Consider here the quandary of critics who imagine that anything significant hangs on believing that it makes a difference whether we say that our knowledge of the Renaissance is "objective" or "socially constructed.") In his discussion of "complete *clarity*" as his goal, Wittgenstein makes this wise suggestion: "The real discovery is the one that makes me capable of stopping doing philosophy when I want to.— The one that gives philosophy peace, so that it is no longer tormented by questions which bring *itself* in question" (*PI* §133). We need not think of Renaissance literature as that part of a historical canon that is mysteriously unknowable, as if the "knowable" past reaches back only to the Restoration or the French Revolution or the Coronation of Queen Victoria or the end of the Vietnam War.

Suppose a critic persists in asking: "What justifies justified assurance? How do we know when 'assurance' is 'justified'?" Well, isn't the important thing that we do? Some of the "helps" in ordinary use come under consideration at various stages throughout this book. Often, we go to the OED, and the word that sent us there has *n* entries, each documented by a dated quotation. In particular, the theme of chapter 6, "Evidence of Renaissance Criticism," is Wittgensteinian: "To be sure there is justification; but justification comes to an end" (*OC* §192). Or as he puts the same practical notion in *Philosophical Investigations*: "Justification ends somewhere." Sooner or later, we close the dictionary. Sometimes we close it after consulting only a few entries, but we do so with the sense that we have answered the question that sent us there. Suppose at just that moment someone braces us with the order: "Go back. You must consult them all to make sure that you have

found the right example." And we follow the order, consulting every entry, only to hear the same order that we
check again. "Well, what is wrong with that? Surely, over-
confidence can lead to error." Perhaps sometimes it does.
But Wittgenstein reminds us that uncertainty, also, has its
pathological dangers: "As if someone were to buy several
copies of the morning paper to assure himself that what
it said was true" (*PI* §265). In due course, we close the
dictionary and move on.

"And yet have we not already agreed that, in the process,
mistakes are possible?" Again, in our dismay about possible error, we are inclined to ask the wrong question. "Justified assurance" means only that we have ruled out the
probability of error in one case, not that no mistake could
occur under any circumstance, or that even in this case
we are not mistaken. "Assurance" is "justified" because,
unless we encounter inconvenient consequences, we "go
on together." So if we feel comfortable in our conviction,
and if our belief encounters little or no inconvenience in
our interaction with others, what function would doubt
regarding that assurance serve? The point is that, like belief,
doubt serves a purpose. I doubt that I can jump from the
top of this tall building to the top of that taller one, and
my doubt helps restrain me from inappropriate testing of
my leaping ability: "I shall get burnt if I put my hand in
the fire: that is certainty. That is to say: here we see the
meaning of certainty. (What it amounts to, not just the
meaning of the word 'certainty')" (*PI* §474). Whether they
are Stratfordians or anti-Stratfordians, critics have confidence that theirs "was *the* William Shakespeare who wrote
a number of the world's greatest literary works" (Matus
13), but this does not mean that any one of them can "offer
incontrovertible proof of his authorship," which is only to
say that incontrovertibility might not serve as a useful
criterion of justified assurance. Critical confidence is "justified" by our surroundings. It is as if Stratfordians say to
Stratfordians, and Oxfordians to Oxfordians: "Ask me. I
answer questions like this all the time. You can do it, too,

and probably have. We are pretty good at this sort of thing."

When we concede that we might be wrong in particular cases, we admit to the relevance of a proper and legitimate criterion of correction. In so doing, we recognize a standard of argumentative coherence. That is, we find fault with the critic who, after excoriating opponents who believe in "facts," points out as grounds for this critical assault the "fact" that *P*, declared recently in so and so's "daring" or "challenging" book, "shows" or "demonstrates. . . ." But this does not mean that incoherent statements are "nonsensical" or that they are never instructive. When a critic gives a factual refutation of belief in facts, it might serve to remind us, not that we should have faith in the ultimate unreliability of our intellectual proceedings, but, on the contrary, that research potentially adds to the factual basis of our understanding. This is not a pronunciamento about the inevitability of scientific progress, but only a reminder that progress, as well as decline, in certain areas of thought has occurred. We do not need to say that because we are sometimes, with or without justification, undecided, therefore notions of "undecidability" and "subjectivity" must inevitably efface "justified assurance" in all of our critical operations. It would not be wrong to think that "justified assurance" is the underlying preoccupation of this study, but it is the central concern of the final chapter, "Evidence of Renaissance Criticism." How do we know when critics are talking about the Renaissance rather than about themselves or about late twentieth century concerns? What constitutes evidence in this matter? What are the assumptions that we encounter in "going on together" with the "justified assurance" that we can recognize statements about the Renaissance as being *about* the Renaissance? This means that "belief" must be an issue throughout the book. Do critics believe what they say? (Chapter 1 considers an alternative possibility.) Critical disputes proceed as if critics did believe the statements they propound. But why should we believe *that*? Given the available evidence, is our belief in a virtually universal critical sincerity justified?

Let me anticipate one objection in advance. It has been said that I am not asking critical questions here, but, rather, philosophical ones. I believe that we have turned the matter around, and that what we call problems of Renaissance criticism are actually disguised philosophical confusions. In this sense, remarks in the following pages are an extension of the thesis of *Nietzsche's Case: Philosophy as/and Literature*. I do not mean that readers of this book must first read *Nietzsche's Case*, but only that I do not think it is necessary to argue anew that the boundary between philosophy and criticism is too tenuous to defend in critical discussions today, which tend toward more general and interdisciplinary perspectives. But in the following pages I proceed on the related though distinguishable assumption that it is too late to keep literary history, the history of criticism, critical theory and philosophy apart, for they have already become melded in the cauldron of critical exchange, along with further confusions introduced from the social sciences as well as from geopolitical and economic fields of interest. The aim here will be to take "Renaissance" talk as it appears in print in representative confusing forms.

1

A Critique
of Pure "Situating"

We say "The expression in his voice
was *genuine*." If it was spurious we think
as it were of another one behind it.—*This* is the
face he shews the world, inwardly he has another
one.—But this does not mean that when his
expression is *genuine* he has two the same.
(("A quite particular expression."))

— Wittgenstein, *Philosophical Investigations*

The matter under discussion was this: Must one situate oneself in order to engage in critical discussion? Two contrary views had emerged in my department—in the hallway, in the mailroom, and at colloquia (but not all at once, as the following account conveniently suggests). Although they hold that their common field of interest is not germane to the critical dispute between them, the

26

principal protagonists of both positions happen to be Renaissance specialists.

"The insistence that we situate ourselves prior to critical discussion is only a custom," said one critic (whom her opponent suspected of positivist leanings).

"You know that you are making a dismissive move when you say that," said the other. ("Dismissive move" is one of his favorite locutions.) "It's a custom, only a custom, and so will pass. But one's thesis is a necessary outgrowth of the epistemological underpinnings of the critique presented. So when I say that it is necessary, I mean to do more than take note of an oddity in the current critical taxonomy."

"Morphology," she said, with some finality, "is not ladled on after the substance of an argument springs into being."

If I recall correctly—I admit that I am paraphrasing now—her argument went something like this: The insistence that one must situate oneself in the conversation in order to engage in criticism amounts to a shift in emphasis from footnote to text. It is as if the old "pocket bibliography," in which, in the first footnote, a critic listed the major predecessor texts, were moved from footnote to introduction in an effort to justify the critical argument. This development represents more than a "block/move" instruction to the critic's hard disk, for it involves a major expansion of the critical text. As long as the discussion was in the footnotes, the matter of "situating" a particular critique was limited, and sometimes even ignored.

Recently, an interest in theory among Renaissance critics shifted the focus from the arguments advanced and evidence adduced to preconceptions and underlying assumptions of the critic. In order for criticism to establish its claim to attention, it must first situate itself with respect to this ongoing discussion, in effect, acknowledge its own philosophical, literary and ethical assumptions and predilections.

"The older practice," she said, "indicated acquiescence to duty. Our predecessors went along with the accumulation of references out of respect for the received system of bibliographic research and rational argument, not because they believed in the inherent value of secondary sources. That is why the footnotes were seldom slip-shod or unprofessional, but, rather, scrupulously checked for accuracy. Pocket bibliographies were meant to be thorough, consistent and fair representations of one's reading in preparation for the critical task at hand."

"But they were still just footnotes!" he exclaimed, "— no more than proof that the critic had accomplished a required, if meaningless, task, and so [here, his words took on a measure of scorn] had paid obeisance to older specialists in the field. The shared assumption was that all of the secondary works taken together were less important than the subject of their conversation—namely, the object of dispute, let us say, Spenser's *The Faerie Queene*. The older practice accepted that object without question. This was not criticism, but an agglomeration of titles read. The pocket bibliography was the generic expression of an institutional practice, which, in turn, expressed a shared system of mindless repetition. Thank God, we are well rid of it."

He knew, I think, that his opponent had sensed an advantage in his annoyance, for he cast a quick but worried glance in my direction. Although I had heard versions of their ongoing debate many times before, I pretended that I had nothing more important to do than listen. Actually, I was taking mental notes on what seemed to me an interesting development in the way critics talked about the Renaissance.

"By acceding to the pocket bibliography," she was saying, "critics accepted that, even as an essay was being written and read, it was already on its way to someone else's pocket bibliography: doomed to the forgetfulness of an obligatory mention. Resistance to so swift a dispatch is not hard to understand. Roland Barthes signals a reaction—retaliation. Insisting that their work is important, literary critics demanded full disclosure—in the text proper—of the philosophical, social, religious and gender biases of the critic. Criticism leaped from drab footnote to bright page: a value in and of itself. And what critic would argue against this expansion from skeletal footnote to full-blown critical discussion, or openly advocate an ignominious retreat to the bottom of the page or to the end of the essay—and this often in a lesser font size?"

"You are missing the theoretical point," he insisted. "Nowadays, critics are more sophisticated about language."

"Maybe," she said. "The problem is that this custom of 'situating' the critic, in turn, is in danger of becoming, like the pocket bibliography, ossified. Having established that criticism is important, even justifiably the focus of critical commentary in its own right, critics find that the requirement that they situate themselves has become hard to explain, and even harder to defend. For once a critical practice becomes predictable, it opens itself to skeptical inquiry."

"You are trivializing the attack on theory, as if it were only a symptom of waning interest. It is more like an orchestrated reaction on the part of a threatened, white, male gerontocracy."

"Careful!" I put in. "Some of my best friends are white men over fifty."

"Is a yawn a reaction?" she went on, ignoring my remark.

"I assume you are a card-carrying, dues-paying member of the Association of Literary Scholars and Critics," he said. "And I am not talking about waning interest, which has been exaggerated by aging apologists of tradition," he added. (His stress on "aging" was a barb aimed at me.) "Postmodern criticism frees us to explore affinities with the social sciences. Just as it helps to know who is looking at what culture, situating the critic's perspective is essential in vetting the critical account."

"I'm not so sure," she said. "Nor do all critics across the age spectrum find the matter of waning interest in theory a trivial concern. For some, it is an inextirpable symptom of intellectual ferment and change. My doubt concerns your 'necessity' talk. If taken too literally, the bias toward situating oneself, and the 'necessity' talk that it seems to encourage, may already have created a literary demand of one genre of criticism (New Historicism), which then lays claim to that generic feature as a norm."

"So?"

"If I am correct in my impression," she said, "then my efforts to situate myself in a conversation in which that genre plays a part may lead to an impasse, or at least to my impression of an impasse. Tell me. How am I to proceed? For even if, in situating myself, I am telling something true about myself (that is, saying with conviction something that *might* be so about my own beliefs: your notion of the critic's perspective), it does not follow that I know where I am situated in the conversation. For before I can know that, first I must know where that conversation is situated in the ongoing conversation, which may require my familiarity with many voices, some of which I have not yet heard."

He tried to break in, but she hurried on.

"Suppose for the moment that our critical conversation concerns directions to and from an abyss. Further suppose that something of value, say, our understanding of the language in which these directions are encoded, were at stake. Then before I act upon instructions to move away from the abyss, I must be able to differentiate the indications (sounds, gestures, facial expressions) of 'toward' and 'away from.' As Wittgenstein put it, I must learn a language and the 'form of life' of which that language is an organizing instrument."

"Then you *are* conceding that we must situate ourselves in the conversation?"

"Not exactly. I could say that I think so, but how would that help elucidate or relieve my concern about the conversation itself, or about the mechanism of my situating myself in it? You might testify that in such and such a case of self-situating you were helped to an understanding of that critical text; but we must allow for individual, even for eccentric, variations. We can easily imagine ourselves confident of where we are at one moment, yet confused the next—even while standing on the 'same' street corner. You have not overcome my doubts about your 'necessity' talk. But suppose I admit that I situate myself even by raising questions about situating myself. So I situate myself by mentioning Wittgenstein."

"Situate yourself? You do more than that. You expose your bias, which is precisely my point. When I say that the critic must do this, I am only pointing out that such exposure will be present, either overtly or covertly. When you mention Wittgenstein, you imply that, before proceeding with any critique you might offer, your audience must familiarize itself with Wittgenstein."

"With *Philosophical Investigations*?"

"Yes."

"And *The Blue and Brown Books*?"

"I suppose so."

"Surely his *Remarks on Colour*? It's a very late work." His eyes narrowed. "And *On Certainty*—written about the same time, as was at least Appendix 6 of *Remarks on the Foundations of Mathematics*." Now he registered a measure of suspicion. "And perhaps Ray Monk's biography?"[1]

I believe she almost smiled herself at that point.

"I didn't hear you say *that*!" he said.

"Perhaps not, but were you listening? And must all communication be verbal? What about my facial expressions? I intended to say such and such, and surely *my* intentions must be taken into *your* account of them."

"Oh, come on, now. Surely no expression is perfect. Even Wittgenstein set the 'picture theory' of language aside."

"Are you sure of that?" she asked. "He may have complicated the picture of his picture theory with his figure of an 'album' of 'sketches.' But in any case I do not intend at this time to argue the picture theory of language. You ignored my comment on nonverbal communication at some peril to the notion of language that I do think relevant here. If you remove my intention from my expression, what is left? Perhaps you misunderstand what I have said. Which books do I think you should read before I have situated myself, and my critical project can proceed?"

"Well, you mentioned *Philosophical Investigations* and *The Blue and Brown Books,* a ... ah ... few other books in the Wittgenstein canon, and maybe Monk's biography. And then your nod at my mention of Wittgenstein's 'picture theory' of language may have implied that we should read the *Tractatus,* too."

"So you did understand me, even though I did not specifically refer to the *Tractatus.* You responded to my intention. Perhaps I can further situate my project by asking what you inferred from my situating myself regarding your acquaintance with Wittgenstein's *Remarks on Frazer's Golden Bough?*"

"Not much. So is it required, then, or only recommended reading before we carry on?"

"You do get my point." She chose to ignore his sarcasm. "In order to proceed, with my thought adequately situated, you must spend the preceding few decades reading and rereading Wittgenstein. And this instruction follows from my following the custom of situating myself. I tell you what I think is important to your understanding of anything I proceed to say about Spenser or about the Renaissance, and this entails demands that are implicit in the demand that I situate myself prior to proceeding with my critique. Thus, I situate myself in such a way as to elucidate the problem of situating myself as a non-problem, which is the Wittgensteinian way. The point is that so-called problems of criticism, which include the problem of situating the critic, do not emanate from the objects of critical study, but from our insistence that we say something unsayable about them: 'The difficulty in philosophy is to say no more than we know'" (*BBB* 45).

"Do you mean to say that, after all the 'problematizing' that has received grant support and reached print during the last epoch, not one critical problem has survived or been created?"

"I did not say that, but—you are right—I meant to say it. You are getting quick on your feet, but you forgot to note that I also intended to say that, just as critical problems vanish under intensive linguistic scrutiny, they also may be called or recalled into being by the generic demands of habitual problematizing."

"Then in effect you do admit that critical problems ex-ist? This must be a moment of weakness! You have never conceded that before."

"Well, suppose I were to say that the sonnet does not exist? Would you not pop right back with: 'Perhaps not, but surely sonnets do?' Do we take love-sick lovers seriously these days? (Somebody somewhere might.) As we approach the twenty-first century, is belief in unobtainable mis-tresses untenable? Must there be such individuals before one can imagine that someone whom someone else cares for is, for that someone, out of reach?"

"If a line of thought confuses me," he broke in, "I am (at least under our form of government) surely permitted to say that this is a critical, or philosophical, or social, or moral, or spiritual dilemma."

"Perhaps so. But then I am no lawyer. I will say that I know few people (and they seem to me harmless) who would exert themselves to stop you."

"Well, whether you admit it or not, you have conceded that no good purpose would be served by stepping around the critical custom of situating yourself."

"I see no purpose in trying to situate my remarks in a conversation which, someone might say, I do not under-stand. Indeed, an ungenerous critic might even say that I do not understand the underlying motives of my own con-tribution to my mistaken drift of the conversation. 'A philosophical problem,' Wittgenstein writes, 'has the form: "I don't know my way about"' [*PI* §123]. If I say, 'Follow me,' does this mean that I know the terrain?"

"I'll bite. Obviously not."

"Well, if I remove my blindfold, will this affect your confidence in my lead? We need not resort to authority to answer the question, 'Is the cliff this way or that?' Or

'Could this figure have meant thus or so in Renaissance England?'"

"Now, this *is* trivial. Everyone knows we have the OED."

"We have the OED and the repository from which the OED was extrapolated. But that is not my point here. We can, if we wish, argue about the generic propriety of insisting that readers acquaint themselves with Wittgenstein, but the practice of 'privileging' certain authors is already part of the custom of situating the critic."

"You are really out of touch," he said. "The focus has shifted. Do you know the volume subtitled *Literary Theory and Seventeenth-Century English Poetry*? The editors explain *why* the New Historicists, for instance, situate themselves. By turning from 'religious history' and 'the history of genres' [Harvey x], they create 'radically new understandings of familiar texts,' thus forcing 'us to reexamine the critical, historical and cultural presuppositions on which our readings are based' [Harvey ix]. The 'new historicists' have overcome discussions of poetry as transcendental objects removed from history, having in effect transcended the limits of criticism unmindful of the 'structures of political authority' (xi), past and present."

"Have they, indeed?"

"It annoys you, but they have."

"Revolutionary rhetoric," she mused. "And how have they so extraordinarily overcome old limits?"

"By situating themselves within a body of readings. Here, read!"

He plunked an open book in front of her and pointed. Her back stiffened as she read in a stentorian falsetto:

> Thus, while quite eclectic in their use of theoretical models, many recent critics find most consistently helpful those writers who can help articulate those [presumably the "new"?] strategies: Marx, Althusser, Foucault, Freud, Derrida, Lacan, Irigaray. Critics now working on Renaissance literature are far more likely than their predecessors to interpret their task as demystification rather than celebration,

maintaining a skeptical distance from the belief structures of the writers they discuss. (Harvey xi).

"This sounds familiar," she added. "Do you see why I worry? These 'New Historicists' claim to be more self-aware—more alert to the presuppositions underlying critical statements as critical statements—than were their predecessors. But this self-situating list of readings, and the claim asserted that these 'helpful' writers 'help' the 'new historicists' articulate their own 'strategies,' seem, by their circularity, to bring the claim of self-situating self-awareness into question. Besides, the list is incomplete. If 'demystification' is a serious interest, why are the names of world-class demystifiers—such as Moore, Russell, Frege, Carnap, Quine, and (above all) Ludwig Wittgenstein—so conspicuously missing? Can't we imagine skepticism extended to the seemingly unexamined and even unrecognized assumption that reading this set of authors ('Marx . . . Irigaray') is relevant to an understanding of Renaissance texts—even more relevant than texts usually cited by the fallacious predecessors? What is the criterion for deciding which texts are 'helpful'—to what purpose—and why? Which 'strategies' are themselves 'helpful' in understanding Renaissance texts? What do we mean by 'helpful'? What do we mean by 'understanding'? Do the commentators mean that the 'new historicists' maintain a uniformly 'skeptical distance' from 'belief structures,' or is their distance only from 'belief structures' of 'writers they discuss'? Are 'belief structures' always irrelevant to consideration of Renaissance poets? Or are privileged 'belief structures' ('Marx . . . Irigaray') *a priori* exempt from the need for 'skeptical distance,' and therefore immune to criticism?"

He snatched the book from her hands, but she persisted.

"New Historicists praise 'New Historicists' 'for counteracting an ideological system that uses aestheticism or spirituality to conceal politically oppressive tactics' [Harvey x] by raising what one of the 'new historicists' calls 'fundamental questions about the kinds of narrativizations that produce conventional literary history' [Goldberg "Dating" 199]. But the question soon arises whether this 'counteracting an ideological system' proceeds as if terms such as 'conventional' and 'literary' and 'history' designate recognizable sets, the boundaries of which can be easily drawn and agreed upon. What information emerges from this ideological situating? The question at hand concerns the date of composition of Milton's Sonnet 19. Was the poem written, as some critics suppose, in 1643–44, or, as others have argued, as late as 1655? Instead of crediting new or old documentary evidence relevant to the issue, the critic (Jonathan Goldberg) asserts the value of what he calls a 'reading' which imagines the 'possibility' ('the possibility that [he is] imagining' [201]) that Milton revised and rewrote the poem over a period of a dozen years."

"Okay," he said. "So you know the collection."

"The issue is 'what constitutes grounds,'" she persisted. "Goldberg expresses impatience with 'conventional' critics because of what he calls their shared 'teleological imperatives' [Goldberg "Dating" 204]. Can you see my difficulty in situating myself in such a conversation? What 'teleological imperatives' *should* they share, and how does my self-situating lead me to know this? I cannot derive the proposed answer from my self-situating in Wittgenstein: An ideological critique must resist the complicities revealed 'in [a particular "conventional" historicist's] essay' [204]. Rather, my self-situating constrains me to ask: Why must it? or, Suppose it doesn't? or, Is a nonideological critique subject to the same necessity? or, Are nonideological critiques possible? If nonideological critiques are impossible, then it seems to follow that all are subject to the unexplained cause of the necessary condition of resistance to the very complicities exhibited 'in [the non-New Historicist's] essay.' But then this would either deny the hypothesis that nonideological critiques are impossible or set the hypothesis concerning the necessary condition of resistance aside."

"The New Historicists," he said, "talk about 'the false

grounds of traditional historical scholarship' [Goldberg "Dating" 205] because they read Freud and Derrida: 'The temporality sketched here could be called, after Freud, Nachträglichkeit, and would insist that what is retrospectively constructed is not necessarily, is necessarily *not* what was; rather, in Derrida's elegant phrase, it would be "a past that has never been present," nor would it be present in its rewriting.' They proffer a critique of naive, reconstructionist historicism."

"Perhaps," she answered. "Although the unaddressed philosophical issue of 'other minds' lurks in this kind of Renaissance talk, I must set that issue aside to question the implied assertion, which you accept, that all reconstructions are necessarily burdened by a supplement."

"The poststructuralist," he said emphatically, "recognizes that we imagine—*re*-present—our way from texts to narratives of the past. We fashion a revised and necessarily altered text. We add our own interest."

"But," she said, "if all reconstructions are, *a priori*, altered by addition, then it follows that we are unable to say what the sum was to which that supplement was added. If we allow for the perception of a supplement itself, we must concede a difference between the original and the original as revised by addition, and so the apprehended 'thing itself.'"

She paused as if expecting him to respond, but he just looked at her with raised eyebrows.

"The New Historicist," she continued, "says that the past was not present and has never been present, but he neglects to tell us to whom it was never present. Now isn't this an odd way of talking? I say that you began hearing this sentence in a past that was not present to you, and that you finish hearing it in a present that is not present to you either. And in this taxonomy of experience lies the means of identifying 'the false grounds of traditional scholarship.' But aren't 'false grounds' evident only in contrast to grounds lacking the defining characteristics of falsity? So by what oracular procedure do we perceive the essence of falsity in 'grounds of traditional scholarship'? Do these grounds differ from those by which we perceive the falsity of grounds for untraditional scholarship? Suppose we concede that we may not be able to say with certitude just when Milton wrote Sonnet 19. Does it follow that during the period between 1643 and 1655 that Milton revised the poem? What constitutes evidence of revision? With *Lycidas* and *The Readie and Easie Way*,[2] we have different texts for comparison, as we do with *Cooper's Hill*, 'Sailing to Byzantium,' 'These are the days when Birds come back,' and any number of other works. So the concept of revision has its uses."

"Of course," he broke in, "but Goldberg could point out that there is no one fixed meaning of the word 'revision.'"

"So which of the many possibilities applies here?" she asked.

"Besides," he said, ignoring her question, "if what you say is true, he only claims to be dealing with an imagined possibility."

"Which necessarily derived, on your analysis, from his situation?"

"Yes."

"The list of readings ('Marx . . . Irigaray') and the like?"

"At last we agree on something. Situating the critic concerns differences of opinion on the sorts of readings one must undertake prior to critical inquiry."

"Which, in turn, reflect the interests that prompted their selection."

"That would follow, yes. So let us suppose for the moment that Freud's theories about human intentions are, for the purposes of situating myself, justified. In this case, I might not know the actual motives behind my ideological confession. I might, for instance, 'consciously' or 'unconsciously' advance a spurious advocacy only to please or to avoid offending someone whose good will I think useful."

"Or, perversely, you might agree with that critic, but falsify your opinions in the matter in an unconscious effort to defeat yourself."

"These scenarios might seem implausible," she said, "but theories of the unconscious being what they are, I am in no position to guarantee that my situating of myself in the conversation accords with the requisite candor of the genre. For precisely the same reason, I may doubt the protestations of the ideological positions of other critics, whose self-situating critiques may likewise rationalize unconscious but contradictory assertions. So what, then, am I to make of the demand for candor implicit in the generic situating of myself?"

"These remarks are nothing but a cynical assault on our integrity," he protested, "and they hold only as long as psychoanalytic theories hold, which, if we adhere to our behaviorist creed, is not for long. As cultural materialists, we answer the Freudians' claims by attending to the arguments themselves, not to guesses, which can vary, about their supposed unconscious origins."

"You could, indeed," she said. "And to this answer I would reply with an unequivocal, yes, no and maybe. I did suggest (though I did not assert) that were we to imagine that psychoanalytic theories were legitimate, we could not be sure that we were not, in situating ourselves ideologically, actually resisting exposure of our beliefs in the matter at hand. You say that we can break off our imagining the world according to those assumptions any time we wish, and I admit that I know of no way to restrain you from thinking so. But you must concede that, should you allow that line of thought to play out a bit further, your effort to break off, indeed, your challenge to psychoanalytic theories regarding unconscious motives, might give strong evidence of resistance to our unacknowledged feelings about motives in situating ourselves in the ideological framework of the discussion."

"You mean that we attempt to break off the game at just the moment we most desire to continue play?"

"Well, play did continue, and yet we have not decided whether, in continuing my attempt to situate myself, I am situating myself or only trying to persuade you that I have done so, while in fact masking my true aim of situating myself from both of us. How, if we are barred from knowing whether we are honest with ourselves, do we know if we are being honest with each other?

"Suppose I situate myself in such and such a way (as feminist or Marxist or historicist or materialist or conservative or radical or structuralist or deconstructionist or whatever) because I rightly or wrongly consider it in my interest to do so."

"Because that is the way the wind is blowing!"

"An appropriate figure, even if you employ it with a hostile edge. Be that as it may, in agreeing that I act in my own interest, are we not perforce imputing rationality to my act of situating myself? And is this not precisely the issue that, as one New Historicist puts it, New Historicism's 'rhetorical-ethical strategies' [Montrose "Essay" 16] want to question?"

"But you said yourself that we could set the presumption of irrationality aside."

"We can, if we wish, imagine a system of thought in which what people say can be equated with what they say minus tergiversation and deception. If we cannot, what follows in our analysis other than some *a posteriori* observation touching the limits of our imagination?"

"This line of thought is getting us nowhere. You are determined to resuscitate the most moribund of hypostatized abstractions, the hoariest of them being 'authorial intention.' We have all witnessed the demise of hypostatized authors, so how can we now allow them hypostatized intentions? And this is all your 'saying less tergiversation and deception' amounts to. Cultural materialists—and make no mistake about it, we are in the strong majority in this department—unanimously reject your basic premise, which is, if I understand correctly, that the new requirement of situating oneself in the conversation is now, besides being old and ossificd, incoherent and irrational."

"It may not help to protest that I did not describe the requirement that I situate myself as necessarily ossified or irrational. I merely expressed my doubt that I am able to meet the explicit demand of the genre for candor, or, less drastically, a pretense of candor. If deception is built into our system of assumptions, then I cannot meet the demand without deception, in which case the more I try to comply with the imperative that I situate my remarks, the more I run the risk of misleading the discussants."

"But you refuse to see that the problem is right *there* in your notion of yourself," he said with feeling. "You refuse to see how thoroughly even your objections to the norms of situating the critic encode and valorize the norms which you exert yourself to discredit. Your project fails to come to grips with the subject/object problem. Just because you say there are no critical problems does not mean that there are none. You have yet to confront those metacritics who have met the challenge of the subject/object problem by recognizing the social determinacy of all cultural artifacts."

"Criticism as symptomatology?"

"Perhaps 'semiotic' would be a better term for what we do with cultural aritifacts," he said. "Or character analysis. But 'symptomatology' does touch the normative aspects of the conversation today. And, after all, it is within the current conversation that we are trying to situate ourselves."

"That sounds right. But does your implied direction not lead us back down the path from which we just emerged? You tell me that metacritics have addressed the problem of the subject/object distinction, and there may be value in what you say."

"We say that criticism cannot disentangle a poet's text from the critic. So it's no good talking, as one critic does,[3] about Milton's reading of Spenser, because unmediated texts of neither poet are available for commentary. This is so because criticism is ineluctably culture-bound."

"Your New Historicists seem less certain," she intruded slyly, "whether this belief is an occasion for joy or for sorrow."

"New Historicists," he shot back, "align themselves with anthropology and cultural materialism. When Stephen

Greenblatt adopts a credo, he turns to anthropologist Clifford Geertz: 'There is no such thing as a human nature independent of culture'" (Greenblatt *Renaissance* 3).

"You repeat yourself," she said, "but you fail to say how this remark helps us situate ourselves. We insist that two objects never appear except in tandem; or that, although two terms are not synonymous in ordinary usage, when applied in what Greenblatt calls 'anthropological criticism' (Greenblatt 4), they designate the same sorts (if not the same set) of artifacts. But the coincidence of the one with the other thing, here, is absolute. Suppose I say that the two triangles that I am now imagining coincide. How, if I imagine their interdependence or convergence as super-imposition, do I know that I am not imagining the convergence of three or more rather than of two? Wittgenstein writes: '"A thing is identical with itself."—There is no finer example of a useless proposition, which yet is connected with a certain play of the imagination. It is as if in imagination we put a thing into its own shape and saw that it fitted' [*PI* §216]. And now the critic compounds the error by imagining the congruity of a set of *n* distinguishable items. The spatial figure has come to lead a life of its own. Odd."

"You," he said, "are confusing the issue, which, even if conceptually muddled to begin with, has its uses. And just when you seemed on the verge of conceding that New Historicism inclines toward metacriticism. Poststructuralist criticism assumes that critics themselves are necessarily the subjects of any thoughtful critique."

"I fear that I must agree with you here. They do appear to assume that."

"Let me give you an example," he said. "In the metacritical mode, one Spenser critic, writing about another Spenser critic's Spenser criticism, describes a turn from 'hard-headed empiricism' to 'tough-minded theorizing'" (Montrose "Essay" 8).

"'Tough-minded theorizing'? An oxymoron. And aren't you now proving my point?"

"Not at all," he insisted. "The critique concerns, not just Spenser or his texts or times, but the critic, Harry Berger, Jr., as well."

"Precisely. And since Louis Montrose asserts that 'the text in which Berger represents Spenser is also the text in which Spenser represents Berger' ["Essay" 15], it follows that, with Montrose's text representing Berger representing Spenser, we have a bracketing function in what, theoretically, we can project as an open-ended set of refigurations of Spenser critics. It is a mark of what Louis Montrose calls 'New Historicism' [15] that it elevates the critic and the critique to something like primary importance (in the sense of something which precedes—perhaps 'prior' would be a better term). Hence, in another context, Montrose is as concerned about his own ideological predisposition as a critic as he is, in the other circumstance, about Berger's. 'In an attempt at methodological consistency,' Montrose writes, 'I begin with a brief and explicit programmatic statement intended to situate my own discourse in relation to some current issues in literary and social theory, on the one hand, and to some traditions and trends in English Renaissance studies, on the other'" (Montrose "Subject" 303).

"Good for him," he said. "The concept of mediation is central to the New Historicist project of historicizing so-called literary artifacts. Montrose is right. There is no such thing as 'Spenser' or a 'Spenserian text' except as these 'constructs' are mediated, that is, *re*-presented by someone or something between the critic and the proposed subject of criticism. It is no good talking about 'a full and authentic past. . . .'"

"Because only partial, unauthentic 'pasts' are available?"

"*Because*," he persisted, "'a lived material existence' does not exist 'that has not already been mediated by the surviving . . . documents'" ("Subject" 305).

"I think Wittgenstein's famous remark on the unknowable state of other minds fits here," she said: "'In one way this is wrong, and in another nonsense' [*PI* §246]. Even if all documents had survived, they would still be mediated by our or someone else's partial perusal and interpretation. The epistemological condition is fundamentally, foundationally, essentially one of 'social imbedment of all modes of writing,' and that includes the genres of 'history' and 'criticism.'"

"Right! And this is what bothers you. Your ideology is exposed. Because, as Montrose points out, 'bourgeois humanism' (self-situating is not devoid of normalization) 'is now (at least in theory) defunct'" (306).

"Perhaps so," she said, "but maybe not. Will you accept your own example of Montrose as a test case?"

"He is one of the more articulate New Historicists," he said.

"And he articulates a very general principle here."

"That 'bourgeois humanism' is 'defunct.' Who would deny this?"

"The question is not whether debunking 'bourgeois humanism' is now a bandwagon or a gravy train, but whether the argument here holds water. Although some critics might applaud the effort to replace an apologetics of discredited Christian humanism with an apologetics of discredited Marxist humanism (Montrose does refer to Marxist antihumanism [334n], thus allowing the inference that at least one species of Marxism has yet to be discredited), I doubt that the metaphysics of the latter in practice offers a measurable improvement upon the former. For instance, when Montrose turns to history, theoretical nomenclature disappears. It is, presumably, only the following kinds of statements that are 'New' or 'Marxist' in their historical perspective: 'At this historical juncture, the body politic inhered in the body of the prince' [307]. Montrose talks about self-situating as an exercise in class consciousness: 'In this sense, of course, Elizabeth Tudor was herself a gendered and socially situated subject' [308–09]. Seriously, now, this is an odd declaration. If a doubt comes over me, how am I to situate myself to make it known? Does this woman have gender? 'Has this room a length?' [*BBB*

30]. Can my doubt about Elizabeth Tudor's gender serve a useful purpose?"

"You have missed the point again," he said. "The issue here is the sense in which documents are 'mediated.' It isn't Elizabeth's gender that counts, at least no more than the historicist's perception of it, for *that* is what 'mediates' or is 'mediated.'"

"Very well, then, by what means do we test the assertion that Mary Tudor's will, as a document, is 'mediated'? By whom? To what degree? I press this question because it might be pivotal in my own self-situating, for, presumably, one mediates wills, poems and critical texts in precisely the same way. As the cultural materialist might say, they are shaped by and shape the viewing subject. But if we know this, then we must also know how to distinguish mediation from nonmediation. So what is the alternative to mediation? Consider this sentence: 'Shortly before she died in 1558, England's Catholic queen, Mary Tudor, reluctantly designated her Protestant half-sister Elizabeth as her successor' [307]. Montrose claims that since all consciousness of the past is mediated, statements which mediate consciousness must also be so. But after I agree or disagree with this principle, how will my understanding alter the mediated or unmediated sense of Mary Tudor's will? Suppose I say that I should have the same mediated or unmediated understanding, regardless of my understanding that my understanding was or was not mediated or unmediated. Would I not, then, be asserting the inutility of the distinction between mediated and unmediated understanding of the past?"

"You *must* admit that Montrose's self-situating approach concerns what he calls the 'rhetorical-ethical strategies of the writer' ("Essay" 16], meaning Spenser, to some extent."

"Even if I must—and 'necessity' talk still bothers me—his emphasis is on the Spenser critic, in this case, himself, in the other, Harry Berger. I have noted the normative feature of critical self-situating, and expressed my doubts and apprehensions. Although he does allude to an 'imaginative community of the text,' Montrose registers disapproval, not of Spenser, but of Berger: 'Some readers may think me churlish, or at least impolite, to criticize the author in my introduction to his work' [16]. Here, social judgment forms itself in an almost Kantian imperative of expectation: one judges, and (or so that?) one may also be judged.

"I dwell on this instance of self-situating metacriticism, not because it is any better or any worse than other such examples, but because of its candid expression of interest in criticism as 'symptomatology.' To clarify this point I might suggest that this critique of Berger as symptomatic of the self-situating process in criticism may be construed, in turn, as symptomatic of an issue confronting meta-metacriticism.'

"Meta-metacriticism? What is that?"

"What I am doing now," she said. "Montrose addresses, not Spenser, but Berger addressing Spenser. I address Montrose addressing Berger addressing Spenser. Montrose directs attention, not to what one critic thinks has been misunderstood as Spenser's 'numbingly' ethical interest [Paglia 171], but toward the 'rhetorical-ethical strategies of the' Spenser critic. Not surprisingly, then, he focuses, not on the Letter to Ralegh, but on Harry Berger's 'confession' that his 'New-Critical' practice delayed his awareness 'of the basic structural forces and cultural changes of which it [the controversy concerning "text versus performance"] is a superficial symptom' ["Essay" 3n]. Montrose faults Berger for a serious lapse of omission: 'What today strikes us—perhaps I should say, what now strikes me—as conspicuously unrepresented in this model is a dimension of historical experience that is tangibly sociopolitical: there is little explicit or sustained acknowledgment of the poet as a gendered and classed subject acting and acted upon in a particular society, or of the poem's production—its writing, dissemination and reading—as a social act' [7]. Whatever this critique of Berger may say about Berger, it seems to require that Spenser criticism, subsumed beneath the general category of 'criticism,' answer to metaphysical necessity: 'The interpretive activity of the critic of Renaissance literature is, like its object, a production of ideology'" (7).

"Okay," he said abruptly. "So we see here a recurrence of the *Zeitgeist* theory. So what? New Historicists are still historicists."

"But this is *Zeitgeist* with a twist," she said. "Poems and critiques are understood as representations, not of thought, but of the origins of thought in a system of production (not spirit but flesh). Time has been replaced by the number of ideologies extant at a given time. The critic cannot escape from the prisonhouse of ideology, in that the critical artifact produced, under whatever guise, 'actively instatiates' those already imposed 'values, beliefs and experiences.'"

"Montrose," he interrupted, "is only saying that this critique, with its internalized expressions, is (like Spenser's poetry) 'itself a historically determinate social act'" (7).

"Determinate," she added, "even if the critic does not know it. So, happily, Montrose cannot lose the argument, although he can also not help making it."

"Not at all. You imply that the stage is set for a psychodrama of moral judgment, but in fact, the action has already transpired in the 'mediated' past. Montrose perceives an evolution in what he calls (paraphrasing Berger) 'Bergerian dynamics' (2). He is praising Berger."

"He does suggest that Berger's criticism is getting better (which may be so), but it is not getting better because Berger any more ably comes to grips with Spenser, Spenser's texts, or the times in which those texts were written. Rather, while on the one hand Montrose congratulates Berger for resisting 'intellectual foreclosure' (3), on the other he praises him for foreclosing (assuming, of course, that reversals are a species of foreclosure) in one area of his critique: 'I must note the androcentric bias of Berger's language here, a bias he has since acknowledged and repudiated' (2n).

"Praise mixes with blame here, as Montrose braces Berger with his past 'bias' of 'androcentrism,' and the issue of moral concern slips from Spenser's 'general intention' to the critic's moral integrity. The issue is ideological bias, with its propriety to be decided by the metacritic. Hence,

Montrose sharpens the impression that guilt is an issue by pointing to Berger's recantation: 'a bias he has since acknowledged and repudiated.' We are to infer that one's recantation may be taken as a sign of guilt; if Berger repudiated a past action, it must have been wrong. We perceive, beyond a streak of pietism here, a pietism parasitic on a deeper insistence that somehow Roland Barthes must have been right all along. If a critic's biases are important, then, *a fortiori*, criticism itself must be important."

"Are you claiming that Berger has not changed or developed in his thought? Are you saying that, even though he confessed, he did not offend?"

"Such questions indicate that my efforts to situate myself have not succeeded, which was exactly what I predicted would be the case. Do we not know of cases where people confessed to offenses they only wish they had committed? I am only expressing doubt, not final judgment, in the matter. If I may retrace my steps and contextualize Wittgenstein's earlier remark more fully: 'The difficulty in philosophy is to say no more than we know. E.g., to see that when we have put two books together in their right order we have not thereby put them in their final places' (*BBB* 45). Remember, then, that I expressed doubts from the beginning about all attempts to situate oneself in the current conversation. I also questioned the practice of reading motives everywhere we look. Not that motives do not matter; they do, especially to those who hold them. It is possible to impute motives, even to extract unsent messages, from many of the sayings we encounter. But what will serve as a guide to discriminating their propriety?

"Ask yourself this question: Is it preternatural candor that leads me to confess that I have no confidence in my situating myself? Is it my uncertainty here that makes the situating of others seem to me doubtful or even spurious?"

"How can you say *that*? By what warrant can *anyone* say that another's self-situating is spurious? With respect to what criterion are they spurious?"

"I did not say that they were spurious, but only that they left me with that impression. Suppose you hand me an example of your situating of yourself—say, an essay—with the request that I offer helpful criticism, and I return the essay to you with the instruction that you make it sincere. You might look at your pages, perhaps even make minor changes, and say—well, what? 'There now, I have made it sincere?' Was the predecessor version insincere? Was the sincere alternative present, but only excluded, as the predecessor version came into being? Then why did you put it forward? Do you now look at it and ask yourself: 'How am I to remove my insincerity?' Do not misunderstand me. I make no claim to insincerity. I only claim to doubt that my situating of myself in the current conversation is either feasible or helpful."

"So how," he asked with distain, "would your critique of the genre assist me in convincing *you*? Your mind is made up."

"This strikes me as a good question, but then I think any question I can't answer is a good one."

"You question the formal demand, but offer no hint of guidance to critics who must, as things now stand, situate themselves?"

"I am not only puzzled by the question, and so think it a good one, but I neither know the answer to it, nor how to suggest that you proceed in situating yourself. You tell me. How do I situate myself without running the risk of a self-serving self-statement? We are both faculty members of The University of California?" He shrugged, and she continued. "The University permits (but does not require) a 'Self Statement' to accompany personnel files sent forward for action."

"So?"

"So will you concede that these documents bear a family resemblance to the self-situating exercises in criticism that we have been discussing?"

"Are you implying that many—or even any—of these self-statements are fraudulent?"

"Do you find them neatly balanced between litotes and hyperbole?"

"So hyperbole is an obligatory trope of self-situating?"

"Not necessarily. Self statements have become a generic, if unhelpful, feature of certain kinds of critical discussion. But hyperbole is not ladled on after the self-serving artifact has been fashioned. We need not deny the veracity of Berger's claim that he offended, nor that of Montrose's stance of forgiveness."

"This is pernicious. Antediluvian! Of course, our perspective on ourselves might look, to a Martian, like something other than a straight reportorial account. So you posit a Platonic, discredited standard of [he uttered this term with scorn] 'objectivity.'"

"Not at all. I'm not sure what such an account would look like. My modest aim is to raise questions about the generic demands of self-situating in criticism. What do you expect to learn about literature from my attempt to situate myself? Remember Wittgenstein's words:

> —And you really get such a queer connexion when the philosopher tries to bring out *the* relation between name and thing by staring at an object in front of him and repeating a name or even the word "this" innumerable times. For philosophical problems arise when language *goes on holiday*. [*PI* §38]

It would be easy for critics who have not proceeded far beyond the *Tractatus* [obviously, she *had* heard that he regarded her as a positivist] to misunderstand this passage, to give it a hard edge, as if Wittgenstein were saying that language must always be about something useful. Guilt is always guilt; confession invariably exposes both culprit and wrongdoing; criticism is serious business. But sometimes language, even critical language, takes a breather. There is no harm in that; sometimes nonsense syllables are just the ones we need to fill an awkward moment. But if we think that the levers of the locomotive engine engage the mechanism when in fact they do not, we may be disappointed in the results of our working the detached levers. If we expect talk about ourselves to do work beyond talk about ourselves, well, Wittgenstein warns that 'an occult process'

[*PI* §38] may find its way into nonmotion, as 'language *goes on holiday*,' and we are left with the erroneous impression that we have encountered a critical problem."

She was still talking, but he had turned away.

"I thought we were having a conversation," he called back in reproach.

"We were," she said. "We still are." Then she turned to me, as if for support from a reasonable and fair source. (Many in the department regard me as a peacemaker—or, as the monists have been known to say behind my back, a fence-sitter.) But, since I had expressed no partisan interest in the conversation, I felt obliged to shrug and change the subject.

"He did have a point. About the vote in the department, I mean." Now her eyes narrowed as she fixed me in her gaze. Aware that a new dialogue threatened to erupt with me as a participant, I looked with feigned panic at my watch.

"Ah, yes," she was saying, "the vote. Was *that* sign of intellectual ennui the unacknowledged topic of our conversation?"

But, almost simultaneously, with another flourish of my watch, I said: "Running late. Will you be around for lunch? I want to talk to you about Spenser. What do you make of Paglia's notion that he wrote pornography?"

2

Blindness and Apperception

Spenser, Pornography and Politics

> In philosophy it is not enough to learn
> in every case *what* is to be said about a subject, but also
> *how* one must speak about it. We are always having to
> begin by learning the method of tackling it.
> — Wittgenstein, *Remarks on Colour*

The critic Camille Paglia claims that "English literary distinction begins in the Renaissance and is the creation of one man, Edmund Spenser" (Paglia 170). This praise is registered with rhetorical verve (Paglia has captured something of the hyperbolic style of her literary mentor, Friedrich Nietzsche), and while we may find the statement amusing, I do not think we can be surprised. In the past few decades, we have seen a surge of interest in critical analyses based on gender differences, sexual proclivities, and their relations—real or imagined—to social and political history. Recently, the Center for Renaissance Studies at The Newberry Library announced a "Program . . . made possible by a generous grant from the National Endowment for the Humanities" with such "lectures" and "pedagogical strategies" as "Gender and Literacy," "Gender and Religion," "Gender and Institutions," "Genders and Sexualities," and (less felicitously) "Gender and Race/Ethnicity." So it seems "normal" when a critic speaks of Spenser's *magnum opus*, not as evidence that "British women" of the period enlisted in and advanced the cause of their own liberty, but rather that "the liberated woman is the symbol of the English Renaissance . . ." (Paglia 178).

Extending her argument of gender difference, Paglia holds that, typically, Spenser's description of Verdant in the Bower of Bliss is the literary analogue of Botticelli's *Venus and Mars*. Accordingly, sex and violence pair naturally, as everywhere in great art as in life "[t]he masculine hurls itself at the feminine in an eternal circle of pursuit and flight" (Paglia 185). Because of our familiarity with Renaissance gender talk, this statement has a topical interest. And supposing for the moment that we accede to the critical estimate of Spenser that Paglia is presenting, we simultaneously elevate Spenser's prestige in relation to other poets. Perhaps we remember pleasures we have taken in reading notable passages from *The Faerie Queene* or *The Shepheardes Calender*, or recall the impact of an influential critical study of Spenser. And so far no apparent harm has been done. But in fact we don't believe a word of it. We accede as if to say, "Well, let us see where this kind of talk leads," and then we pause and take that line of thought no further. But why is this? Because a simple compunction built into the literary tradition restrains even ardent Spenserians from characterizing Spenser's work as other than important but derivative (revised Chaucer, recycled Ariosto), and so to hold him beneath the trinity of the highest (Chaucer, Shakespeare, Milton). We have been taught that Shakespeare represents the apex of the English Renaissance, that his achievement defines and shapes our sense of the period.

In chapter 3, we will investigate that teaching, but even at this juncture we must ask "Why should what we have been taught constrain us in what we think about Spenser in relation to Chaucer and Shakespeare?" Perhaps this is the question that Camille Paglia's brash style is meant to address. For not only does Paglia defy the canon, ranking Spenser above Chaucer in the poetic hierarchy, but she makes Spenser the shaping figure of the Elizabethan Age: "His influence upon later writers, beginning with Shakespeare, was incalculable" (170).

1.

Suppose we take Paglia's adjustment of the literary canon as a healthy correction of an overly determined ethical outlook. How do we then explain why Spenser is so widely unread? Conveniently, Paglia takes that fact as proof of her thesis, which is, simply put, that proper admiration of *The Faerie Queene* runs counter to established critical taste. As Paglia perceives the state of Spenser criticism, poorly guided literary dolts publish their Spenserian misprisions in academic journals that (mercifully) nobody reads. Indeed, the argument goes, professional Spenser critics are responsible for the low esteem in which Spenser's great poem is held: "At the moment, *The Faerie Queene* is a great beached whale . . . [and] Spenser is a hostage of his own critics, who have thrown up a thicket of unreadable commentary around him" (Paglia 170). This is harsh criticism. Probably only a minority of critics will believe that Spenserians move, herdlike, in the single direction of distorting Spenser's great poem, but Paglia's statement can, nevertheless, too easily be caricatured as self-serving. A more charitable characterization might hold that Paglia perhaps overstates a justifiable concern that the prose of Spenser critics sometimes obfuscates interesting and even useful observations on Spenser. The problem with this gambit of "evenhandedness" is that it does not really do justice to Paglia's critique, and it leaves unanswered the charge that how Spenser critics talk affects the nature of what they say. Paglia claims that, even if Spenser critics could write clearly, it would do no good, because (and here she reiterates a charge made by John Upton in 1758),[1] they egregiously misread Spenser. In their misunderstanding, academic critics turn *The Faerie Queene* into a "numbingly moralistic" imitation of Chaucer (171), and they do so because they are incapable of grasping "what Spenser was about."

Obviously, this is a serious charge, which, if credible, means that Spenser criticism no less than the hierarchized canon is, at the very least, in need of adjustment. But is Paglia's metacritical assertion fair? Is it reasonable to believe that no more ludicrous a misreading can be imagined than a "numbingly moralistic" Spenser? Does Paglia's characterization of *The Faerie Queene* as a masterpiece of equivocal values merit assent? Questions like this go beyond a critic's lively writing style, touching, in fact, the relation of a critic's "belief" to the critical canon. It is not a matter of an isolated decision regarding one's reactions to Paglia's characterization of the relative merits of Chaucer, Spenser and Shakespeare that is solely at issue. We cannot separate the valuation of the sexual content of *The Faerie Queene* from our sense of the work's literary value, for the simple reason that thematic interest is integral to the literary value of *any* poem. Paglia writes: "Pornography and art are inseparable, because there is voyeurism and voracity in all our sensations as seeing, feeling beings. The fullest exploration of these ideas is Edmund Spenser's Renaissance epic, *The Faerie Queene*" (35). And we want to know what governs reasonable assent or dissent from this assertion and assertions like it.

Wittgenstein warns that we are sometimes misled by language, as if "A *picture* held us captive" (*PI* §115):

> "The general form of propositions is: this is how things are."—That is the kind of proposition that one repeats to

oneself countless times. One thinks that one is tracing the
outline of the thing's nature over and over again, and one
is merely tracing round the frame through which we look
at it. (*PI* §114)

It is as if the grand sweep of Paglia's statement must tell
us something about Spenser—and even about his critics
(Paglia's remarks are aimed at "secondary" as well as "primary" sources). But why must "pornography" and "art" be
inseparable? What does it mean to say that "there is voyeurism and voracity in all our sensations as seeing, feeling beings"? Would it be a mistake to say that, "This is
an odd way of talking about all, or even any, of my 'sensations'"? In criticism, hyperbole invites a perception of
unfairness. Surely not all Spenser commentary is unreadable, for if it were, Paglia would be unable to object to
its unread contents, and we would not be talking about
Paglia's perspective either. Of course, Paglia could always
answer: "This objection depends on too lame a literal understanding of a metaphoric expression. I mean, isn't it
amusing to think of Spenser criticism as a thicket surrounding the reified body of Spenser's works, or of the
naive Spenser critic as a 'to that [good] quite contrary'
Agdistes of moralistic misprision?" Perhaps so. But, again,
the question is: Would that characterization be fair? Should
we believe it? "Well, what do we have in the way of stated
or implied criteria of credibility?" Now, I suggest, we are
in quandary. We may in fact be amused by Paglia's characterization of Spenser critics, but we can neither consent
to nor dissent from the significance of what she says about
them or about *The Faerie Queene*. This is so because,
although her heterodox reading challenges the traditional
canon, her views of sexuality in Spenser are not actually
at odds with entrenched thought on Spenser's poem.
Rather, her remarks are much like many that have appeared from the time of Spenser's "Letter of the Authors
expounding his whole intention" (*Var* 3.167).

I am talking now about the popular view that Spenser

didn't know what his poem was about. If I understand the thinking here correctly, regardless of how strenuously the Spenser critic strives to write "against the grain," the underlying question posed by orthodox and heterodox critics alike concerns the poet's "whole intention." Even if Paglia could "read" (tolerate? decipher?) the prose of Spenser's critics, she would perceive only that they leave out of account the peculiarly Spenserian features of *The Faerie Queene*, namely, its deeply "chthonian daemonism," its "mystic hieraticism of power latent in western sexual personae" (Paglia 170, 171). Hence, the critic's charge against mistaken Spenserians is that, while stressing the ethical, and now even "Protestant," elements (173) in Spenser's poem, misguided critics ignore its wanton features:

> A) *The poetically strongest and most fully realized material in* The Faerie Queene *is pornographic. (Paglia 190)*

Proposition *A* sorts well with Paglia's argument that, in stressing the ethical and religious purpose enunciated by Spenser, Spenser critics have failed to recognized what is "strong" and "fully realized" in the poem. But it follows that if they have been taken in by Spenser's rhetoric ("The generall end"), so has Spenser; for, as this line of argument requires, Spenser's claim that his "generall end" is "to fashion a gentleman or noble person in vertuous and gentle discipline" is palpably false, which is to say incredible.

There is a methodological problem here—a matter, I think, of authority, of whom to believe. A critic emphasizes the erotic content of *The Faerie Queene*, which she imagines to be at loggerheads with Spenser's stated plan. And yet it is this plan that misleads: "Spenser wants good to come out of noble action. But sexual personae have a will of their own" (Paglia 192). Spenser failed in his "generall end," but this cannot be taken as a sign of fault. Rather it is the *sine qua non* of his greatness. Presumably, it need not concern us that the wills of "sexual personae" are steered by critics who have imagined their deeply seated origins in the human psyche. What is important here is the claim that Spenser's "whole intention" in writing *The Faerie Queene* entails elements that he may not have imparted (or, rather, may not have thought to impart) in his own conception of the "generall end . . . to fashion a gentleman." Spenser did not himself recognize that part of the "whole" which now emerges as the dominant value of his great poem. This may seem odd, but Paglia explains why it is so: "Criticism assumes that what Spenser says is what he means. But a poet is not always master of his own poem, for imagination can overwhelm moral intention" (191).

As Wittgenstein suggests, one of the challenges we face in criticism (as in philosophy) "is to say no more than we know" (*BBB* 45). Once we accept (if we do) the idea that Spenser did not say what he meant, or know what he said, we can easily think that he said other, more interesting things instead. For instance, arguing that "Spenser is history's first theorist of aggression, anticipating Hobbes, Sade, Darwin, Nietzsche and Freud" (172), Paglia proclaims that *"The Faerie Queene* is the most extended and extensive meditation on sex in the history of poetry" (188). Although she portrays *The Faerie Queene* as "an encyclopedic catalog of perversions, like Richard Krafft-Ebing's *Psychopathia Sexualis*" (189), she nevertheless recognizes Spenser's affirmation of "Marriage [as] the sanctified link between nature and society," and so concedes that "[s]ex in Spenser must always have a social goal" (189). Here Paglia seems, as her mentor, Harold Bloom, might say, "to veer" from her own thesis, for if Spenser's poem is "always" answerable to "a social goal," then Spenser's supposedly "pornographic" poem must have a moral purpose. In effect, this assertion does not follow from Paglia's statement that Spenser's "generall intention" never gets made. If Spenser included *something* of what he meant to include in his "whole intention," then something of his "generall intention" must remain intact. Paglia claims that, perhaps without "knowing" it, Spenser included a less "humanistic," "chthonian daemonic" element in the poem, and that this element, once introduced, came to lead a life of its own. Moreover, in leading a life of its own, this motif came into destructive conflict with the poet's intention. Spenser was unaware of the contrariness of this "chthonian daemonic" element because he could not recognize it. At the same time, he was also everywhere advancing the cause of such non-"chthonian daemonic" elements as marriage and social good. Now, this seems odd, not because we lack instruction on the "density of language" or the "ambivalence of human attitudes," but because the claim for a "mystic hieraticism of power latent in western sexual personae" (171) implies so univocal a rhetorical force as to render the claim of Spenser's effort to find "the sanctified link between nature and society" unbelievable. Is it possible to focus so completely on "unconscious thought" that one's awareness of conscious expression is impaired?

2.

Returning to the question of fairness, we might be grateful to Paglia for elevating Spenser's place in the canon and still wonder if it is fair to say that Spenser critics are so blinded by prudery that they fail to recognize Spenser's acquaintance with, and exploitation of, the devices of Renaissance sexuality, and even of pornography. Are Spenser critics such prudes that they erroneously find prudery in Spenser's poetry? For many, this seems like an odd notion, because Spenser critics have made notable contributions to this very area of thought. For instance, not long before Paglia's book appeared, David O. Frantz's extensive survey of the subject discussed Spenser's indebtedness to Renaissance pornography. I doubt that anyone who has read this study of the erotic works of Poggio Bracciolini, Francesco Berni, Giulio Romano, Aretino, Nashe and others, would characterize it as "moralistic," and the designation "prudish" would seem even more out of place. This is not to say that Frantz places *The Faerie Queene* cheek by jowl with Aretino's sonnets on the *posizioni* of Giulio Romano.

Instead, he considers "problems of definition, especially the definition of pornography" (Frantz 5), this apparently because "Renaissance writers themselves struggled to differentiate what they saw as wanton or bawdy from what they termed obscene" works. The implication is that how words were used in the Renaissance bears on the fidelity of our characterization of the literary works of that time. For instance, Renaissance writers scrupulously differentiated between types of erotic expression: "Aretino, Poggio, Nashe and the epigrammatists" (Frantz 6) were usually designated as pornographers. In marked contrast, Spenser's name is never listed. Should our characterization take this fact into account? In the Renaissance, commentators discriminated among four authorial aims (pornographic, obscene, bawdy, erotic), and the first of these concerned "'autoerotic desires'" (Frantz 4). Then must we take "autoerotic desires" as a criterion for application of the term "pornography" in discussions of Renaissance pornography today? That would depend, some will say, on how rigorously we wish to use the term "pornography." Would rigor help in this case? Obviously, it would affect our sense of the propriety of Proposition *A*. When Frantz admits that the definition of Renaissance "pornography" is tricky at best and certainly "'not entirely foolproof'" (Frantz 4), we would be justified in withholding judgment in the matter.

Frantz argues that inquiry into historical discriminations assists our understanding of Renaissance perspectives on these artifacts. We could, of course, say the same of Paglia's critique of Spenser critics. Is she using the term *pornography* in the way Renaissance critics, including Spenser critics, use the term? Suppose the answer is "No, but then she is using it in a different way that suits her purpose." Then we could argue that, as long as we know what that purpose is, no harm is done. But, as Wittgenstein's example indicates, this strategy runs the risk of being misunderstood: "Imagine someone pointing to his cheek with an expression of pain and saying 'abracadabra!'—We ask 'What do you mean?' And he answers 'I meant toothache'. You at once think to yourself: How can one 'mean toothache' by that word?" (*PI* §665) "Well, so be it; the risk is minimal, and the possible gain considerable. If we ask too much rigor of our critical language, we create a kind of verbal claustrophobia. A variety of expressions enriches the reading experience: 'But—can't I say "By 'abracadabra' I mean toothache"'? (*PI* §665) It's a free country. And besides, we invent new uses for old sounds all the time." We do, but even so, effective communication depends on the surrounding and supporting help that is given in particular cases. Communication involves *n* tradeoffs, large and small.

Although Frantz and Paglia appear to disagree in the way Renaissance critics should talk about pornography, to a certain extent the two are in accord on Spenser, for Frantz writes: "Perhaps no poet of the English Renaissance recognized more clearly the power in the sense of sight to arouse erotic impulses than Edmund Spenser" (Frantz 245). Like Paglia, he thinks of Spenser's reader as well as of his characters as "enticed," tempted and tested by the allure of "female nudity" (245). Specifically, Frantz mentions the naked maidens in the fountain in the Bower of Bliss, the Serena episode in book 6, and "Venus' obsession with Adonis" (248) in book 3:

> And whilst he slept, she over him would spred
> > Her mantle, colour'd like the starry skyes,
> > And her soft arme lay underneath his hed,
> > And with ambrosiall kisses bathe his eyes;
> > And whilest he bath'd, with her two crafty spyes,
> > She secretly would search each daintie lim. . . .
> > > (*FQ* 3.1.36)

Returning to the criterion of "autoerotic desires," I want to ask: What, if anything, is "pornographic" about this passage? A critic cites these lines as evidence that Spenser recognized the role of sight in sexual excitation, but forgets to say which Spenser critics have been sexually aroused by reading them. Instead, the critic talks about allegory, recalling Britomart's vision of Artegall in the mirror (Frantz 248), then turns to another critic's discussion of the House of Busirane. Noting that Thomas Roche describes the tapestries in the first room visited by Britomart as "one of Spenser's greatest poetic achievements" (Roche 84), he points out that Roche remarks on the "debasement" and "bestiality" of the visual effects of Spenser's diction. Now, the effect of Spenser's poetic tableau is just the opposite of Agostino Carracci's pornographic designs: "These are not depictions analogous to the drawings of a Guilio Romano, an Agostino Carracci, or a Perino del Vaga" (Frantz 249). The critic adds: "As anyone who has read Spenser carefully knows, such an omission does not stem from any reluctance on Spenser's part to celebrate human sexual love" (250). Following the predecessor critic (Roche), Frantz argues that, because the loves of the gods (such as Carracci's "Jupiter and Juno") are "negative exempli," neither the reader nor Britomart is "enticed or tempted" (252). From this point of view, then, since the aim of *The Faerie Queene* is not pornographic, it would not be proper to describe Spenser as a failed pornographer. And yet in such passages Spenser's poetic effects depend on his readers' awareness of the *context* of pornography—that is, of the positive exempla—of erotica.

So is the Spenser tableau "pornographic" or not? Setting aside notions of "positive" and "negative exempla," we want to know what happened to "autoerotic desires." We remember that somehow the visual dimension of Spenser's description entailed some species of sexual arousal, but it wasn't clear whose. Although we recognize the qualifications here, the critic has left the impression that the scene in the Bower of Bliss meets the test of pornographic composition: "*That* [sexual arousal] is the test of Cissie and Flossie in Acrasia's pool" (Frantz 249). How do we construe the lexical item, *test*, here? The reader's reaction has something to do with sexual excitation, which is "the test ," presumably, of Spenser's description "of Cissie and Flossie in Acrasia's pool." If true, then the case has been made for the historical applicability of the term *pornographic*. We recognize *that*, but applicability of the term *test* presents a problem. Perhaps out of generosity we concede that the passage is lovely, and even that some readers will empathize with Sir Guyon when the Palmer interrupts his concentration, betrayed with "secret signes of kindled lust" (*FQ* 2.12.68). We know, when the Palmer speaks, that Sir Guyon is enjoying himself, and that at the very least the "naked Damzelles" have momentarily distracted him from the high purpose of his quest. Whether or not they have actually "kindled lust" in Sir Guyon, the "naked Damzelles" have certainly attracted his attention for the moment. Spenser's ethical focus is on the inappropriate lack of intimacy in the scene. The contrived sexual attraction of impersonal nudity has a momentary appeal. The two women remind us of Phædria, but there is greater distance here, partly because there are two "Damzelles" now, and they are already "naked." Even the presence, if momentarily forgotten, of the Palmer, fits here, for his intrusion interrupts Sir Guyon's absorption in momentary visual stimulation.

Once the standard of sexual arousal is raised for the application of the Renaissance notion of *pornography*, it is hard to see how the passage from the Bower of Bliss will work as an example. To my knowledge no one—not even Sir Guyon—provides a single instance of anyone's being sexually aroused by the encounter at Acrasia's fountain. To the contrary, Spenserians can probably add anecdotal evidence of more subdued reactions to this very passage. So does this mean that Spenser was, Frantz's apology notwithstanding, a failed pornographer? Well, we can follow Paglia's thinking in another direction and say that Spenser didn't fully know his intentions, so he can hardly be blamed for not achieving them. The power of his theme took control, but not complete control, which explains why some readers (but we admit that no one has identified them) react as they would to a candidly pornographic text. Roche's notion of positive exempla suggests that readers do know what is happening to Sir Guyon; he is, as a man, visually interested, tempted, so to speak. But this does not mean that Sir Guyon is sexually stimulated. Then as now, readers recognize stages in the psychology and physiology of sexual excitation.

It seems fair to say, then, that Paglia is mistaken in her belief that Spenser critics ignore the poet's interest in erotica. We need only point to Frantz's book to say this with some confidence. As has already been suggested, we cannot blame Paglia for not knowing details of a book that came out only a year before her own, but we can say that Spenser's interest in sexuality is not now, nor has it ever been, a well-kept secret. Stephen Greenblatt pointed out some time ago that Romantic critics of Spenser, who have been in so many areas of thought "discredited" by their twentieth century descendants, "had the virtue of fully acknowledging the Bower's intense erotic appeal" to readers (Greenblatt *Renaissance* 171). In fact, Frantz himself builds on remarks made by C. S. Lewis and Thomas Roche, two of the most influential Spenser critics of the twentieth century. For instance, Frantz refers to this passage from Lewis (245):

> The reader who wishes to understand Spenser in this matter may begin with one of his most elementary contrasts— that between the naked damsels in Acrasia's fountain and the equally naked (in fact rather more naked) damsels who dance round Colin Clout. Here, I presume, no one can be confused. Acrasia's two young women (their names are obviously Cissie and Flossie) are ducking and giggling in a bathing-pool for the benefit of a passerby: a man does not need to go to fairie land to meet them. (Lewis 331)

Lewis makes a distinction here between the literary effects of two Spenserian tableaux, to both of which he attributes sexual content—neither of which would meet the test of pornography as Frantz defines it, based on examples from Aretino, Romano and Carracci. As the tone of C. S. Lewis's remarks suggests, it looks as if Spenserians think of sexuality as a rather obvious subject of Spenser's poem.

And rather than anomalies in the field, Frantz, Roche and Lewis are representative of mainstream Renaissance and Spenserian criticism. It would be fair to say that the very routine aspect of this perspective on Spenser's sexual motif is more and more evident in the literature. So I want to ask: Don't recent critics (Hendrix, Krier, Berry) take Spenser's strong interest in sexuality for granted? The answer is: Yes. Like many of their predecessors, they recognize that sexuality is part of Spenser's conception of the natural order, which he subsumed beneath an overarching divine order.[2]

Not only do many, if not all, Spenserians seem quite at ease with notions of sexuality in *The Faerie Queene*, but, rather than being inclined to suppress the sexual content of the poem, they are more likely to find sexual content where none exists (that is, none that Renaissance readers apparently perceived). Consider The April Eclogue, for example. Frantz doesn't mention the April Eclogue as an example of pornography, and neither Lewis nor Roche thinks of the poem as particularly sexual in content. Probably most Spenser critics would agree that Sir Guyon—I am tempted to say even Malecasta and Busirane—could read the April eclogue without betraying "signes" of "kindled lust." But a rhetorician could argue that this remark coercively attempts to normalize too narrow a range of responses to the poem. Critics, the argument goes, too easily generalize from obvious examples, but in the "hard cases"—in cases that resist such efforts to normalize responses—perception of sexual interest becomes "problematic," and will very likely reflect no more than the interests and proclivities of the perceiver. This sounds reasonable. So then is the April Eclogue a "hard" or "easy" case? One critic writes:

> B) *The block shows three events in the text and is to be read sequentially in a counterclockwise direction starting at the upper left and ending in the center. Accordingly, we see (1) Thenot with Hobbinol, who recites (2) Colin's lay to (3) Eliza and her attendants. (Luborsky 30)*

We note perhaps that Proposition *B* makes no mention of the "absence" of men in either Spenser's poem or its accompanying woodcut. This is significant, in that another critic finds the absence of men in the scene indicative of a more sexually nuanced poetic expression. For her, the emphatic presence of women is a sign of the absence of men, and therefore evidence of the "intimate association [of woman] with her own sex" (Berry 78). Accordingly, the critic "sees" masculine and feminine genitalia: The absence of men in the text reveals that "the solid phallic authority . . . emblematized by the wild man's club" has been "hollowed out and transferred to the female" (Berry 79).

Suppose that I look closely at the woodcut for "Aprill". Rather than agree with Berry, I observe how hard it is to bring her perception into accord with Paglia's insistence that Spenserians unjustly strip Spenser's poetry of sexual content:

> C) In Spenser's eclogue, the place of the decentred and sexually thwarted father, Pan, is assumed by his own persona of the shepherd poet Colin Clout. Like Pan, Colin has replaced phallic sexual desire with the pipes of Pan: the hollow and musical maternal phallus (which is also multiple rather than singular). (Berry 79)

Although the claim here is not that "Aprill" is pornographic, for Berry, the poem does convey an explicitly pronounced sexual motif.

The argument supporting Proposition *C* goes like this: There is a father in the eclogue, and he is "sexually thwarted," but why or by whom Berry does not say. Colin has taken the father's place, and he has "replaced phallic desires"—his, presumably, so we must assume that he had them at one time, and then, willingly or unwillingly, surrendered them—with "the pipes of Pan." In turn, these pipes, which have become "multiple" phalluses, change their sexual demeanor and function, transformed from masculine to feminine; they are "hollowed out," but, again, how or why we are not told. Nor do we learn what masculine phalluses are not "hollowed out," so that we might compare them with those "hollowed out" in "Aprill." Finally, Berry offers no evidence that Proposition *C* deserves assent on the grounds that readers in Elizabethan England actually read the poem that way. So the question becomes: What makes assent or dissent appropriate in this case?

Well, the critic argues, Spenser's "emphasis upon the colour red . . . should alert us to the fact that even if the male is excluded from this scene, it [the April Eclogue] is none the less far from devoid of sexuality" (Berry 80). With this statement, we are in a position to see how wrong Paglia is in claiming that Spenserians ignore the sexuality in Spenser's texts. But more important than that recognition, we can see that the assertions of Berry and Paglia, although different in detail and emphasis, are similar, in that the arguments are characteristic of the vocabulary and assumptions of late twentieth century Renaissance talk. And in both cases, it is hard to see what the arguments have to do with the language of Spenser's poetry. Given this fact, the critical question is, What evidence do we consider relevant in evaluating these claims? "Whether a proposition can turn out false after all," Wittgenstein reminds us, "depends on what I make count as determinants for that proposition" (*OC* §5).

3.

It is possible to dismiss the objections raised in section 2 by saying that critics are sometimes blind to meanings that more sophisticated readers easily perceive. They are, so to speak, "meaning blind," unable to grasp a certain aspect of an expression, as if, no matter how hard they try, they cannot attain the required perspective on the subject. In the section of part 2 of the *Investigations* in which he discusses the famous "duck-rabbit," Wittgenstein writes:

> Aspect blindness will be *akin* to the lack of a "musical ear".
> The importance of this concept lies in the connexion between the concepts of "seeing an aspect" and "experiencing the meaning of a word". For we want to ask "What would

you be missing if you did not *experience* the meaning of a word?" (*PI* 214)

The concept of *meaning blindness* is relevant to our critical problem. For suppose I am constrained to admit that I do not perceive a sadomasochistic motif in *The Faerie Queene* (Paglia) or sexual overtones in "Aprill" (Berry). One could infer that I am "blind" to these motifs in these settings. On the other hand, I could take this inference as evidence that critics who perceive these motifs are merely imposing on Spenser the diction and assumptions of Freud and his disciple, Lacan. Having internalized post-Renaissance vocabulary from these sources, they have come to think of a particular kind of "sexuality talk" as "natural" or "necessary" or "liberating" or whatever, and proceed to discover sexuality everywhere in Spenser that they look. My analysis would, in effect, rationalize my blindness; if I don't perceive X in Spenser's works, X isn't there.

It could be objected that, regardless of any impediment to perception that I may suffer, I should not take the remarks of Paglia and Berry seriously, since they do not represent mainstream Renaissance or Spenserian critics. This is not a weighty objection, but since it is widely disseminated, it deserves an answer. In a period in which the literary canon is being reshuffled, it is odd that critical arguments should be considered in terms of such matters as the number of notices it receives in the *Citation Index*. Important methodological problems do not disappear when a book is reprinted or frequently cited. On the contrary, promulgation of error increases the likelihood that misinformation will establish itself as trendy insight and, eventually, as the accepted norm. Of course, not all citations are favorable; and even frequent favorable citations may indicate no more than intellectual credulity, malaise, or worse. Chapter 1 dealt with the dubiousness of taking the motives of critics into account when considering their arguments; and, when favorable or unfavorable mention is made of a critic's work, more considerations than listings of even the most influential work in the *Citation Index* come into play.

In any event, problems that arise from unshared critical perceptions do not go away when we nail to the mast the rule that we attend only to the arguments of "influential" or "trendy" critics. For instance, we read the following lines:

> ... oft inclining downe with kisses light,
> For feare of waking him, [Acrasia] his lips bedewd,
> And through his humid eyes did sucke his spright,
> Quite molten into lust and pleasure lewd.
>
> (*FQ* 2.12.73)

Should we dismiss Paglia's assertion of a connection between this tableau from the Bower of Bliss episode and Botticelli's *Venus and Mars* on the grounds that it doesn't mesh with the claim of Stephen Greenblatt, leading exponent of the Geertzian school of criticism? He says of the same passage:

> D) *Even cannibalism and incest which are the extreme manifestations of the disordered and licentious life attributed to the Indians are both subtly suggested in the picture of Acrasia hanging over her adolescent lover.* (Greenblatt *Renaissance 182*)

It seems to me clear that Proposition *D* raises, and even compounds, many of the same questions of unshared perceptions seen in Paglia and Berry. While most Spenserians would concede that Verdant is a "young man" (*FQ* 2.12.79), his kinship with Acrasia is less clear or, as Greenblatt puts it, more "subtle." Even Greenblatt's claim of subtlety is confusing. For surely that aspect of the assertion concerning incest is not intrinsically subtle. If it were, we could not ask, "What in these lines makes Acrasia Verdant's mother or older sister?"

We are talking now about what Wittgenstein calls "seeing as." Although some critics think that awareness of a critic's conditioning is an epistemologically necessary component of serious discussion, we need not resort to "necessity" talk to make a modest point about "justification" in critical argument. First ("cannibalism" aside, for the moment), let us suppose that "in the picture of Acrasia hanging over her adolescent lover" the theme of incest is "subtly suggested." In Greenblatt's formulation, the issue is not historical actuality; nobody in the history of the world need ever have committed incest for his point to hold. Nor does his argument depend on evidence that incest was an Indian custom, but rather on showing that English accounts of Indians "constructed" it so, which is only to say that Greenblatt talks about his subjects (poetry and culture) in figurative language. He claims that this sexual subject ("incest") is *in* Spenser's text, and it is this spatial figure that interests me. If the suggestion is "in the picture," it must be "in the picture" in some place, in which case we can imagine moving that part while leaving the others untouched. Were we to do so, what would remain of the lines quoted? Everything would remain except language suggesting copulation between family members. The alternative possibility—that the incest theme is an aspect of the passage in its entirety, extrapolated, as it were, from the "whole"—requires that the incest motif exists apart from the text, as an epiphenomenon or mental accompaniment of the text.

Now, again, Greenblatt claims that the incest motif is "subtly suggested." Suppose it is so "subtly suggested" that we are unable to perceive it. How do we know that it is there not to perceive? Can the perceiver teach perception to nonperceivers, say, by urging a closer look at the text? Just as in the test for color blindness the examiner might trace a finger across the plate of colored spots where the color-sighted examiner claims to see a number, perhaps we need only be shown the segment of the passage that "subtly suggested" incest to Greenblatt. As I have indicated, Wittgenstein talks about meaning blindness as well as color blindness (*PI* 213–18).[3] If a critic fails to perceive an incestuous tableau in the Spenser passage, and if coaching doesn't help, how can the matter be resolved? The very evidence that Greenblatt cites to support his claim prompts the nonperceiver's doubt. Even the argument that the analogy between the lovers and Indians lends credence to Greenblatt's reading because it is based on historical observations and descriptions seems murky. For even if we concede that English explorers attributed incestuous behavior to New World inhabitants, it would not follow that Acrasia and Verdant are family relations. Rather, the assertion that English explorers attributed such behavior to Indians constitutes a new and discrete claim concerning the observational skills of New World explorers.

Expanding upon Wittgenstein's figure of "meaning blindness" might help here. If we can imagine meaning blindness, we can imagine its opposite: meaning apperception, a hyperawareness of thematic material "in" the text, but neither put there by Spenser nor perceived by contemporary readers (Ralegh, Bryskett, Dixon, Jonson).[4] In order for a theme to be muted or amplified, subtle or obvious, first, it must be expressed in some language. Suppose Greenblatt were the only reader who ever perceived incest in this passage. We have John Dixon's annotations—and now Ben Jonson's—but they do not infer incest from the passage, and, try as we may, we find no sign of the inference anywhere in the Renaissance archives. Would it be fair to say that Spenser and his contemporaries were meaning blind?

Even if we assume that a poetic motif is only "subtly suggested" it does not follow that it is necessarily opaque or inaccessible on the basis of historical evidence. For example, suppose I assert the following proposition:

> E) *In Elizabethan England, the Redcrosse Knight was construed as the Earl of Leicester.*

I claim that this topical allusion is "subtly suggested" because I recall that, on first reading the opening stanzas of *The Faerie Queene*, I was not put in mind of the Earl of Leicester. And yet I know from the annotations decoded by Graham Hough that John Dixon recognized this very connection (Dixon 2). Although, as I ponder Dixon's inscriptions, I cannot be sure that he found Spenser's expression "subtle," his comments serve as evidence—though by no means the only kind of evidence—to support statements about one way in which readers in Spenser's time construed the Redcrosse Knight. Sharing certain grammatical features, *B* and *C* seem alike to characterize similarly obscure meanings in Spenser's text. In fact, the documentary evidence from Dixon supports *E*. The words of Wittgenstein's "common sense" interlocutor come to mind: "'If I don't trust *this* evidence why should I trust any evidence?'" (*OC* §672) But then *On Certainty* is a volume of rejoinders to the idea that justified confidence is predicated on some unshakable, uniform, common sense ground: "To be sure there is justification; but justification comes to an end" (*OC* §192).[5]

I want to say that the burden of proof is on Greenblatt to show that anyone in the Renaissance considered the possibility of an incest motif in the Verdant passage, but I know that someone might respond:

> *Renaissance readers clearly read for different things than modern readers do [F]—or at least they thought it worthwhile only to record different responses and impressions [G].*[6]

Proposition *F*, along with *G*'s milder ("or at least") excursion into genetic explanation ("they thought it worthwhile to"), takes differences predicated on historical interest to be the plenary grounds for inferences such as those drawn in Greenblatt's perception of the Verdant passage. Here, the appeal is to readers' motives—the "different things" that modern as opposed to early modern readers "read for" or "thought it worthwhile . . . to record." That is, the grounds on which defense of such assertions lies derive from the assumption that reading motives—the "different things" that modern as opposed to Renaissance readers "read for" or "thought it worthwhile . . . to record"—are members of sets differentiated by acts of will (reading "for") or of

valuation ("thought . . . worthwhile"). But without the evidence of a "record" of responses, on what grounds do we
say what is willfully included or left out? I can understand
how a modern reader might read a Spenser poem "for"—
that is, to elicit or to affirm—a Freudian interpretation. But
it is not clear what evidence we would need to show that
Dixon or Ralegh or Jonson or Digby "read for" or "against"
anything resembling such an interpretive possibility.

4.

Suppose we agree with Wittgenstein here: The grounds
for deciding between propositions that are "false" and
those that are not so have already been decided when we
proceed to look for certain kinds of evidence to "prove" or
"disprove" an assertion about a Spenser poem. When Renaissance critics talk about "the false grounds of traditional historical scholarship" (Goldberg "Dating" 205), they
invoke a traditional distinction between truth and falsity,
which, in literary criticism, implies that there are appropriate and inappropriate accounts of historical texts. So the
question for Spenserians would be: What "counts as determinants" in choosing between competing Spenserian
claims? We think of the examples in sections 1–3 as instances of ideas and attitudes which are, in Greenblatt's
locution, so "subtly suggested" that no critic (not Paglia,
Berry or Greenblatt, for instance) claims to have evidence of
Renaissance readers actually inferring the notions asserted
in their late twentieth century critiques. Greenblatt's discussion of Freud's *Civilization and its Discontents*, with
its belief in the concept of sexual repression, is relevant
here. Although critics inclined to talk of the "unconscious"
often speak of a general or universal sexual repression,
neither Freud nor they explain what their "repression talk"
represses. And yet, to be fair, Spenserian critics of this kind
must agree that Spenser's text did—or does (the difference
in tense affects the claim)—suggest as well as repress these
"subtly suggested" possibilities; and universality being

what it is, the same must be said of their critical accounts,
which repress what?

It appears that the "incestuous" aspect of Greenblatt's
reading of the Verdant passage and other "overdeter-
minedly" sexual readings of certain Spenser passages
present intractable difficulties, and that these probably derive from assumptions of psychoanalytic theory. But what
of the other aspect of Greenblatt's assertion: that "cannibalism," also "attributed to the Indians," was likewise
"subtly suggested" in the Verdant passage? On its face, this
inference might look more amenable to historical analysis. The textual association seems less strained; Acrasia
does "sucke," which sounds at least remotely like a gus-
tatory figure. On the other hand, she sucks Verdant's
"Spright," and she does this "through his humid eyes,"
which wouldn't seem to fit the ordinary description of
cannibalistic fare, at least not as Spenser probably thought
of it. The relevant passage from *The Faerie Queene* is
in book 6; "a salvage nation" (6.8.35) follows the "most
accursed order, / To eate the flesh of men" (6.8.36), and,
happening upon Serena asleep, they plan to eat her. The
only question is when, to "her eate attonce; or many meales
to make" (6.8.37).

As the Spenser *Variorum* notes indicate, the term *can-
nibal*, like *savage*, had more than one meaning in Elizabethan times (as in our own). In a letter to Lord Grey, for
instance, when Sir Henry Sidney describes the Irish rebels
as "those Cannibals in Goulranell" (6.233), he is being
merely abusive in general, not saying that the Irish of that
province eat each other. On the other hand, we do have a
contemporary account of the Irish of "[t]he poorest sort"
consuming "dead men's bodies which was cast away in
shipwrack." It seems obvious that members of the "salvage
nation" are cannibals in this more specific sense; and,
Greenblatt could say, that is the point. Because it is obvious, the example has no bearing on the argument in question, which is, after all, that Spenser's motif is here only
"subtly suggested." The problem with this rejoinder is
that it seems to require that we retrace our steps with

"meaning blindness" to answer it. Since the objection in this case is so similar, we are tempted to employ the same method of response, this despite the fact that cannibalism and incest are not very similar acts (unless, as in *Titus Andronicus*, one dines on a family member). One is surely less private than the others. The examples we have of humans consuming the flesh of corpses are something like communal efforts to survive under the most dire of circumstances. And this fact leads us to consider the social elements of Greenblatt's argument. For his remarks on the Verdant passage emerge as part of a wider discussion of Elizabethan *travel narratives*, which are often characterized by "the threat of effeminacy" (181) and a recurring sense that in exotic surroundings one might be "engulfed" by feelings and impulses ordinarily kept in check. That is, European—and especially Christian—values are "complicit" in an untoward colonial spirit, and, worse, in an actual imperial mode of conquest and victimization. Thus Spenser has a "field theory of culture" (187) which requires that "to *reform* [a native] people one must not simply conquer it—though conquest is an absolute necessity—but eradicate the native culture: in this case Ireland" (187). What many of us think of as "[p]itiless destruction" Spenser finds "not a stain but a virtue" (187). According to this analysis, the razing of the Bower of Bliss is imaginatively tantamount to destruction of another's culture, and the same line of thought "links this episode to the colonial policy of Lord Grey" and to "the destruction of the Catholic Church furnishings" (188). Accordingly, literary figuration is a species of "colonialization."

We can return now to the question raised by Greenblatt's perception of cannibalism in the Verdant passage, which includes talk predicated on the notion that Elizabethan English in general, and subsets of the language in particular, may usefully be regarded as "colonized." "Colonization" talk flourishes, not because of an upsurge of interest in westward expansion of European cultural, commercial and military interests (indeed, there is a paucity of research in these fields by literary critics these days), but because of the lure of the language, especially when it assumes an aura of science: "Philosophy," Wittgenstein writes, "is a battle against the bewitchment of our intelligence by means of language" (*PI* §109). Literary critics import the language and assumptions of a certain kind of anthropology (Clilfford Geertz's *Interpretation of Cultures* is very popular), forming what Greenblatt calls "anthropological criticism" (Greenblatt *Renaissance* 4). The assumption is that the language does the same work in criticism as it does in anthropology. It seems reasonable to say that belief in the methodological relevance of this crossover has something to do with the way in which Greenblatt is able to extract not only "subtly suggested" incest but also Indian cannibalism from the Verdant passage of *Thee Faerie Queene*. That "something," I suspect, emanates from Greenblatt's reading of the episode as an allegory of "Otherness" constructed within a matrix of assumptions of economic determinism (a model or paradigm) derived, not from Renaissance ethnography ("travel narratives"), but from twentieth century characterizations of cultures quite far removed in time and space from Elizabethan England. The protocols of this dislocation of descriptive procedures lead, in critical practice, to the transformation of the narrative of Sir Guyon, a "Legend of Temperance," to one about real and/or imagined evils of colonialism. Thus the Bower of Bliss episode is not about youth caught in the clutches of sexual indulgence at the hands of a wily temptress, but about sexual deviance and inhuman dietary habits of New World Indians. Above all, the Verdant passage is not about individual, moral vacillation and subsequent resolve. But why not? Because political aggressions and fears appear to be their "real"—that is, their hidden—motive.

As with the observations of Paglia and Berry, so with Proposition *D*, the "aboutness" raises questions for literary theory and practice that have not only not been satisfactorily answered but in recent times have hardly even been addressed. We need to ask: How can a text which, on its face, depicts the vulnerability of a young lover after a banquet of the senses turn out to be about so lifeless a thing as a political comment on "colonialism" and Indian mores? Is the idea simply that Spenser didn't know how to write political allegory, and so, wittingly or unwittingly, disguised his sentiments about the plantation movement in a retelling of the Circe myth? If so, the idea would not seem to fit the predominance in book 5 of *The Faerie Queene* of political allegory.

The issue concerns what will count as a "political expression," and, again, we might not need, and should not expect to find, unanimity among critics. But in my judgment, book 5 comes as close as we get in the poem to a Spenserian vision of statecraft; it is in the dispensing of justice by the power of government that individual and group conflicts are resolved. In this connection, most critics have little trouble identifying the political significance of the reversal of sexual roles in the Amazon empire.[7] Radigund dresses Artegall "[i]n womans weedes, that is to manhood shame, / And put before his lap a napron white, / In stead of Curiets and bases fit for fight" (*FQ* 5.5.20). More shocking still, Radigund assigns Artegall unmanly tasks:

> Amongst them all she placed him most low,
> > And in his hand a distaffe to him gave,
> > That he thereon should spin both flax and tow;
> > A sordid office for a mind so brave.
> > So hard it is to be a womans slave.
> > Yet he it tooke in his owne selfes despight,
> > And thereto did himselfe right well behave,
> > Her to obey, sith he his faith had plight,
> Her vassall to become, if she him wonne in fight.
>
> > > > (*FQ* 5.5.23)

Dressed as a woman, Artegall is forced to spin and sew. Spenser makes clear that this situation humiliates Artegall; but, as the narrator's instruction at the opening of the following canto indicates, the blame for his condition doesn't fall on Radigund:

> Some men, I wote, will deeme in *Artegall*
> > Great weaknesse, and report of him much ill,
> > For yeelding so himselfe a wretched thrall,

To th'insolent commaund of womens will;
That all his former praise doth fowly spill.
But he the man, that say or doe so dare,
Be well adviz'd, that he stand stedfast still:
For never yet was wight so well aware,
But he at first or last was trapt in womens snare.

(*FQ* 5.6.1)

Yes, Radigund possesses a "snare" or "snatch" or "trap," but that snare works only because there exists "[s]ome weaknesse" in Artegall. If readers, men in particular, judge the administrator of judges harshly, they do so only by forgetting Radigund's beauty for the moment. Artegall's situation is both a challenge and a warning: Judges are not immune to the beauty of woman. In this case, the physical asymmetry typical of most earlier episodes in book 5 is reversed, and Justice becomes manipulable. The powerful quester finds himself "a wretched thrall."

The test of Artegall's character is not yet over. Radigund's persistent attempts to seduce him do not succeed. Paradoxically, it is as if imprisonment renders Artegall immune to sexual desire, which was the source of his vulnerability in the first place. After he is conquered, Artegall perseveres in refusing Radigund, but his "strength" derives from his social transformation to woman's attire and woman's work. What has happened to his sexual impulse? In some way, Radigund is responsible for the atrophy of his libido, but then it was Artegall who, like Sir Guyon, became distracted by Radigund's magnificent, uncovered femininity in the first place. Her beauty, compounded with his vulnerability to it, creates a sexual and therefore (because of Artegall's calling or quest) a judicial impasse. We may recall what Artegall was like on that fateful morning, when his mettle as a true knight of Justice was first tested against the Queen of the Amazons. As T. K. Dunseath sees it, in details reminiscent of those describing the Diana-like snowy Florimell, Spenser depicts Radigund in terms rich in "ambiguous sexuality" (Dunseath 130). The fight, like Artegall's earlier joust with Britomart, is both terrible and

splendid: sexuality and violence, Mars and Venus, love and
hate, with the sexual component of male/female conflict
ever present. Then, just as the battle seems to be going
Artegall's way (he exposes but does not yet penetrate
Radigund's bare flesh), the Queen of Amazons draws blood.
Even so, having managed to destroy her shield, Artegall
strikes "Upon her helmet" with such force that Radigund
falls into a "sencelesse swoune" (5.5.11), whereupon he
"unlaces" her helmet. At just this moment, the conflict
between human Justice and male "weaknesse" becomes
clear:

> But when as he discovered had her face,
> > He saw his senses straunge astonishment,
> > A miracle of natures goodly grace,
> > In her faire visage voide of ornament,
> > But bath'd in bloud and sweat together ment;
> > Which in the rudeness of that evill plight,
> > Bewrayd the signs of feature excellent:
> > Like as the Moone in foggie winters night,
> Doth seeme to be her selfe, though darkned be her light.
>
> At sight thereof his cruell minded hart
> > Empierced was with pittifull regard,
> > That his sharpe sword he threw from him apart,
> > Cursing his hand that had that visage mard:
> > No hand so cruell, nor no hart so hard,
> > But ruth of beautie will it mollifie.
> > By this upstarting from her swoune, she star'd
> > A while about her with confused eye;
> Like one that from his dreame is waked suddenlye.
>
> > > > > > > > (*FQ* 5.5.12–13)

Astounded by Radigund's beauty, Artegall is literally trans-
fixed—immobilized. He is no longer a warrior. To him,
Radigund's presence is pure femininity, "voide of ornament," except for the aphrodisiacal traces of "bloud and
sweat together ment" (stanza 12).

Spenser characterizes a powerful dilemma here. In many
cases in book 5, Spenser's protagonist of Justice stands
firm. He adheres to his duty with absolute circumspection

in confrontations with Pollente, who extorts outrageous tribute by controlling the sole means of conveyance (a bridge); he destroys the "mighty Gyant" of communism, who would haul everything down to the lowest level; he sorts out the maritime law dividing the brothers Bracidas and Amidas; and in these and other situations he functions without any sign of personal interest. The test of his character comes only when Artegall, the true knight of Justice, must deal with an attractive participant—a complainant or defendant with the sexual appeal of Radigund: "But ruth of beautie will it mollifie." In these lines Spenser undoes the narrator's portraiture of Artegall as universally even-handed. When brought face to face with a beautiful woman wholly in his power, Artegall becomes, like Verdant and all men including Prince Arthur, for that matter, vulnerable to the controlling attributes of Florimell (feminine beauty, "womens snare") in Radigund. Of course, in Radigund, those attributes are physically exaggerated—"writ large," as it were, in the ample dimensions of her Amazonian splendor. But her very dimensions emphasize that Radigund is real: large, athletic, forceful, perspiring, bloody, combative, and (best of all) at least for the moment, present and apparently available. All these features only heighten the sense of dramatic reversal, in which, like Verdant, Artegall casts his weapon aside. Overcome by the power of female beauty, he loses his grip on the capacity to judge. The change of clothing that follows only externalizes what has happened to Artegall because of his response to Radigund's uncovered face. He cannot judge because he sees Radigund not as a combatant (not as a proper litigant) but as the immediate object of his sexual desire. Thus, in this passage Spenser imagines a legal system governed by men rather than by laws. Perhaps Lear's indictment comes to mind: "Thou rascal beadle, hold thy bloody hand! / Why dost thou lash that whore? Strip thine own back, / Thou hotly lust to use her in that kind / For which thou whip'st her" (4.6.160–63).

"Unconscious" motives can bedevil us here, and raise

again the problem of "meaning blindness." A critic may think of the Radigund episode as a sign of Spenser's "submerged anxiety" concerning "female sexuality" (Wofford 351) or say that this theme of sexual "anxiety," "unacknowledged by the narrator" (Wofford 311), amounts to a "psychological allegory." But such talk only encourages the illusion that an intractable critical problem exists. For suppose I agree that some allegories lack a psychological dimension. That would mean that, for me, the concept of a psychological dimension makes sense. But even then the question of my blindness to "submerged anxiety" concerning "female sexuality," in the Radigund episode, might remain. It could remain despite the fact that I perceive "anxiety" in the passage and see that "female sexuality" is involved in it. "Well, one says, this is not so hard to do; we have a scene of mortal combat, so 'anxiety' is customarily associated with it. Besides, Radigund is so compelling a figure of 'female sexuality' that Artegall, 'anxious in the extreme,' loses his composure, and with it all sense of judicial purpose. If he had wits about him equal to his quest he would cut Radigund's head off." But Spenser portrays a different perspective on the justice system. The episode suggests that perhaps there is no such thing as the perfect conduct of a legal case in which one of the litigants is so attractive a woman as Radigund (assuming, of course, that the sitting judge is a man or a woman). It may not be possible to eliminate such motives as desire or resentment from human judgment. For judges render only human judgments, not, in Nietzsche's phraseology, "immaculate perceptions." One who insists on inhuman performances in human endeavors is like the infant who cries for the moon. The Radigund episode represents the human limits of human institutions. The sexual politics of Artegall's "unmanning" sequence characterizes, not so much a flaw in the justice system, as the human dimension of sexuality, which, by its indomitable presence, threatens to frustrate some judicial functions.

So what is the problem of "meaning blindness" here? In

dealing with the sexual and political aspects of the critic's assertion, we have ignored its spatial aspect. The critic argues for a "submerged," presumably hidden, feature of the sexuality in the Radigund episode. The question is: Why would anyone think of Spenser's treatment of "anxiety" concerning "female sexuality" here as "submerged"? Are we to take this figure literally, or is the critic's point only that in this case Spenser's diction is so complex that we might miss its particular elements ("female sexuality," "submerged anxiety"). This is of course possible. On the other hand, isn't it strange that one should talk of something sexual in this Spenser text that many see quite readily as "submerged"? How would we, should we be so inclined, inquire further into such an assertion? What I question is the notion that "what is hidden from us" is what makes Spenser's text sexual and political. Why wouldn't what we perceive exercise that moral and intellectual suasion? I think again of Wittgenstein: "Philosophy simply puts everything before us, and neither explains nor deduces anything.—Since everything lies open to view there is nothing to explain. For what is hidden, for example, is of no interest to us" (*PI* §126). Why would Spenserians be interested in the unperceived, "submerged" feature of the Radigund episode?

5.

Since we talk about the formal arrangement of parts in book 5 of *The Faerie Queene*, answers to this question will vary. But what about the value, the relevance, the social significance of what *we* say? Responses here have something to do with the adversarial aspect of Spenser criticism. No good purpose would be served by denying that Spenser criticism has in recent times taken on an ideological edge. One critic talks about the "propaganda potential" of a politicized vocabulary, of "the postmodernist, poststructuralist climate of the 1970s and 80s, particularly among the so-called 'new historicists,'" and adds that, "Current scholarship suggests the futility if not the impossibility, of reading the poetry of Spenser and his contemporaries, outside its political context" (Bernard 1). This comment concerns the fascination of some Spenserians with government. For them, political considerations dominate reflections on the Renaissance—so much so, in fact, that they will take any evidence, even evidence of indifference to political concerns, as a plenary sign of intense "underlying" preoccupation with this one interest.[8] For example, one critic thinks of Spenser's apparent lack of interest in governmental matters in the Letter to Ralegh as an "exclusionary deferral" of what "is itself an inescapably political act" (Helgerson 49). In what sounds like a mantra marking a certain ideological perspective (Gayatri Spivak: "No nomenclature is ideologically pure" [366]), Richard Helgerson proclaims:

> H) *None can escape the particularity of time and ideol-*
> *ogy—certainly not chivalric romance. (Helgerson 50)*

I want to ask: What work does the locution *ideology* accomplish here? Such comments on the development (or stasis) of literary forms appear weighty. If we are curious, we want to know how we might prove or disprove them. What grounds would justify such a declaration? Wittgenstein writes: "The work of the philosopher consists in assembling reminders for a particular purpose" (*PI* §127). His observation might suggest a rhetorical—the logician would say a modal—difference between a reminder and a principle. If the point of *H* is the modest assertion that authors and their literary forms are part of the history of language and culture, there would be little cause to object and less need to consent to an unexceptional truism. But the claim here seems to be stronger. Helgerson advances a theory of social conditions as the agency of artistic creation, not just of literary forms but of their creators too.

How far can we proceed on the basis of (in one critic's

jaundiced locution) faith in the "fashionable shibboleth derived ultimately from Marx—that individuals are incapable of penetrating the sealed dome of ideology under which they are born"? (Patterson 109) Skepticism intrudes with respect to Helgerson's claim about the Letter to Ralegh, and a sense of conceptual confusion emerges. It is not clear what work Helgerson thinks the concepts of "political" and "act" and "inescapability" are doing in this context. In a world of inescapable consequences, how do we familiarize ourselves with the notion of escape? "None can escape the particularities of time and ideology—certainly not chivalric romance"? In an effort to salvage Helgerson's project, we might ask: Would trying harder help? If no one has ever escaped, how do we know that anyone was ever trapped? We hear that a Spenser critic emerges, claiming to have escaped the choices determined by the received culture. And we wonder: How will we persuade that misguided critic otherwise?

It is "natural" and even "admirable" that critics wish for a serendipitous wedding between literary and political understanding, but when the conjunction is too vigorously forced, inconveniences inevitably mar the outcome. Critics like Helgerson and Greenblatt claim that it is impossible to imagine Spenser criticism without some ideological purchase on the critic's loyalties. Greenblatt writes:

> 1) *In all my texts and documents, there were, so far as I could tell, no moments of pure, unfettered subjectivity; indeed, the human subject itself began to seem remarkably unfree, the ideological product of the relations of power in a particular society. (256)*

Suppose that, attracted by the orderliness of the social scheme implied by this line of thought, we concede that such an assertion conveys information, and that under certain conditions it is helpful to talk this way (although at the moment perhaps we cannot think of one). We wonder about "unfettered subjectivity," knowing that to understand its significance we must first establish the dimensions of "fettered subjectivity." We recognize the difficulty: This might be like convincing the critic who claims to have "escaped the particularities of time and ideology" to feel "unfree," to feel bound, as if fabricated by some agency—for Greenblatt, "the relations of power in a particular society." In this context, choice has an "unfree" feel about it, as if, when ideological production does its work, it alters the critic's sense ("the human subject itself began to seem") from "free" to "unfree." But this is odd. Imagine that one dreams of being in danger and of wanting to run, but being unable to do so. In relating the dream to the analyst, the subject says, "I was free to move—not chained or bound in any way—but I couldn't move. I seemed 'unfree,' willing to move but unable to do so." This makes sense. But suppose the same subject said, under the same circumstances—but recounting an incident rather than a dream: "I felt like running, willed to run, but I seemed 'unfree.'" Would "feeling," "seeming," and "willing" function in both cases in similar ways? In the dream the subject wants to—wills to—run, but can't. In the account of the actual incident, when the danger is "real" (the neighbor's Rottweiler, under quarantine, has broken loose again, and is chasing the subject), imagined agencies ("feeling," "seeming," "willing") understandably have less bearing on our interest than "running," *simpliciter*. We want to know if the subject got away.

And yet we cannot and need not deny that how one feels about "relations of power" may affect one's sense of the subject's "free" or "unfree" condition. Critics insist that every "choice" made by Spenser and his contemporaries was made "among possibilities whose range was strictly delineated by the social and ideological system in force" (Greenblatt 256). And since there is no exception to this rule, they will argue that we must accede to its implicit claim. Unfortunately for advocates of "inescapability" talk, prospects of confirming Helgerson's assertion and Greenblatt's corollary are not promising. The question is: How do Elizabethans imagine the "possibilities whose range was strictly delineated by the social and ideological system in force"? How do they articulate problems, solutions and beliefs, which include notions of a critic's political "being"? I realize that the critics in question could easily cite a number of examples—the whole field of "anthropological criticism," perhaps—to show support for the "none can escape" proposition, which is only to say that this belief shows a definite upward curve in the approval rate of Spenser critics. And yet, while conceding the demographic point about consensus, we might hold it prudent to doubt what follows from that shared belief and the critical practices associated with it. We need not believe that advocacy is a stranger to Spenser criticism to suspect that, somehow, pointing to the persistence of a belief is not the same as providing grounds or justification for it.

About a hundred years ago Karl Marx caricatured Spenser as "Elizabeths arschkissen poet," ironically suggesting that such an "unprejudiced and disinterested fellow" as he could not be a poet,[9] but his remark would not be far out of place in Spenser criticism today. The "fashionable shibboleth [of a 'sealed dome of ideology'] derived ultimately from Marx" is fashionable for a reason. Like Hamlet, earnest critics may yearn for unassailable ground for belief and action; in Spenser criticism, signs of that longing appear in the lure of "a stable and monolithic discourse" (Dubrow 214). Thus, we read of "colonial ideology" in the "Mutabilitie Cantos" (Coughlan 57), of "radical contradictions" in Spenser's texts, and of the "internal contradictions of a discourse of colonization" (Fogarty 75, 77). Understandably believing with Louis Althusser that "Marx founded a new science: the science of history" (Althusser 18), "materialists" talk about parliamentary politics extending all the way back to the 1530s, deriving from these "facts" the comfort of "scientific" historical interpretation.[10] No one doubts that comfort is a value, but we cannot say that it is an unassailable criterion of judgment. Documents surrounding the debate during the sixteenth century on England's involvement in Ireland provide supporting evidence for nonideological no less than for ideological formulations.[11] There is an ethical point here. Evidence provides the opportunity, not the necessity, for a perspective uncontaminated by late twentieth century interests and beliefs—for an awareness of historical voices other than our own, including Spenser's. We talk about *colonial ideology* and *radical contradictions*, and such notions exhibit belief in "the sealed dome of ideology." But surely, while pondering notions of determinism for whatever explanatory value they may provide, we can think of "none can escape" talk as optional.

Perhaps the greatest inconvenience of "inescapability" pronouncements in practice is that they rely on reference, not to evidence of Renaissance texts, but to secondary sources, which, in turn, embroil literary criticism in controversies of related fields. Ill-equipped to sort out competing claims in, say, anthropology, sociology or history, the critic accepts one as against other explanations on faith. This works well as long as the critic guesses right, but a flip of the coin does not provide proper grounds for historical statements. And when literary critics guess wrong, the consequences for literary analysis can be serious. For instance, David Cressy warns literary critics against relying "uncritically" on the "musings of Michel Foucault or the scholarship of Lawrence Stone" ("Foucault" 122). Cressy points out that historians disdain Foucault because his work is "ungrounded in evidence" and so "unhistorical" (124). Likewise, Brian Vickers thinks of it as pathological "paranoia" (218). As for Stone, Cressy insists, literary critics often "prove their points by a reference to *The Family, Sex and Marriage in England, 1500–1800*, "the most dangerous and controversial" of Stone's works, now "rejected by social historians" (Cressy 128).[12] "The case against Stone," Vickers writes, "seems unanswerable": "Every detail in Stone's thesis has been questioned by competent historians" (Vickers 333). Even critics sympathetic to "the movement" warn that the work of Lawrence Stone and Michel Foucault has "proved problematical" (Dubrow

212, 217). But such doubts have not discouraged critics like Richard Helgerson (see, for instance, Helgerson 214–15). Nor does it matter much what secondary source Helgerson relies on, when the secondary source merely asserts that medieval society was "'essentially pluralist'" (Helgerson 311–12n). Worse, the sentence misleads by implying that Spenser's figurative expression constitutes a "monarchic claim." It might be true that any Elizabethan—Spenser, for instance—could make such a claim. But a "monarchic claim" could also be asserted, probably with greater conviction, by Mary Stuart (or even Elizabeth I).

Helgerson implies that *The Faerie Queene* is complicit in establishing and defending an "absolutist regime," and this view pairs nicely with Greenblatt's insinuation that the "incestuous" Acrasia/Verdant passage (discussed above) entails contempt for Indians encountered in the New World. In this instance, Helgerson's secondary source suggests that the predecessor "pluralist" regime permitted one to change employers, while, alas, that empowerment vanished under Tudor and Stuart rule. Hence, contrary to all the available evidence suggests about Spenser, Shakespeare, Donne, Jonson, Traherne and Milton, in theory, they worked for one and only one employer throughout their lives. Why? Because everybody did. What is missing here—in both Helgerson's critique and in the shaky secondary source on which it depends—is convincing evidence that nobody in Elizabeth's time changed jobs, or at the very least that they did so in significantly reduced numbers as a result of governmental, "absolutist" regulation. As for "absolutist" claims by government, legal complications in the lives of Giordano Bruno, Joan of Arc, Thomas à Becket, Savonarola, Galileo, hundreds of victims of the Inquisition and many others, suggest that they—the "absolutist" claims—were hardly an Elizabethan invention.

Even if we assume that the term "absolutist" fits in the context of Elizabethan usage, it does not follow that it justly applies to Spenser. Annabel Patterson argues that Renaissance poets, including Spenser, are not victims of a

Hegelianesque metanarrative, and that even *A View of the Present State of Ireland* cannot fairly be read as a univocal endorsement of England's military policy in Ireland: "It would be so much simpler ... to imagine that Spenser's own eloquent social criticism was being expressed, all the more eloquently for its symptomatic evasion of censorship, in the enigmatic forms he thought he could get away with" (Patterson 109). Accordingly, Spenser's writings on Ireland register "discomfort" (he "backs away into allegory") with the relentless use of force entailed by the Crown policy that Spenser presumably supported (Patterson 110). The point here is not whether the views of Helgerson/Greenblatt or Patterson on "none can escape" talk are incompatible, or even that we need to develop criteria for deciding on the basis of evidence between them. Rather, by investigating "none can escape" talk itself, we might learn to "go on together" without expecting such language to do the work of historical description, an outlook meaning that we need not be puzzled or disappointed when it fails to do so.

* * * * *

This inquiry into Spenser criticism began by focusing on the hidden motives of Spenser and his critics, moving on to consider belief in hidden societal dynamics, not of the individual unconscious, but of "culture," the dynamics of which control the means and motives of production (expression, dissemination), known *and* unknown, of both Spenser and his critics. In fact, it appears that, for critics who propound "none can escape" talk, "culture" determines what *counts* as Spenser criticism. I want to inquire: In every case? Does "culture" as agency never sit one out? If not, it is not clear what sense the notion that "culture determines what counts as Spenser criticism" makes. Nor is it clear that this way of talking—this method (to use Wittgenstein's figure) of "tackling" the problem—works (*RC* §43).

3

Shakespeare's "Singularity"

> It may be that the essential thing with
> Shakespeare is his ease and authority and that
> you just have to accept him as he is if you are going
> to be able to admire him properly, in the way
> you accept nature, a piece of scenery,
> for example, just as it is.
> — Wittgenstein, *Culture and Value*

It seems clear that "seeing" in the sense of apprehending the marks on a page is a necessary but not a sufficient condition of understanding a printed expression. We orient our sense of sight and correct errors by comparing our impressions with those of others, as through the years we move about the world without bumping into things or each other. Because confidence in our visual skills is constantly reinforced by experience, we act on the justified expectation that we see what others see. Ordinarily, when discrepancies occur, they are of little consequence. Until I applied for officer training in the U.S. Navy, I didn't know I was color blind. Prior to that, my range of color perception made no difference to anyone, but at that point I was told that I am blind to a certain sector of the color spectrum. I do not recall registering any doubt regarding my examiner's diagnosis. Rather, the experience helped teach me that clinical distinctions are made for a purpose: I wasn't known to be color blind until I tried to do something with my eyesight that would affect others. The "fact" of my "deficiency" emerged from a process of shared experience: a standardized test. If there is a critical question here, it might be this: In what was I believing when I registered no doubt of the diagnosis? Perhaps the confident manner in which my examiner traced out what he claimed to be figures on the colored plates convinced me of his veracity. I couldn't see the numbers, but I believed that my examiner and others did, and so, that the figures were really "there."

1.

The fact that, once we learn to read, we most often read in private probably reinforces the sense that there is something deeply personal about the activity. Occasionally someone may ask us to read aloud, or we may volunteer to do so, but, since ordinarily we read by ourselves, even when in public places (say, in a library or a doctor's office), we are tempted to think of the reading experience as private. The concept of reading as a private act has theoretical implications for Renaissance criticism. As I. A. Richards once pointed out, as long as criticism concerns itself with "reader response" in the sense of private as distinct from public experience, it will be hard to separate out the "misleading effects of the reader's being reminded of some personal scene or adventure, erratic associations, the interference of emotional reverberations from a past which may have nothing to do with the work in question" (Richards 5). Even practitioners of the method will acknowledge that its emphasis on "interior" experience makes it vulnerable to "the charge of solipsism" (Fish *Artifacts* 425, 407). On the other hand, we recognize the strategic advantage of that admission, for, presumably, the private aspect of the practitioner's "response" probably shields the utterances made about it from intellectual scrutiny, and surely from challenge.

We can say we believe or doubt a critic's protestation of "interior" experience, but we can offer no legitimate correction to the claim, because the matter in question is private. We might find a critic's "response" to Shakespeare's *Sonnets* dull or timid or offensive, but we have no basis for asserting that it is inappropriate or incorrect. Admittedly, statements derived from the "interior method" can be defended as a cultivated connoiseurship, in effect, a "controlled subjectivity" of "the *informed* reader" (Fish 406).[1] "Well," the proponent of "reader response" theory could say, "what is wrong with *that*? When we read, we *are* experiencing something private. Finally, all experience is private. That is, after all, what the word means: '*Experiri*,' doing something, putting something personally to the test, a state or condition of consciousness (OED). Reading is personal activity. Thus, when reading, I experience my state or condition of consciousness—my sensory impressions or pleasure or pain—not yours. Even supposing that, by some empathic means, you experience *my* 'reading' of Shakespeare in your consciousness, it would still be your experience of my reading in your consciousness, not mine. So in this literal sense, one reads by oneself."[2]

In accord with that analysis, then, suppose I concede that I have experienced pain in public (as in a dentist's office), and that these episodes might not have been accompanied by such public displays as furrowing my brow or soliciting the dentist for painkillers. Mental states are not necessarily accompanied by signs that others perceive and can interpret. If I concede this, however, it would seem that I recognize the reading experience as private, even when in the public space of the waiting room of a dentist's office. But what if, at the same time, I recall experts saying that our tongues and lips move when we read silently? Even though we are not aware of this movement, it is possible for others to observe it, by means of sophisticated electronic equipment, for instance. Would this fact not require that I rethink my concession? The answer might come: "I doubt that empirical data on involuntary movements of our lips and tongues will be acquired under the conditions mentioned. We are talking about libraries here, where customs and protocols militate against such an inquiry. But even if they did not, it is hard to see how evidence of these micromovements of lips and tongue would bear on the theoretical issue involved. It would be easy to suppose that one retired to a remote alcove, and read Shakespeare in complete isolation, unobserved."

Then I admit that when I read Shakespeare in a library, in isolation, no one else knows, strictly speaking, exactly what I am reading or how I am reacting to what I read. "If you admit that, you concede the major premise of reader response theory, that the reading experience has a private dimension, as if in reading, say, *King Lear* in a library alcove, you in effect performed that play in your imagination—silently spoke it to yourself." What I *do* concede is this: that *dimension* is the key term in this characterization of my concession. Perhaps no one—not even I on another occasion—will ever read the text of *Lear* that I am now reading in exactly the same way. But it is hard to see what follows from this, and easy to make a mistake here. We are tempted to think of this modest assertion as a general "truth" of some consequence, and to say something like this: Since no reading of *Lear* is identical to any other, none can be replicated. The problem then is that, by taking the pronouncement too seriously, we are inclined to overreact, with euphoria or dismay. For on the one hand, we are encouraged to think of the critic as creating something "singular" and important, but, on the other, to imagine that something as vanishing the moment it comes into being.

The question is: Are there protocols of caution that would enable us to avoid extreme reactions here? Surely it is not necessary to think of *identical* and *replicable* as irreconcilable opposites. Indeed, if taken too seriously, the concept of *identity* loses something of its purchase on sensible usage. Wittgenstein's cautionary remark aims at avoidance of the lure of the serious mode: "'A thing is identical with itself.'—There is no finer example of a useless proposition, which yet is connected with a certain play of the imagination. It is as if in imagination we put a thing into its own shape and saw that it fitted" (*PI* §216). To be useful, a proposition should tell us more than that a certain object fits nicely into its own shape. But sometimes critics forget caution and, stumbling on, assert general but not well considered "truths," for example, that "utterance" necessarily falsifies "experience," that "experience is immediately compromised the moment you say anything about it" (Fish *Artifacts* 425). This is an example of the critical "dismay" just mentioned; in frustration, the critic decides that the only alternative to distortion of that reading "moment" is the authenticity of silence. The same critic might protest: "I should think you would find this decision a source of relief. Doesn't Wittgenstein say: 'What we cannot speak about we must pass over in silence'?" (*TLP* §7).

Wittgenstein does say that, but quite early on in his career, besides which it isn't clear how we should employ that instruction here. We are talking about critical theory now, and silence is not one of its distinguishing features. Admittedly, if we "pass [the matter] over in silence," only a very zealous—and clairvoyant—critic would bother to disagree with us. But the demands of the genre nevertheless apply; "reader response" criticism does not, to my recollection, "speak about" literal "silence," but about the way in which its opposite—the assertive mode—sullies or distorts something—a perception or whatever—that was, in its original state, pure and authentic. It is this notion of something authentic and irreplaceable that interests me, since it implies something like a Platonic purity of consciousness, an unsullied, undistorted "response," which is coterminous with the true "reading" experience. Not having experienced one myself, I cannot confidently deny that such perceptions might occur in other people, or that, if they do, they might appear to be of value. But I do suspect that an inconvenience accompanies the overvaluing of that "phenomenon" (which would be no more mysterious to me if it were an epiphenomenon). The inconvenience stems from the fact that we don't seem to have such a pure reaction to compare with its impure representation. In order to preserve the pure phenomenon, the critic must surrender replicability: "It follows, then, that we shouldn't try to analyze language at all" (Fish 425). Since reader responses to Shakespeare texts are like theatrical performances of his plays, and since representation distorts those reactions, the only way to avoid distortion is to avoid utterance. Although the critic might admit that various responses sometimes resemble each other, that resemblance can be no more than the happenstance occurrence of apposite consciousnesses intersecting under apposite circumstances with the "same text," and so producing similar distortions. As individual enactments, representations remain unique renditions; and since this is so, representations of these "performances" are not only distortions, but also distortions with no empirical or rational purchase on the assent of unbiased arbiters of the matter. It follows that the "facts" of the reading experience require individuated interpretation and valuation of Shakespeare's works.

Although the "reader response" critic's admission that the method is vulnerable to "the charge of solipsism" (407) implies that "solipsism" is a chargeable offense, probably as long as the "affective" line of thought is limited to mentation, no intractable critical problem should appear. But when a conception of a Shakespeare play based on that method is made public (as, for example, when it appears in print) it might seem to pose a critical or philosophical

problem: If one's experience is by nature radically individual, it follows that, arising as they do from radically
individual circumstances, assertions about those experiences must be radically individual, too. The consequences
of this view are easy to see if we imagine that every reading experience were accompanied by a descriptive declaration, in which case characterizations of a Shakespeare
play must exceed the number of critics making them (for,
as we have already noticed, as conditions change, the
"same" reader experiences the "same" Shakespeare text
in different ways). The practical and theoretical inconveniences of adherence to such a critical view are likewise
evident and considerable. Not only would it provide for an
unwieldy canon of critical interpretations, but it would
also allow for no discrimination between them. For if we
concede that the notion of "the *informed* reader" (Fish 406)
is so vague that it must render valuation of the reader's
response untenable, and with it the utility of an authentic response that includes "everything" (Fish 424) in the
reader's experience, then the characterizations of Anne
Barton and Robert Ornstein must enjoy no greater claim
to critical assent than those of the most untutored novice
in Shakespeare studies.

It is probably fair to say that, however loudly individuals
proclaim the virtues of pluralism, in practice, Shakespeare
critics will tolerate no such antinomianism. Moreover,
even if they would, university trustees and elected politicians would probably bar them from implementing so utopian a nonjudgmental system. This is only to say that no
matter how "private" critics imagine the experience of
reading a Shakespeare play to be, when characterizations
of that experience are made public, Shakespeareans insist
that they answer to public rather than to private standards.
This does not mean that standards are themselves always
publicly recognized or even often discussed, but only that
they are overtly or covertly imposed (when Shakespeareans
prepare lectures, grade examinations, referee essays, and
review books). Even so, the distinction between covert and

overt literary standards is important in Shakespeare criticism because, when publicly exposed, standards become "fair game," and may be praised or impugned as political, apolitical, arbitrary, coercive, naive, essentialist, relativist, positivist, universalizing, patriarchal, feminist, masculist,[3] traditional, conservative, subversive, nihilistic, pluralistic, monistic, hegemonic, bourgeois, elitist, decadent, popular, simplistic, obscurantist, and so on. Honorific and adversarial tags readily replace thought, and critics encourage each other to assent to or dissent from arguments and the beliefs that they support. Some critics even challenge the existence and/or the value of the Shakespeare canon. Caught up in the affirmative mode, critics declare that there is no more reason to value Shakespeare than any of an array of lesser known authors (Taylor 377), and that universities should replace courses in Shakespeare with others on authors more tractable to such political interests as Marxist feminism (Howard 1).

Given the stature of Shakespeare in the public mind, such a curricular initiative might seem hopelessly misguided. Of course, this doesn't mean it is not worth trying. Critics inclined to advocacy assertions might argue, for instance, that, as a "cultural icon" (Howard 10), Shakespeare is the ideal figure on which to focus a worthy social agenda. The assumption is that, if Shakespeare can be politicized, then any author can be politicized, for Shakespeare is the test case of the critical tendency toward a "universalizing and overtly apolitical pedagogy" (Howard 1). Here, critics-as-advocates echo the Coleridgean maxim "that to judge aright, and with distinct consciousness of the grounds of our judgment, concerning the works of Shakespeare, implies the power and the means of judging rightly of all other works of intellect, those of abstract science alone excepted" (Coleridge 4.52–53). Thus, Shakespeare criticism becomes the proving ground *par excellence* for assertions about literature in general. Often with disarming candor, advocacy critics aim at an "enabling discourse for political activism" (Howard 10) that would make Shakespeare

criticism "of *use* in changing specific practices" (Howard 5).
With literary criticism, they would alter social and institutional practices.

Despite its ingenuousness, this critical outlook raises
ethical and epistemological questions. On its face, any
argument in favor of "change" assumes, of course, that
stasis is a possible alternative. Then too, it is not clear just
how advocacy critics will decide which Shakespearean or
societal practices should be changed, or in what direction
change should be directed. Nor is it clear how teaching
Renaissance authors of secondary or tertiary literary interest will prompt society toward goals held forth as desirable.
Which authors of negligible literary interest should be produced and read, and why? (Why not drastically revise the
canon before it can oppress anyone by simply not establishing it? Why read anything in particular? Aren't interests uniformly coercive?) Unless it can be shown that a
shift in the object of study will actually effect desirable
goals, the shift would run the risk of sacrificing literary
values to no purpose. Worse, even if that sacrifice of literary value could be shown to encourage society toward
beneficial goals, it would not follow that those goals could
not be achieved more readily by explicit political action,
and this without any sacrifice of literary value.

Given the uncertainty encountered in these matters,
philosophical reflection might help. One need not be, as
Jean Howard claims to be, a Marxist to believe that what
we read or say about Shakespeare involves interpretive and
valuative standards, and that these limit the range of assertions about Shakespeare and his works that critics take
seriously. Wouldn't we think it strange if they did otherwise? The inconvenience of providing for no intellectual
limits on critical assertions seems obvious, in that no basis
for evaluating statements or for instructing a novice on the
subject of Shakespeare would be available. At the same
time, we know that many Shakespeare critics believe the
question of what constitutes legitimate grounds for such
judgment or limitation remains unresolved. Indeed, some

would say that it is not at all clear that it *could* be resolved. So the question is: When critics tender or withhold assent to a proposition about Shakespeare or a Shakespeare "text" or the society in which such a text exists as a linguistic and moral possibility, what grounds for decision do they think relevant in deciding the matter?

2.

Some critics hold that the question of grounds for decision regarding statements about a Shakespeare "text" itself presents a problem. We cannot reasonably discuss assertions about such a "text" until we have a "text" to talk about, and these critics believe that the concept of a Shakespeare "text" is in and of itself "problematic." As it is used in criticism today, they argue, the concept of a *text* (and, because of the myriad variations possible in performances onstage, *a fortiori* that of a theatrical *text*) is irretrievably ambiguous. For instance, many critics "refer to literary works as 'texts'" (Tanselle 1), and this usage lends to a belief that difficulties of determining the meaning of a poem ("interpretations of the significance of words") are related to, or even coincident with, the problems of establishing the "text" of a poem (the "text" as an "arrangement of words" [Tanselle 5]). Because of the possible confusion between these two uses, many critics hold that different critical aims require different terminology:

> *A) When new historicist, deconstructive, semiotic, psychoanalytic, or feminist and gender critics discuss and analyze the "text" of a Shakespearian play, they are, in great measure, creating the "text" as they interpret it; for them, the word "text" is synonymous with "literary work" and is concerned with that work's inherent meaning and possible interpretations. (Ioppolo 161)*

According to Proposition *A,* certain classes of Shakespeareans ("new historicist, deconstructive, semiotic . . .") use the term in a hieratic sense that presupposes and elicits "inherent meaning" and value. Not only do these critics impute "literary value" to the "text," but they *invest* those values in the text by the very process of their interpretive intervention, becoming, in effect, collaborators with the author and all other agents in the history of the "text's" production. They are all of them "creative" in the sense that, from the textual scholar's point of view, the product of their imaginative venture with the "literary work" exists quite apart from the physical results of the editorial process.

Textual scholar think of the linguistic artifact as "being there"—as an interpretive possibility in time and space—prior to any critic's apprehension of the text. This makes them different from the critics catalogued in Proposition *A*, since they aim at different ends:

> B) *For a textual scholar the "text" is primarily the physical object and that descends from the author in all its various forms and permutations, and is also in some measure created by the editor and other agents who reproduce it in print. (Ioppolo 161)*

It appears that only in a very narrow sense do textual scholars resemble literary critics in being participants in an interpretive process. Bibliographical scholars are "creators," but their domain of creative operation is temporally and spatially distinct from that of literary critics in that editors limit the realm of their creativity to demonstrable actions and objects. They "construct" (in the sense of reconstruct) rather than "interpret" a "text." In so doing, they assume that, as a physical object, a "text" has already been shaped in the past by someone other than themselves, and that the apprehensible product of the "text" may have no aesthetic value whatsoever and still exist as a physical artifact apprehensible on paper, vellum, parchment, fabric, stone, metal, film (and we can imagine "cyberspace" adding new pathways for preserving "arrangements of words" [Tanselle 5]). So one asks: In preserving physical artifacts produced in a variety of ways, given the fact that editors may begin and end their task without reference to "literary values," in what way does the "textual scholar," like the literary critic, "intervene" in the sense of alter the work? In what way, that is, does the editor participate in the "creative process?" Clearly, formulation of the question in this way forecloses other possibly productive lines of thought: The locution, "in what ways," presupposes that, among *n* possible "ways," the textual scholar does "alter" the text specifically from one state to another. But this assumption begs the question of whether, before that alteration, there was a text to "alter." I think it might be more helpful to pose a different question: In describing the editorial function as *creative*, do we use the term in the way it is used when we talk about the literary critic's task? Wittgenstein writes: "Misunderstandings concerning the use of words, [may be] caused, among other things, by certain analogies between the forms of expression in different regions of language" (*PI* §90). He means to alert readers to an unrecognized dislocation of meaning; there is nothing wrong with the importation of a use from one region of the language to another (from editing to criticism) unless critics unwittingly allow a subtle form of equivocation to take place in the process, taking a metaphorical analogy as a statement of equivalence. The danger arises from the expectation that a word will work in its new environment as it did in the old.

By holding apart two "regions of language" sometimes conjoined in critical discussion, we are able to emphasize that the textual editor, in contrast to the literary critic (less "creatively," as it were), intervenes at a certain time, not to interpret a phonemic structure, but to adjust its physical presentation in accordance with physical standards of bibliographic practice (*B*). This doesn't mean that the task undertaken exerts no influence on contemplation of that object as a literary work once it is available as a coherent or incoherent expression. *Coherence* and *incoherence* suggest literary judgment. The editorial task may aim at and facilitate contemplation of the text as a literary artifact.

And yet descriptive bibliographers like Grace Ioppolo will argue that aesthetic judgments about "texts" established by erroneous editorial procedures are necessarily skewed, and may even be "about" the critics rather than "about" the "text that descends" from Shakespeare. But this doesn't mean that, for the textual scholar, *literary* judgment is a necessary concomitant of the bibliographic *process* in establishing a text.

Just such a philosophical assumption leads some critics to argue that textual questions concern "the intellectual division of general from specific, of the category division of contingent and absolute" (Trousdale 218). Accordingly, differences between Quarto and Folio printings of *King Lear* inevitably affect the speech and, hence, the presentation of "characters" in the play (Taylor 220). Indeed, these critics say, differences distinguishing the texts of Quarto and Folio versions—of *King Lear*, for instance—are such that they sum quite literally to two distinct plays, the later being a revision (not necessarily in its entire "authorial") of the former. Indeed, for some critics, these differences justify a sweeping proposition with respect to Shakespeare plays:

> C) *There never has been, and never can be, an unedited Shakespearean text.* (Goldberg "Properties" 213–14)

Here, "intellectual division of general from specific" and "the category division of contingent and absolute" take on theoretical significance. Critical argument turns philosophical in the sense that, when one disagrees with the "never has been . . . an unedited . . ." locution, one tacitly affirms "the notion that there might be a single Shakespearean text behind *King Lear*," which is tantamount to expression of belief in an "unrecoverable Urtext" of *Lear*. In turn, by assenting to such a view, one philosophically commits oneself to an "unfounded Platonism" (Goldberg 213), which would be, if this view is correct, a mistake. In accord with this argument and in contradistinction to "unfounded Platonism," the critic declares:

D) [T]here never was a King Lear. (Goldberg 213)

This surprising assertion raises further questions: How does the "ever was/never was" opposition extricate criticism from the supposed dangers of "unfounded Platonism?" Indeed, wouldn't assertion *D* be likely to dismay proponents of "founded" as well as of "unfounded Platonism?" My puzzlement here, whether "founded" or "unfounded," may yet serve a purpose, for it seems to me reasonable that someone interested in Shakespeare should ask: How would a critic informed by "founded" or "unfounded Platonism"—or by any other philosophical system—discover that "there never was *a King Lear?*" When was it that this member of the null set (the *"King Lear"* that "never was") failed to appear? What sense are we to make of "there never was *a King Lear"* talk? What use *can* we make of it?

We could consider reasons given why "there never was *a King Lear."* We would find, I think, belief that Shakespeareans are barred from the prize of *"a King Lear"* because they have no "originals, only copies" of the play. This would serve, of course, as a serious limitation. If this postulate is believed, then all Shakespeare plays represent a "dispersal of authorial intention" (Goldberg 214). But is the statement credible? It should be easy to see that introduction of the contrast between "original" and "copy" does not clarify the textual problem, but in fact only deepens the confusion. To take "We have no 'originals, only copies'" talk seriously, we must first imagine that the terms "originals" and "copies" are doing the significant work of disjunction in this context. But this is a strange undertaking. It is as if a historian were to declare that there never were tribes of Hebrews in the Holy Land, and then, for proof, point to evidence of diaspora. What theoretical sense does the concept of diaspora make without the notion of a prior condition of nondispersal? Similarly, a critic insists that Q1 is a copy. Fair enough. Because we have heard of prompt books and memorial reconstruction and the like, the assertion passes as unexceptional. But then the critic claims that, if any "texts" preceded Q1, they were copies, too. This must be so on the grounds that "there never was *a King Lear*," and there "never was *a̱ King Lear*" because there never *could* be "*a̱ King Lear*." The grammatical problem here can be traced to the fact that the notion of "*a̱* [= one] *King Lear*" implies the existence of an "original" we do not possess. Proceeding on the unwarranted assumption that this fact entails an eternal condition of an absent "original," the critic accuses critics who talk about "originals" (authorial intention) of "Gnosticism," which appears to be an occult belief in a "universal and transcendent" text "saturated with meaning" (Goldberg 214) in such a way that it defies the ravaging power of "history" to shape the past as it wills.

Again we perceive the strength of the claim here, as the critic of "unfounded Platonism" proceeds: "The historical construction of Shakespeare is not a statement about the intrinsic value of the Shakespeare text" (Goldberg 214). It might appear that the critic wants to distinguish "intrinsic" from "extrinsic" value perceived in Shakespeare's works, but the drift of the argument is in a less historical, more philosophical direction. The critic of "unfounded Platonism" wants to say, "There is no Shakespeare." Because there are so many editions of Shakespeare's works, so many copies of copies and all of them "critical interventions" with no two alike, we are compelled to dismiss the idea of *textual authority*. Hence, the popular reiteration of "death of the author" talk. But this is odd. When we use the term *intervene*, don't we imagine something opposing or emerging between temporal or spatial elements or forces or phalanxes? If the first copy was itself a copy of a copy, with no original "behind" or beside or over or under it, then how would "intervention" be possible? In asking this question, I do not mean to defend "an unfounded Platonism." (I am not attacking it either, for, as we shall see, supplied with a proper foundation of an "ordinary language" context, "Platonism" might have its uses.) Rather, it seems that the argument imposes its own version of hypostatized "reality," disguised as an attack on "unfounded Platonism": one hypothetical copy hypothetically intervening "between" itself and a hypothetical absence of an "original." The critic imagines a sequence of copies emerging, like Athena from the head of Zeus, as a First Form of "Intervention" or "Copy." But why would the essence of a "copy" be easier to perceive than that of an "original?"

Let us imagine how this concept would work in a more ordinary, less philosophical context. At the close of act 3 of *Othello*, as Bianca comes on stage, Cassio says that he was just on his way to her house. Then he asks for a favor: "Sweet Bianca, / Take me this work out." Customarily, Cassio gives Bianca the handkerchief that Iago has suborned from Emilia. But let us suppose that now he offers Bianca no "original" to "copy." "O Cassio," Bianca says (referring, presumably, to Cassio's abrupt request for a service), "whence came this?" Given the new circumstance, she cannot be indicating a handkerchief she has never seen. Rather, Bianca imagines that she knows the "cause" of Cassio's recent absence from her life: He has found someone else and now wants Bianca to make "some token from a newer friend." In response, Cassio accuses Bianca of being foolishly jealous. But does this make sense? Wouldn't we, as readers or auditors, think Cassio obtuse? Why should he infer that Bianca is merely jealous? Without the stage prop of the handkerchief, she could be frustrated as well, wondering how she could, lacking an "original" to copy, follow the instruction "to copy" it. In this case, the reference of Bianca's "this" ("O Cassio, whence came this?") is, to use a popular if overworked expression, "indeterminate," like the "it" of Cassio's rejoinder: "I would have it copied. / Take it, and do't." Bianca could be jealous, of course, but she might also feel put upon: "Take it," that is, the request for a service, "and do't." Without the original, at the very least, the interlude between Cassio and Bianca would take on a different emotional cast than the one we are used to. From what materials will Bianca shape the love "token," and how will she select and distribute colors? Even more problematic, given the play's "two hours' traffic," how long will it take for Bianca's "vild guesses" (3.4.184) to produce a copy of Desdemona's "first remembrance from the Moor?" (3.3.291) Although the scene might strain audience credulity, think how amusing it would be when, by a lucky guess, Bianca shows up in act 4 with a "copy" of an "original" she has never seen.

Not only are the implications of Propositions *C* and *D* far reaching, but they are also vulnerable to investigation. First, supposedly, there exist "only composite texts" (Goldberg 216) of *Lear* or of any Shakespeare play. If true, it would pose a serious limitation, but it appears to entail a second: "No one can own the text. No one can clean it up." Assuming that the first of these assertions concerns proprietary interests in Renaissance texts in general, it doesn't help with our understanding of how things worked at the time. For it would not distort circumstances as we know them to say Sir Kenelm Digby did in fact "own" the text of Ben Jonson's annotations to *The Faerie Queene*. He "owned" it in the legal sense that, along with Jonson's other literary remains, he came into full possession and control of it. We "know" that Digby became Jonson's literary executor, and it looks as if he took advantage of his possession of this particular 1617 Spenser Folio, with its copious Jonsonian annotations.[4] So, in the ordinary sense that most people will readily understand, someone "*can* own the text," and as anyone who has ever written for permission to reprint copyrighted material will tell you, often someone does own it. The question is why anyone would *say* that "no one *can* own the text." If people *do* own or *have* owned "a" text, they *can* own "the text"— *that* one, the one we are presently talking about. So the general proclamation, which appears to imply the existence of a figurative, if not a natural, impediment to ownership of "the text," appears mistaken—at loggerheads with the facts, false.

Second, the assertion that "the text," whether of *Lear* or of any other Shakespeare play, is in a state of corruption, is likewise dubious. Proprietary interests aside, it is an odd thing to worry that someone else might "clean it up." The critic claims that it is impossible to "clean it up," that is, that "the text" is corrupt in a way that prohibits "clean[ing] it up." Since cleaning is a figure for editing, the sense is that no one can establish an unsullied, authoritative text of *Lear*. But why, if a "text" requires cleansing, shouldn't it be cleansed? If editing will help clarify a point that has confused someone, what is wrong with providing appropriate editorial assistance? Wouldn't the propriety of an editorial intervention depend on the question that has been asked? Obviously the term "editing" is flexible enough to apply to a wide range of activities that might serve in answering a wide variety of questions about both the accuracy and the significance of a text: glosses, explanatory notes, critical commentary—any sort of help one gives to others in a literary context. Textual variants, marginal comments, footnotes, companion volumes, articles, books—all may have explanatory functions.

"Cleaning," "owning," "editing"—these are just words like other words; they can be useful in certain contexts. Surely efforts to clean texts up have been helpful: "A babbled of green fields." Editors decide what to print, and their decisions "are not absolutely dead things." For instance, an editor decides that a compositor reached for one piece of type, but unwittingly withdrew another (here the shape of the "type case" used in Renaissance print shops matters). The most minute question—say, even of punctuation—matters. In *The Riverside Shakespeare*, an "eclectic" edition of Shakespeare's plays and poems which enjoys a place of honor right next to the First Folio in the North Library of the British Museum, just as Macbeth emerges from the death chamber, Lady Macbeth, hearing something, calls out: "My husband!" (2.2.13) With the trochaic rhythm of the line, and the stress on the first syllable of "husband," the exclamation serves as a stage direction, telling readers, directors, and actresses how to read the line. With exuberance! Lady Macbeth is pleased with *her* husband. Her doubts about him have been set to rest. She proudly claims Macbeth as a prized possession. It is as if suddenly their marital love has been tested and renewed, with the ultimate power of the throne as an achievable bond between them.

But a gifted actress could place the metrical stress on the first syllable of "husband" and still, as if thinking aloud, ask a question: "My husband?" By what warrant does *The Riverside Shakespeare* reproduce an exclamation point at this juncture in the play? On what "authority?" "I suppose one could say that the distinguished textual editor, G. Blakemore Evans, backed up by a host of contributing editors to the *Riverside* edition, *is* the 'authority': Harry Levin, Anne Barton, Frank Kermode, Hallett Smith and the others reinforce our sense that we can rely on the text. Moreover, the Signet editors—including Norman Holland, Richard Hosley, Alvin Kernan, Clifford Leech, Kenneth Muir, Russell Fraser and Sam Schoenbaum—agree with the punctuation, and so does Yale editor Eugene M. Waith. The *Arden Shakespeare*, which has only recently been redone, shows an exclamation point here, and so do the Kittredge-Ribner and Bevington editions. But if these 'authorities' do not seem sufficient, we could look for the earliest instance of the exclamation point, and take that instance as the 'authority' for the relevant editorial choice, in which case the term *textual authority* would mean something like 'precedent.'" In a modest sense, this use would not be normative, or, in Wittgenstein's sense, "important" or "absolute." For Wittgenstein, such uses are no more than shorthand expressions of factual conditions: "Instead of saying 'This is the right way to Granchester,' I could equally well have said, 'This is the right way you have to go if you want to get to Granchester in the shortest time'" (LE 6). Similarly, we may use the term *authoritative* to do no more than designate a history of a particular textual practice. Or we might point to the institutions with which the editors responsible for the practice were associated, or indicate the honors they have received and the titles they have held, in which case *authority* suggests a factual condition: institutional assurance of professional prestige.

Obviously, these factual conditions hold sway in various circumstances (classroom adoptions, scholarly citations, professional standing), but they do not crowd out other facts. "Authorities"—Nicholas Brooke, Stanley Wells and Gary Taylor, for instance—disagree. Of the same line in *Macbeth*, similarly reputable modern editions—The Shakespeare *Variorum*, the Oxford Clarendon "Original-Spelling" edition—show a question mark rather than an exclamation point: "My husband?" The dramatic difference could prove significant, in that a question mark might suggest an entirely different state of mind in Lady Macbeth. In this context, an actress might reasonably read the line in such a way as to suggest dubious feelings toward Macbeth, and these, in turn, would dramatically foreshadow her descent into madness. In this interrogative mode, Lady Macbeth exhibits the persistence of her uncertainty regarding her husband's determination: Is it he, or someone else, who has emerged from the king's chamber? Has Macbeth failed in the venture? Moreover, rather than claiming Macbeth as her spouse, she questions their relationship: Is this *her* husband? Even if he has returned, is this vacillating fellow worthy of belonging to *her*? Worse, has he perhaps been caught in the very act of an attempt on the king's life, and would her life as well as his be ruined? A decision on the punctuation of this line, then, makes a difference in the play's mood and direction.

Since the decision has consequences, the question persists: By what "authority" do editors put a question mark here? For that matter, by what "authority" (or factual condition) would we decide between editors, who are as a matter of fact "authorities," and who reproduce question marks *and* exclamation points? "Well, editors must choose, and in this case, editors did just that. To tell the truth, the exclamation works very nicely. So why ask 'by what authority'? when in fact the editor *is* the authority. By custom, the editor is selected on the basis of presumed or demonstrated training. It is a matter of competence, on the one hand, and trust, on the other. The question of 'authority' is, after all, no more mysterious than our practice of giving 'reasons' in any practical matter of choice. In this case, our reasons tell us of the picture we have in mind of the origins of Shakespeare's text. Someday, a manuscript of *Macbeth* in Shakespeare's hand could turn up, with the exclamation point clearly in place." All the same, isn't it more likely that, in this instance, *The Riverside Shakespeare* is in error, and the line from the 1623 and 1664 Folios and the 1673 Quarto and the *Variorum* are correct? Isn't it in our thinking about such decisions that we configure our standard of correctness? As for "competence," don't we imply by the use of that term the ordinary skills acquired in literary training? And don't they tell us not only that "authorities" do choose, but how they ought to choose as well?

3.

It seems that in the context of textual criticism the concept of *correctness* is linked to the concepts of *original* and *copy*, and the latter terms seem to involve ideas of *variation* or *difference*. But recognizing these connections may not help us sort out problems entailed by assertion of the absence of *King Lear* in history: "There never was a *King Lear*." Albeit there are productive ways to ponder the "being" or "nothingness" of "*a King Lear*" "Original" or "Copy," suppose for the moment that the utility of "never was" or "never will be" talk eludes us. This might be because, ordinarily, we think of something as missing only in contrast to the possibility of its appearance. So when someone asks, "Why was 'there never . . . a *King Lear*'?" what would serve as a reasonable response? The answer given is Proposition *C*: "There never has been, and never can be, an unedited Shakespearean text" (Goldberg 213–14). I think we can perceive in this assertion a sense of strong conviction, of confidence. The "never . . . never" combination hints at surety, allowing as it does for not even the occasional deviation into being of an "unedited" text. The magisterial, prophetic scope and tone of the assertion does the work here: There never was and never will be *"a King Lear"* means that, this side of Doomsday, the world will never know a single, authentic, "unedited" text of this or any other Shakespeare play.

Now, the talismanic indefinite article (*"a"*) helps by suggesting the absurdity in this context of the concept of singularity. How could there be *"a"* "text" when there are so many *texts*? We think of hypothetical holograph manuscripts, actors' sides, various quartos, the 1623 Folio, facsimiles of the 1623 Folio, and of all the variables that could have affected what Ioppolo characterizes as the "descent" of the "text" from the playwright's written or dictated composition to the printed word in front of us or the spoken word resonating from the stage: memorial reconstruction, occasional interpolation, *ad libs*, compositors' errors, intuitive emendations, blind chance. On reflection, we may decide that there is a benign and modest sense in which Proposition *C* is uncontroversial: "There is no avoiding edited Shakespeare, the question is only what kind of editing. A Shakespeare play first assumed material form as the author's bundle of manuscript sheets" (*First Quarto* v). And although this qualified assertion sounds right, Proposition *C* implies a stronger claim. It aims to convince critics that a theoretical, as distinct from an editorial, problem has been generated by the "two text hypothesis" (*First Quarto* 1). This concerns the origin of the text of *Lear*, which goes to the core of the larger issue of Shakespeare's singularity, including the theory of Shakespeare's revision of the play:

> Briefly stated, the hypothesis maintains that the quarto and Folio texts do not derive from a single, lost exemplar of the play; instead, they represent two related but significantly distinct versions—an original one, most likely printed from Shakespeare's foul papers, or a rough draft, and a revised version adapted for presentation in the theatre. (*First Quarto* 1)

Intelligent textual scholars may disagree on the matter, but the strong inferences permitted and encouraged by

Propositions *C* and *D* suggest rhetorical aims and philosophical assumptions concerning the general application
of a principle unaddressed by the editorial questions surrounding *King Lear*. *C* and *D* are ambitious statements, for,
if I understand correctly, what applies to *King Lear* applies
also to *Twelfth Night* and to the Shakespeare canon in
general: "An examination of the textual properties of Shakespearean texts ... will never produce a proper, selfsame
Shakespearean text" (Goldberg 217). Accordingly, "it is the
lesson of recent textual criticism that there is no such
Shakespearean text."

We are assuming, remember, that Propositions *C* and *D*
are puzzling locutions. How, without a "proper, selfsame
Shakespearean text," can a critic propounding *C* and *D*
discuss *"a"* Shakespeare play without *"a"* Shakespeare
text? The answer seems to be: "By handing you an edited
one, of course." But now we must suppose that the term
edited cogently distinguishes between an "edited" and an
"unedited" text of the play in question, in this case,
Twelfth Night. The critic quotes "from the Arden edition"
("Ourselves we do not owe"), explaining that "Olivia testi-
fies after her first interview with Viola (I.v.314)" (Goldberg
216). When I check the Arden edition, an allegedly non-
"selfsame Shakespearean text" appears, more or less as the
critic quoted it. The critic has capitalized "ourselves,"
presumably because the word stands in initial position in
the sentence. Does this, then, amount to a "textual variation?" Still puzzled, I peruse the Bevington and Kittredge-
Ribner editions and *The Riverside Shakespeare*, and find
that they agree with the Arden. So I look at the Oxford
"Original Spelling" edition of *Twelfe Night, Or What You
Will*. At last I perceive variance. Not only do line numbers
differ (we have scene divisions rather than divisions into
acts and scenes), but here the "selfsame Shakespearean
text," although looking somewhat "selfsame," looks less
"selfsame" than it did in the previously consulted editions:
"our selues we do not owe" (5.584).

Of course, nothing compels the critic of "unfounded
Platonism" to consider such a divergence as characteristic

of textual problems in Shakespeare studies. Some but not all variations of Shakespeare texts are trivial orthographic inflections. For instance, although the list of "Works Cited" at the back of this book follows the card catalog at the Huntington Library in listing *The History of King Lear Acted at the Queene's Theatre* (1681) under "William Shakespeare," it would make just as much (or more) sense to list it under "N[ahum] Tate," whose "Alterations" are announced on the title page; and neither option precludes crosslisting a collaborative effort. This is, in effect, what the publisher does in 1681, announcing that the play was "Reviv'd with Alterations. By *N. TATE.*" That is, the play, which lay dead or dormant, was brought back to life "with" (as if by means of) "Alterations." As Tate declares in his Dedication, Thomas Boteler's "Zeal for all the Remains of *Shakespear*" (A2) led him to suggest "Revival of it [*King Lear*] with Alterations," as if the reason the play required resuscitation lay in the fact that it required a "New modelling of th[e] story." Of course, this observation imputes a deficiency to "Shakespeare's" unaltered play; but it also implies that it existed in a form that could be altered, that is, that Shakespeare's *King Lear* was a recognizable and integral, if dormant, text that *could* be changed into a vivified something other than the "original."

For Tate, justification of the particular changes imposed is ethical, or as some prefer to say, aesthetic (as we shall see, for a different purpose, Wittgenstein collapses the two categories). Tate believed that the unaltered *King Lear* lacked "Regularity and Probability." Specifically, "*Love* betwixt *Edgar* and *Cordelia*, that never chang'd word with each other in the Original" (A2ᵛ) was a missing dramatic possibility of "Regularity and Probability." From the beginning, in fact, a romantic attachment between Edgar and Cordelia is exactly what Shakespeare's play needed: "This renders *Cordelia's* Indifference, and her Father's Passion in the first Scene probable" (A2ᵛ). At the same time, by developing Edgar's hopes of marrying Cordelia, his feigned madness is saved from expressing only a craven desire to "save his Life" (A2ᵛ). At the same time, the audience will

enjoy the vicarious satisfaction of "Success to the innocent distrest Persons" (A3). Here is the key ethical point:
"Otherwise," Tate insists, "I must have incumbred the
Stage with dead Bodies, which Conduct makes many Tragedies conclude with unseasonable Jests" (A3). Tate admits
that at first he was diffident of altering a word the great playwright had written, but audience reactions to his changes
reassured him that the difficulties which he overcame were
those that Shakespeare ignored by taking the easy way out
and simply killing everybody off. Alluding to Dryden's Preface to *The Spanish Friar*, Tate explains—or justifies—his
intervention, not only as interpretation of Shakespeare's
play, but also as a sensitive appreciation of the interests of
his own audience. In his own prefatory remarks, Tate provides the source of his quotation:

> Neither is it so Trivial an Undertaking to make a Tragedy
> end happily, for 'tis more difficult to Save than 'tis to Kill:
> The Dagger and Cup of Poyson are alwaies in Readiness;
> but to bring the Action to the last Extremity, and then by
> probable Means to recover All, will require the Art and
> Judgment of a Writer, and cost him many a Pang in the
> Performance. (A3)

Along with Dryden, "Tate evidently felt that his audience
was ready for the happy ending" (Black xxvi). And this is
more than mere criticism of Shakespeare's play. In revising *Lear*, Tate faced up to difficulties that Shakespeare
avoided; and the implication is that he did so because he
wrote for a more discriminating audience. He comments,
too, on the growing influence of theatre-goers, and, of
course, flatters their tastes as well as his own talent.

Obviously, we are talking now about social change and
public mores. In the Prologue, Tate justifies this venture
into the dramatist's hieratic function by charging that
priests have already intruded on the playwright's "Province
of Intrigue." Not only have they practiced the art of deception, but they have been successful in their attempt to
poach on the dramatist's territory:

Morals were alwaies proper for the Stage,
But are ev'n necessary in this Age.
Poets must take the Churches Teaching Trade,
Since Priests their Province of Intrigue invade;
But We the worst in this Exchange have got,
In vain our Poets Preach, whilst Church-men Plot.

(A4)

Life has imitated art so well that the clergy have perfected the playwright's skill of complicating plots. But all the while, as the need for moral instruction increases, the clergy have abandoned their role of pulpit instruction, thus creating a moral vacuum, which playwrights now only feebly fill. Tate's revisions, then, not only correct generic deficiencies in Shakespeare's play, but also address a social need in a way that Shakespeare's "old honest Play" (A4) could not. Shakespeare unaltered would leave "innocent distrest Persons" unsuccored and the stage piled high with wronged victims. The theme of Tate's "Altered" version of *Lear*, then, is "Regularity and Probability," which he and his audience recognized in the morality that melodrama supplied to the dramatic action. Not only are Tate's alterations a critique of the mores and the clergy of his time, but given the tastes and social conditions of Restoration England, they are also a critique of the propriety—and perhaps even of the economic viability—of Shakespeare's tragic drama.

Given this line of thought, the question is: When does "Alteration"—or editing of any sort—of a play's text become production of a different play? What do we mean by textual "difference" in literary study? Can we have "difference" without having "sameness"—even Shakespearean "selfsameness"—too? Tate admits that he doesn't wish to produce a tragedy. Does it make a difference whether we designate the titles of the 1608 and 1619 Quartos as well as Tate's "Alteration" of *Lear* as *The Historie of King Lear* or *The Tragedie of King Lear*? What real difference—and here I mean in the Wittgensteinian sense "significant" or "important" difference—would it make? Except for the absence of the King of France, the Dramatis Personae list of Tate's version is "roughly" that of preceding editions. Some critics will say that this remark skirts the issue: "Doesn't the 'roughly' in the assertion do most of the work here, and with it all of the damage to the standard of clarity that we seek?" It is just the matter of clarity about such terms as *intervention, edited, unedited* and *altered* that concern me. Wittgenstein writes:

> If I tell someone "Stand roughly here"—may not this explanation work perfectly? And cannot every other one fail too?"
> But isn't it an inexact explanation?—Yes; why shouldn't we call it "inexact?" Only let us understand what "inexact" means. For it does not mean "unusable". And let us consider what we call an "exact" explanation in contrast with this one. Perhaps something like drawing a chalk line round an area? Here it strikes us at once that the line has breadth. So a colour-edge would be more exact. But has this exactness still got a function here: isn't the engine idling? And remember too that we have not yet defined what is to count as overstepping this exact boundary; how, with what instruments, it is to be established. And so on. (*PI* §88)

Aren't we inclined, with Wittgenstein's interlocutor, to be puzzled by the notion of exactness, as if *that*—the notion itself—were an idea with precise dimensions? The direction comes, "Stand roughly here," and we don't know how to behave. So Wittgenstein tries again:

> Now, if I tell someone: "You should come to dinner more punctually; you know it begins at one o'clock exactly"— is there really no question of *exactness* here? because it is possible to say: "Think of the determination of time in the laboratory or the observatory; *there* you see what 'exactness' means?"

Perhaps the critical interlocutor begins to understand the point, and with it the Wittgensteinian enigma: "If a lion could talk, we could not understand him" (*PI* 223). There is a purposiveness about language which, although not epiphenomenal, is often hard to articulate, because it involves a vast array of experiences that go into understanding an expression. What is needed, Wittgenstein suggests, is useful discrimination, not between exact and inexact estimates, but between the functions of various synonyms and antonyms, and this means understanding a whole system of values:

> "Inexact" is really a reproach, and "exact" is praise. And that is to say that what is inexact attains its goal less perfectly than what is more exact. Thus the point here is what we call "the goal". Am I inexact when I do not give our distance from the sun to the nearest foot, or tell a joiner the width of a table to the nearest thousandth of an inch? (*PI* §88)

Let me elaborate on the point by returning to the instruction, "Stand roughly here." Imagine that the photographer giving the order is a famous professional, whose skillful portraits and landscapes have been widely reproduced and distributed. The photographer looks at the subject, points almost without looking up from the camera, and says, "Stand roughly here." The subject moves about, complaining that the instruction is not clear, but the photographer, again without looking up, says, "Right! That's right!" and shoots the picture. The subject complains: "Where was I supposed to stand? I never got set!" Hasn't the subject made a good point? Where did the photographer want the subject to stand? And why did the photographer shoot the picture before the subject had settled into place? Wittgenstein suggests that, in some cases, exactness—even clarity—might not be what one is looking for. We can easily imagine that, in the situation just described, the photographer might have no particular spot in mind in saying, "Stand roughly here or there." "Nevertheless," one might insist, "the instruction is still vague." Imagine, then, that the photographer shot the picture at just the moment of the subject's greatest discomfort, just as the subject appeared most annoyed and restless, shifting from one foot to the other, and not even looking at the camera. The photographer smiles and, without looking up, says, "Perfect!"

"Is the point then simply that the criterion of exactness in textual studies is not very strict, but that it is all we want or need?" We might have our reasons for keeping track of textual histories, and the taxonomy involved might help us understand differences that seem to us important. Many Shakespeare critics will say that Nahum Tate's deletion of France is so structural a change in the text of *King Lear* as to amount to creation of a separate play. "That sounds right." But by the same token, France is much reduced in the Folio version of *Lear*. "Then the play was revised." Perhaps so; the term is flexible. The question is: How do we account for the differences? The deletion of France in Tate allows for swift development of romance between Edgar and Cordelia, the absence of which, in Tate's mind, vitiates the original play. When Lear withdraws Cordelia's dowry, and Burgundy declines to press his suit for her hand, Edgar says:

> Has Heaven then weigh'd the merit of my Love,
> Or is't the raving of my sickly Thought?
> Cou'd *Burgundy* forgoe so rich a Prize
> And leave her to despairing *Edgar*'s Arms?
> Have I thy Hand *Cordelia*, do I clasp it,
> The Hand that was this minute to have join'd
> My hated Rival's?
>
> (6)

Cordelia reassures Edgar, and he delivers lines paraphrased from the original France's speech: Cordelia is herself a dowry. In Tate's version, Burgundy's declination permits Cordelia to launch into a sermon against greed: "This Baseness of th'ignoble *Burgundy* / Draws just suspicion on the Race of Men, / His Love was Int'rest" (7). By lodging France's integrity in matters of the heart in Edgar, Tate establishes symmetry ("Regularity") where, in his mind, Shakespeare had imparted its opposite.

The asymmetry of male/female distribution in Shakespeare's *Lear* (seen in the struggle between Regan and

Goneril for Edmund's affections) goes hand in hand with the emerging sense in the play that the cosmos itself is out of order. For Tate, the fact that in that play Edgar and Cordelia never meet, and so cannot marry, represents moral as well as theatrical disorder. In act 5 of *Lear*, Shakespeare emphasizes the gap between aims and results. In the end, Edmund repents ("Some good I mean to do") by rescinding the order (from Goneril and himself) to "hang Cordelia." But in the world of Shakespeare's play, repentance is meaningless. Edmund urges them to hurry, and Albany prays for divine intervention ("The gods defend her"), but to no avail, as before another word is uttered onstage, Lear enters "with Cordelia in his arms." The dramatic sense is that, in this instance, neither prayer nor repentance have any bearing on the senseless machinations of Fortuna. This cosmic outlook, also, Tate sets right, as Edgar observes, "Lucky was the Minute / Of our Approach, the Gods have weigh'd our Suffrings; / W'are past the Fire, and now must shine to Ages" (63–64). Likewise, as Tate's Albany orders the chains removed from Lear and Cordelia, he says: "The Wheel of Fortune now has made her Circle, / And Blessings yet stand 'twixt thy Grave and Thee" (64). Moments later, Cordelia with matchless assurance responds: "Then there are Gods, and Vertue is their Care" (65). These lines are tantamount to a rejoinder to the "original" Gloucester's pessimistic remarks on Edgar's condition as both "madman and beggar too":

> He has some reason, else he could not beg.
> I' th' last night's storm I such a fellow saw,
> Which made me think a man a worm. My son
> Came then into my mind, and yet my mind
> Was then scarce friends with him. I have heard more since.
> As flies to wanton boys are we to th' gods,
> They kill us for their sport.
>
> (4.1.31–37)

Most readers will say that the differences in tone in these contexts exceed differences generated by compositors' errors

or shifts in printing practices. By "alter'd," Tate means
altered in a significant or important way. For instance,
even Edgar's closing speech in Nahum Tate's revision of
the play evokes a quite different dramatic effect than that
of the earlier version:

> Our drooping Country now erects her Head,
> Peace spreads her balmy Wings, and Plenty Blooms.
> Divine *Cordelia*, all the Gods can witness
> How much thy Love to Empire I prefer!
> Thy bright Example shall convince the World
> (Whatever Storms of Fortune are decreed)
> That Truth and Vertue shall at last succeed.
>
> (67)

Before Mrs. Barry delivers her Epilogue, Edgar encapsulates
the significance of Tate's "Alterations." His reference to
"Gods" veers ever so slightly from Christian monotheism,
but not from the overriding faith in God's Providential
guidance of events. Life is not intrinsically unfair; the cosmos is not indifferent to human suffering. To Tate's Glos-
ter, whose counterpart in the earlier version thinks the
"gods" "kill us for their sport," Lear offers assurance that
he has "Business yet for Life" (66). Nor will their mutual
"calm Reflections" (Kent will join them) be only on "For-
tunes past," but also on "the prosperous Reign / Of this
celestial Pair" (67). The love between Edgar and Cordelia
is all important in this new scheme of things. The Glou-
cester/Lear lines, in Shakespeare cut off (in the Jacobean
Lear, Edgar, although alive at the end, survives in a world,
albeit a fictional world, with no women in it), are here
restored. Not only does the new order promise a more
humane rule, but the honorable blood lines will continue.
So there is reason for revelry, which is the underlying rhetorical mode of comedy. Tate's generic "Alteration" presents the triumph of *The History of King Lear* as an orderly
conception of the way Shakespeare should have dramatized
these events. It is too late to say that Tate created new

events to dramatize. He believed that his audience would recognize and refuse to accept the unresolved moral antinomies of Shakespeare's play. By reconciling these conflicting emotional needs, Tate creates a "history of King Lear" not at all like that of the Quartos. In comparison, the Quarto *True Chronicle History of King Lear* seems closer to *The Tragedie* of the First Folio than to Tate's *History*. On the other hand, Shakespeare's audience would have recognized an affinity between the 1608 Quarto *History* and *The Tragedy of Richard III*. But dramatic "history" is linked, also, with comedy in *The comicall Historie of the Merchant of Venice*. These literary terms can be helpful, but if we rely on them with too much credulity, we might think of them as designating boundable literary sets. It is probably less misleading to see how these categories were understood in Tate's and Shakespeare's times than to conclude that, when the norms of comedy replace those of tragedy, even if the outcome is called *history*, we have *melodrama*. And even though that term might say something about Tate's "Alterations," we can use it without believing that it designates a form impervious to other forms.

We do not need intractable principles to make ordinary judgments. In a recent edition of Tate's *Lear*, there is an obvious printer's error in the speech just quoted. In Edgar's final line of the play, the text reads "viture" instead of "[v]ertue." Is it worth wondering how, if at all, this minor slip-up adds to or detracts from the significance of the rewriting that Tate accomplished, including the "Alteration" of the cast of characters? Nowadays, critics regard Tate's revisions as evidence of eighteenth century resistance to the un-Christian close of Shakespeare's *Lear*. In doing so, they in effect insist that these changes go beyond "free emendation." Every Shakespearean remembers Theobald's confrontation with the "authority" of the First Folio ("A table of green fields" > "A [babbl'd] of green fields"). Is there a difference between "restoring" and "altering" Shakespeare's language? What do our practices say about this?

Nahum Tate removes the King of France from the play, and by so doing he rights, as Shakespeare forgot to do, the many wrongs perpetrated against the righteous.

Whether we agree or disagree with "free emendation" as an editorial practice, we should be able to see that Tate's "intervention" is not, in the ordinary sense, textual. Rather, his "Alteration" is aesthetic and ethical: "all the Gods can witness" that Edgar's and Cordelia's suffering—and old Gloucester's and Lear's, too—are not in vain. Edgar and Cordelia are, as Mrs. Elizabeth Barry's "Epilogue" to *Lear* suggests, "true Lovers." "Poëts kill 'em," she claims, "in their own Defence," but she insists that Shakespeare's play transcends any criticism that the audience could make. These lines suggest that neither Tate nor Mrs. Perry thought they were "changing" Shakespeare's play, but only altering its text to make it clearer, to make it more effectively avoid the charge of "Inconstancy, the reigning Sin o'th'Age" (68).

This distinction is, of course, not only taxonomic. By assigning these revisions to Tate as playwright rather than as editor, critics affirm the singularity of Shakespeare's *King Lear.* Just as audiences are not likely to confuse Tate's *King Lear* with *Macbeth* or *Love's Labour's Lost,* neither will they fail to recognize how different that play is from Shakespeare's *Lear.* But given the fact that many critics adhere to the notion that no "text" of *Lear* has been or could be established, isn't this odd? We can say that the notion of "a different play" applies in a way that it does not to versions based on the 1608 Quarto and the 1623 Folio. Then let us look again at the closing quatrain of *Lear* in *The Riverside Shakespeare:*

> *Edg.* The weight of this sad time we must obey,
> Speak what we feel, not what we ought to say:
> The oldest hath borne most; we that are young
> Shall never see so much, nor live so long.

As with the line from *Twelfth Night,* the Arden, Bevington, and Kittredge-Ribner editions exhibit no apparent difference. Phonemically, even the Oxford Clarendon Press "Original-Spelling" edition is pretty much "selfsame":

> EDGAR
> The waight of this sad time we must obey,
> Speake what we feele, not what we ought to say:
> The oldest hath borne most, we that are yong,
> Shall neuer see so much, nor liue so long.

But we discover, too, that these lines represent only the close of *The Tragedie of King Lear*. *The Historie of King Lear* is less "selfsame":

> ALBANY
> The waight of this sad time we must obey,
> Speake what we feele, not what we ought to say,
> The oldest haue borne most, we that are yong,
> Shall neuer see so much, nor liue so long.

Again, the speech itself is pretty much the same; but it does make a difference when "roughly" the "same lines" are spoken by different characters. How does this variation come about, and what are we to make of it? On what "authority" would we choose, should we decide to choose, between them, say, in selecting a play text for a production company or in making a reading assignment for a class? Perhaps we resort to the Quartos themselves:

> *Duke.* The waight of this sad time we must obey,
> Speake what we feele, not what we ought to say,
> The oldest haue borne most, we that are yong,
> Shall neuer see so much, nor liue so long.
> (HEH 1608)

> *Duke* The waight of this sad time we must obay,
> Speake what we feele, not what we ought to say:
> The oldest haue borne most, we that are yong,
> Shall neuer see so much, nor liue so long.
> (HEH 1608 [1619])

Even with the help of the Hinman Collator, one would find negligible variation here: a different spelling of "obey," a period after the character's name in one but not in the other, a comma in 1608 where a colon appears in 1619. So we check the four Huntington copies of the 1623 Folio:

> *Edg.* The waight of this sad time we must obey,
> Speake what we feele, not what we ought to say:
> The oldest hath borne most; we that are yong,
> Shall neuer see so much, nor liue so long.

Obviously, the eclectic editions we have examined follow the First Folio in assigning the play's closing speech to Edgar. This fact leads to another question: Are the variations we see here of the sort that lead some critics to think that there isn't, never has been, and never will be a "proper, selfsame Shakespearean text?" Assuming that this is the sense of Propositions *C* and *D*, perhaps we breathe a sigh of relief, and, after referring to the Oxford companion edition of the "selfsame" text in non-"selfsame" modernized spelling, we remind ourselves that, when read aloud by actors, these differences in orthography vanish into the "reality" of phonemic articulation (idiolect > dialect > language).

If we focus on a particular utterance, trivial variations appear to be ordinary and nonproblematic. In order to assent to Proposition *D* with conviction ("[t]here never will be a text of *Lear*"), one must first forget that in every performance there was, is, and always will be one and only one "text" (i.e., script) of *Lear*. Likewise, even with an "eclectic" edition (*The Riverside Shakespeare*, for instance), selection of lines from Quarto and Folio versions will be the "one" reader's "experience." This is only to say that, for the moment, more than one version isn't supposed useful or convenient or to the purpose. (Can we in practical terms imagine the Quarto and Folio versions of *Lear* being staged at the Barbican simultaneously?) Once the choice between versions is made—by a stage director, for instance—it is made on that occasion for all time (think of Zarathustra's gateway "Moment"). One cannot retroactively insert Albany's attempt to intervene between Lear and Kent in scene 1 ("Dear Sir forbeare") from the Folio after having omitted it by following the Quarto; and other differences in the presentation of Albany will also appear in choosing between *The History* and *The Tragedy of King Lear*.[5] Suppose we proceed as if today were Doomsday. Then we imagine the *n* accumulated choices among oral or written *Lear* "texts" made to date to approximate the total group of arrangements recognizable—as family members might be through "family resemblances"—as *King Lear*. We have Japanese, Russian, German and English versions. We have Nahum Tate's revision and legions of editions and performances with myriads of major and minor differences. Now, with all this variation, is it likely that knowledgeable critics will ever mistake any one of them for "*a* text of" *Love's Labour's Lost*, or with any other Shakespeare play? If not, what is the significance of "there never will be a text of *Lear*" talk?

4.

"We cannot evade the charge of 'unfounded Platonism' by breezily introducing Wittgenstein's hoary figure of 'family resemblances.'" Even so, perhaps we can agree that Shakespeare criticism still grapples with the philosophical problem of the One and the Many. Sometimes it seems that the myriad of linguistic details must overwhelm any hope of validating useful generalization about literature. We talk about the "Petrarchan" and "Shakespearean sonnet," but we know that in the Renaissance "sonnets" ("little songs") have 8, 16, 18 and even 96 lines.[6] Just as the "texts" of *Lear* or *Twelfth Night* do not exist in any authorized form, some would say, so is "the Shakespearean sonnet" an illusory figment of the critical imagination. On the other hand, experience teaches that the term *sonnet* is flexible enough to do its work regardless of such anomalies as Francis Quarles's *Sions Sonets*. But the objection to establishing textual genealogies or literary genres can be met more directly. Albeit that the pictures we have in mind of talk about them as different activities may serve

a purpose; in an important sense, talk about literary *texts*
and talk about literary *genres* have much in common.

In the only public lecture that Wittgenstein ever delivered, he spoke on "the subject matter of Ethics" (LE 4).
Using the term much as G. E. Moore had used it in *Prin-
cipia Ethica*, Wittgenstein nevertheless sought to expand
it to include what he called "Aesthetics," and what today
is often referred to as "critical theory." But Wittgenstein
was not interested in niceties of wording. Rather, he wanted
to show how any of a large number of synonyms might
serve as well:

> And to make you see as clearly as possible what I take to
> be the subject matter of Ethics I will put before you a num-
> ber of more or less synonymous expressions each of which
> could be substituted for the above definition, and by enu-
> merating them I want to produce the same sort of effect
> which Galton produced when he took a number of photos
> of different faces on the same photographic plate in order
> to get the picture of the typical features they all had in
> common. And as by showing to you such a collective photo
> I could make you see what is the typical—say—Chinese
> face; so if you look through the row of synonyms which I
> will put before you, you will, I hope, be able to see charac-
> teristic features they all have in common. . . . (LE 4-5)

Wittgenstein's allusion to Sir Francis Galton[7] provides, I
think, a helpful perspective on the related practices of textual and genre theory, both of which involve the "problem"
of "singularity." Sir Francis Galton believed that the human
mind was not very adept at formulating generic images:
"Our mental generic composites are rarely defined; they
have that blur in excess which photographic composites
have in a small degree, and their background is crowded
with faint and incongruous imagery" (Galton *Generic* 9).
Wittgenstein was interested in Galton's project of sharpen-
ing generic impressions. In turn, Galton's idea of physical
impressions was much like I. A. Richards's conception of
eccentricities in individual interpretations, including "*mnemonic irrelevances*" (Richards 15), sometimes inappropriate

associations from individual pasts intrude on representations of generic features.[8] Because they are isolated, they tend to be irrelevant: They blur the focus on the work in question. Sir Francis wanted to clarify impressions of the features shared by members of related groups, especially those that were genetically related. "Our general impressions," he wrote, "are founded upon blended memories" (Galton *Generic* 1), which are like "Composite Portraits." Thus, Galton's work on inherited characteristics—"family resemblances"—was instrumental in the foundation of what we now call genetics. He sought to establish concrete evidence of what Thomas Huxley called "generic portraits."

In the early 1880s, Galton began experiments with photographs of people linked by family, race, disease and occupation. He aimed to classify members of groups in much the same way as biologists would later on (with photographs of individuals grouped under such categories as mesomorphic and endomorphic). He thought it feasible to capture a "picture" of the "typical" Chinese face. In order to produce the evidence for such a typology, Galton experimented with numerous ways of focusing several faces on a single photographic plate. He used a sextant with a telescope attached (Pearson 2, 285), focused glass slides together through "magic lanterns" on the same screen, and photographed photographs of individuals scaled to proportion, dividing the optimum shutter time by the number of component subjects. The result was a picture, not of an abstraction, but of the physical features shared by the subjects.

Galton used this technique to resolve what some critics now regard as a literary problem: namely, the apparently illusory appearance of an integral "self" (of authors, critics or anyone in particular). For instance, Galton understood that individuals change over time. Indeed, they exhibit different impressions even in the briefest passage of time. Pictures taken of the "same" individual at the "same" sitting capture aspects or impressions which might not be typical. For instance, the subject is smiling in this photograph, and yet friends regard the person as typically reticent and reflective. What was needed was a picture of what is typical about that individual. Galton got the idea of representing typicality from the numerous medals that had been struck of Alexander the Great (Pearson 2, plates 37 and 38). Although a composite of them all lacked the particularity of each, it nevertheless captured something unique to the medals in tandem, namely, what they had in common. Photography enabled Galton to capture that element of a shared characteristic of the "same person" at different times. Among Galton's papers in the Manuscript Room of the Library of University College, London, is a statement, signed by two photographers, two print sellers, an ornamental carver and a "Practical Surveyor," swearing that two photographs and one "Blended Photograph" are of the same individual. One photograph is of Mr. Roger Tichborne, a thin, rakish young man with a mustache, the other of a rather mature Sir Roger Tichborne, who has, along with his title, acquired a lowered beard, but is otherwise clean-shaven. A third—the "Blended Photograph"—is a portrait of a man somewhat less jowled than Sir Roger, but less callow-looking than Mr. Tichborne.

With the technique that he settled on, Galton achieved his "Composite Portraiture" by superimposing photographs scaled to proportional size of the group. In open letters to the public, he solicited families to send such photos to him in London. He gave very detailed instructions to participants to assure proportionality, and he insisted absolutely on full face and profile shots only. Setting aside the technical questions that arise here (I am no expert in photography), the important point to recognize is that the product of the procedure was a photograph (Pearson 2, plates 28–35), which is, in its composite segment, neither of an individual nor of nothing at all. That is, the picture was a picture, not of an abstract concept of "family resemblances," but of the family resemblance itself: the shared features of the family members participating in the "composite." In this way, Galton sought to establish, so to speak, a "founded

Platonism": "A Galtonian photograph is the picture of a probability" (*PG* "Appendix" 229). One cannot say that these "Composite Portraits" are of imaginary configurations, because the photographs are as "real" as those of the individuals included in the composite. The difference is simply that the "many" have been apprehended as the "one" by the technological capacity to register light waves on photographic plates.

We know from his numerous references that Wittgenstein was intrigued by Galton's conceptual framework; and Wittgenstein had such a "Composite Portrait" taken of himself and his sisters (Koeb 156).[9] The result is a picture of Wittgensteinian "family resemblance," neither markedly male nor female, but unmistakable. The method, with superimposition of one portrait upon another, resulting in pictures of pictures, with the process repeatable many times over, suggests, I believe, something about the method of composition of *Philosophical Investigations*, which does not so much depart from as develop Wittgenstein's "picture theory" of language as laid out in the *Tractatus*. In the Preface to the *Investigations*, Wittgenstein writes:

> After several unsuccessful attempts to weld my results together into . . . a whole, I realized that I should never succeed. The best that I could write would never be more than philosophical remarks; my thoughts were soon crippled if I tried to force them on in any single direction against their natural inclination.—And this was, of course, connected with the very nature of the investigation. For this compels us to travel over a wide field of thought criss-cross in every direction.—The philosophical remarks in this book are, as it were, a number of sketches of landscapes which were made in the course of these long and involved journeyings. (*PI* v)

As with Galton's project of multiplying exposures on the same photographic plate, Wittgenstein came to realize that, to "investigate" philosophical problems in a way that did not distort the effort, he needed to escape from the formal design of the argumentative essay. Rather than a single "finished" picture, he offered an expanded "album" of impressions of the "same" landscape.

I have suggested that Galton's method relates to textual and genre theory. Employing a technique very much like that of Galton's "Composite Portraiture," Michael Warren produced a photographic facsimile product, *The Complete King Lear: 1608–1623*, which purports to be a comprehensive (*Complete*) textual production of Shakespeare's *King Lear*. It is "*Complete*" in the sense that anything less than is included in it would be lacking, and anything more, by exceeding "completeness," would introduce extraneous material. This text, "Prepared by Michael Warren," is divided, like one of Galton's group of photographs, into several parts: a "General Introduction," an "Annotated Bibliography," "Parallel Texts" (of Q1, Q2 and 1623), and "Photographic Facsimile" reproductions of the 1608 and 1619 Quartos and of the First Folio. For this production, Warren worked with thousands of pieces of text cut from photographs of the Quarto and Folio versions of *King Lear*. He not only presents facsimiles of the individual artifacts, but a composite of their matching parts. Warren places pictures of matching lines from the play side by side, so that users can see, not only how they differ, but in what ways they do not *significantly* differ. Implicitly, lines cannot differ in an important way unless they are sufficiently similar to make the juxtaposition sensible or useful. It is clear why, then, in the "Parallel Texts" section of *The Complete King Lear*, Michael Warren uses the term *authority* in a way quite different from that implying a factual condition of the credentials of the scholars discussed in section 2. Wittgenstein would say that Warren uses the term in an "ethical" or "absolute" sense.

We have agreed that editors choose. For Warren, the term *authority* in the context of Shakespeare's text entails application of a rule to be followed in choosing. Thus Warren has in mind a hierarchy of claims with respect to the *n* available *Lears*. He does concede that his "book demonstrates the problem of the term *King Lear*," but it is clear that the very ambiguity of the term drives the ethical design of his editorial project. Recognizing the difficulties of even the most minimalist effort—to juxtapose photographs of different versions of "the self-same *Lear*" text—Warren concedes that the editor must select from a range of photographs of the same line from the "same edition," for they are not "identical." For instance, the inking is not uniform, and, of course, all sorts of things happened during a print run. Still, Warren projects resolution of the problem through a "minimum of editorial intervention" (1, vii). Since it is a mistake to think "that all that can be known is known already" (1, vii), presumably, Warren would not rule out the possibility that someday someone might turn up a manuscript of *Lear*, written, like the holograph of Jonson's *Masque of Queenes*, in the author's hand. But in the interim, Warren adheres to the textual editor's version of the Hippocratic oath: "First, do no harm." Insofar as it is humanly possible, Editor Warren seeks "to avoid editing" (vii). The aim is both a motive and a rule to be followed.

Warren's minimalist method is to reproduce photographic "copies" of the earliest "originals" (printings of *King Lear*), and by that means to render apprehensible the physical artifact—*The Complete King Lear*—"before the historical document" (vii), that is, before *King Lear* became an object of presumably obfuscatory intrusions. In this context, we can see the ethical implications of the figure of "descent" in Proposition *B*. Limiting his project to photographs of the two Quartos (Q1, 1608, Q2, 1619) and the First Folio (1623), Warren declares:

> E) *All subsequent editions of the play derive directly or indirectly from these editions and therefore have no authority. (Warren 1, xii)*

Now, the sense of "completeness" implied by the title of Warren's edition of *Lear* can be seen. It is "complete" because everything that is not included is excluded by and from "authority." Since all later editions derive from Q1, Q2 and 1623, all lack "authority." Obviously, Warren is using the term *authority* in a strong sense here, for many of the names and reputations implied by the factual, institutional sense of the term, discussed in section 2, are eliminated from "authority." Thus, in the Wittgensteinian sense, Proposition *E* establishes an "ethical" or "absolute"—today we would probably use the term *normative*—definition of the status of various Shakespeare texts of *Lear*.

It seems clear that this ethical norm requires focus on the physicality of the "text," and that this focus proceeds from a purchase for correction of error. For if we assent to *E*, mistakes are possible, and so is correction of error. As a matter of practical procedure, we may compare a given text with any of the three authoritative sources of all *Lear* texts. This assumption has important consequences for criticism, for in emphasizing the "how" or the "method" of investigation, the textual editor precludes appeal to such individualized concepts as *insight* or *intelligence* or *relevance* or *prestige*. We have already seen that not all Shakespeareans agree with such a limitation. It is one thing to say that even intelligent critics have been mistaken in their statements about Shakespeare, but quite another to erect a standard of judgment able to separate correct from incorrect assertions. And yet no error can be perceived except in a context of correction, even if the *means* of correction (as in the case of Q2's "dram of eale") are not presently available.

It is not hard to imagine an opponent of "unfounded Platonism" talk responding: "With respect, this is an odd way to defend the 'singularity' of *King Lear*. Instead of one *Lear* you would give the one name to a whole clan of plays. And then at your convenience you would have the individual members collapse into a single verbal structure. In this way, *King Lear* oscillates between temporal annihilation and immortality. Is this fair? Don't you, in an effort to have it both ways, indulge in a bit of critical flim-flam? Wouldn't it be more forthright to say that you have either one or many *Lears*, and that neither one or all of them are 'original' or 'authorial' in any case?" Candor aside, the point of this objection seems clear enough. What is less clear is how we are to investigate and test the proposed constraint implicit in its claim. Is it the statement of limits itself, or something in the nature of things, that restrains critics from deciding the "one" or "many" issue, either/ or? What do we gain by acceding to the broad assertion that it is either "one" *or* "many?" Wouldn't the propriety of any claim in the matter depend on the work that it does? If the proposition only tells us what we already know, why would we think it useful?

The problem here is, to paraphrase Wittgenstein, that "a picture holds us captive." We insist—as if there were something important at stake—upon the absolute separation between one and many. But in so doing, we assume that the locution, *Lear*, is subject to an arithmetical schematization, and cannot exist without it. In acquiring the skill of manipulating our number system, I did not learn that, because there are millions of oak trees in the world, therefore there is no such thing as "one" of that kind. The single oak in my backyard changes from year to year, season to season, moment to moment; and when I get home tonight it might not even be there: My wife may have ordered the arborist to cut it down, in order to permit more sunlight on the flower bed. But of one thing I am certain: The oak tree in my backyard will never become the Aspen in front of my neighbor's house. "So is it the arithmetical classification system that is in question here?" I add one more performance of *Lear* to my experience; I see or read the play again, and talk or write about it. Is there a critical problem of how many times I experienced this additional performance last night? I recall Wittgenstein's remark regarding whether a particular "sentence consists of four or of nine elements." The interlocutor wants to know the correct way to characterize this "selfsame" block of words. Wittgenstein's response may seem elliptical and even indirect: "Does it matter which we say, so long as we avoid misunderstandings in any particular case?" (*PI* §48) We would be surprised if an order for "Two tickets to Saturday night's performance of *Lear*" produced one ticket to two different versions of Shakespeare's play. In the context of practical communication in ordinary circumstances, the concepts of *singularity* and *plurality* work sufficiently well. It is in the effort to find some final method of articulation that we are tempted to go astray. Wittgenstein's suggestion can be helpful here: "The real discovery is the one that makes me capable of stopping doing philosophy when I want to.—The one that gives philosophy peace, so that it is no longer tormented by questions that bring *itself* in question" (*PI* §133).

"Nevertheless," one could object, "if we say these productions are 'selfsame,' surely we contradict ourselves." This articulation of a familiar theme is, in and of itself, indicative of that longing for a species of "Renaissance talk" that demands so much of the vocabulary that it "brings *itself* in question." Not only is the utterance itself doubtful, but even if it were "true," it need not necessarily undermine our justified confidence in the way we talk about Shakespeare, when that talk proceeds as talk usually does in ordinary circumstances. After all, "contradiction" is just a word like other words. In his *Remarks on the Foundations of Mathematics*, Wittgenstein writes:

> [I]f a contradiction were now actually found in arithmetic—that would only prove that an arithmetic with *such* a contradiction in it could render very good service; and it will be better for us to modify our concept of the certainty required, than to say that it would really not yet have been a proper arithmetic.
>
> (401)

Again, the question concerns function, what communication is *for*. Here, Wittgenstein draws attention to the role the arithmetic system plays in our lives. Earlier on, he shows how other systems work coherently, even though they might seem to us contrary to all logic and experience.

In everyday life, as we conduct business, buying products and paying bills, what counts is how things work within an order of things. The notion of the "Petrarchan sonnet" is useful if and only if "non-Petrarchan sonnets" are available for comparison. *King Lear* may be, in certain contexts, as Michael Warren claims, an "ambiguous" term, but it is not so under all circumstances. When one attempts to book seats for a staging of *Lear*, it's no good, even with a forthcoming inflection, to proclaim Proposition *D* ("There is no *King Lear*"), for the simple reason that the statement would not likely be understood, and it might even lead to social unpleasantness. In this context of purposive utterance, textual theory is closely related to genre theory. We can distinguish a Petrarchan from a Shakespearean sonnet in the same way we recognize the difference between Quarto and Folio versions of *Lear*, which, in turn, is like the way we discriminate between the varieties of ways the play may be interpreted. As Sir Francis Galton put it, "The word generic presupposes a genus, that is to say, a collection of individuals who have much in common, and among whom medium characteristics are very much more frequent than extreme ones" (Galton *Generic* 2).

5.

Critics familiar with the recent literature know that, even if we could set the textual difficulties perceived in discussion of Shakespeare's text aside, the concept of Shakespeare's *singularity* would still bedevil critics. For not only does the idea of the *singularity* of a given Shakespeare text create the impression of a problem for some critics, but for others the notion of Shakespeare's *singularity* is, in and of itself, "problematic." They will say that Shakespeare is "like us," and that claim, if accompanied by appropriate signs of irony, might merely amuse or be brushed aside. But when it seems that the assertion is serious, it arrests our attention. Even then, in a charitable effort to "go on together," we might reasonably think of ways in which the remark is unexceptional: "All men are mortal; Shakespeare is a man; therefore," and so on. We agree with the assertion because the modesty of our construction allows assent.

But suppose that the absence of irony in the remark becomes the basis of our characterization. We have reason, beyond the bare locution itself, to believe that the critic has a more ambitious aim in mind: Shakespeare isn't just "like us," he is *more* "like us" and *more* like other writers of his time than most people think, or most Shakespeareans imagine. Suppose, as we examine the context of the utterance, we find that the statement ("Shakespeare is like us") resists a benignly modest characterization. For instance, contrary to the argument that Shakespeare stands out from the playwrights of his time, the critic asserts that Thomas Heywood was "'the most complete man of the theatre of his time'" (Taylor 376). Thus Shakespeare is "like us" in a strong sense of the assertion; "like us," he is undeservedly thought "singular." Thus, the critic asserts:

> F) Nothing in the facts of Shakespeare's life can define or support his alleged supremacy among the world's writers. (Taylor 377)

Clearly, if this view is credible, Shakespeare is "like us," and he is "like us" because, although his works are given much attention in the here and now, we can't be sure that his plays will survive (Taylor 378). Indeed, because he is "like us," his works are "disappearing before our eyes" (Taylor 378).

I want to ask: What bars me from surety that Shakespeare's plays will survive? Am I not as sure of this as I am of most things that I am sure of? Would changing my state of mind in the matter (by taking a drug known to induce feelings of anxiety or uncertainty, for instance) alter my understanding of Shakespeare or of the Elizabethan *zeitgeist* or "paradigm" or "social construct" involved in my statement of belief in the persistence of interest in Shakespeare? Proponents of Proposition *F* could answer: "It might well challenge unwarranted confidence, and elicit a healthy skepticism regarding Shakespeare's 'singularity.' There should be no objection to *that*." Agreed. But the hard part comes in gauging the difference between "warranted" and "unwarranted" confidence. If my confidence is unwarranted, can I expect some gain if I cultivate feelings of uncertainty in the matter? I mean, what would doubt in this matter amount to? What work could I do with it? How would doubt alter the production or understanding of, say, the five Shakespeare plays running concurrently in London? What difference would doubt about the persistence of interest in Shakespeare make to our *"way* of living?" (*RFM* 6.34). For instance, I pretend to doubt Shakespeare's "singularity," but see no change in the world. But in fact, I have no more reason to doubt that English-speaking audiences will be flocking to Shakespeare plays a hundred years from now than I do that water at sea level will continue to boil at 100°C. I have "experienced" neither condition first hand, but, as Wittgenstein puts it, my expectation that this boiling will occur just seems to "hang together with" everything else I believe (*OC* §313). "But then one can easily 'test' the one and not even with difficulty the other." I know this, too, but that knowledge doesn't shake my confidence. Is my assurance in this matter irrational? Some people might think so, but then some people say that "society is sick" and that my assurance of Shakespeare's "singularity" is symptomatic of a more general social malaise. Proponents of "nothing supports Shakespeare's supremacy" talk could still say, "You can't *know* that anyone will be reading Shakespeare a hundred years from now. Your expectation about water boiling at such and such a temperature is rooted in our experience of the physical world; Shakespeare's reputation is just a social convention. And, anyway, a hundred years! What kind of immortality is that? Aristophanes and Sophocles and Euripides have lasted for thousands of years."

Now, the argument is that only the ancient predecessors, who will always be more ancient than their less ancient descendants, are "immortal" or "singular" and not "like us." Shakespeare's dates (as presently understood: 1564–1616) are clearly a limiting factor. But, if I understand correctly, our contemporaneity also figures here, for "after all, despite our fondness for fools' prophecies, we cannot really *know* what kind of reputation Shakespeare will enjoy, in the theatre or the library, two thousand years from now" (Taylor 378, italics mine). The implied distinction here, I assume, is between "really knowing" something and only knowing it provisionally or as a hunch or a guess. One critic is sure that, a thousand years from now, Shakespeare will be going strong; another says that crowds will be flocking to Thomas Heywood, because he was "'the most complete man of the theatre of his time.'" How can we be sure, and yet be sure of what we agree no one can know for a certainty (namely, the future)? As Wittgenstein points out in *On Certainty*, sometimes we invest too much emphasis on the concept of *knowing*—so much so, in fact, that the conversation easily slips from *certainty* to *knowledge*. Assurance of Shakespeare's "immortality" might have an entirely less millennial horizon than that of "really knowing" something about the future, such as the site of the next Winter Olympics. But just because the criterion of *immortality* might be modest and flexible doesn't mean that it has no use. By *immortality* one might only mean to indicate the opposite of *ephemeral*—*timeless*—that is, not like the remarks printed on this page: *immortal*, but not necessarily *Immortal*. Sacred, not Sacred.

Suppose that, notwithstanding my effort to limit expectations surrounding ordinary use of the term *immortality*, the critic insists that I have not addressed the question of how assurance of Shakespeare's longevity fits with the assertion that his words are disappearing before our very eyes. *Are* his words "disappearing before our eyes?" If so, how do they deceive us into perceiving that they don't disappear as they are read or heard, but—to the contrary—that it is at that moment of our reading them or hearing them performed that they become most evident? Admittedly, to emphasize the evanescence of some aspect or other of an expression, a critic metaphorically exclaims that words are actually "disappearing before our eyes," it is reasonable to lend assent. For, again, "going on together" would be rendered ever more difficult if metaphor were barred from communication. But if an emotional investment is at stake, then this question remains: Even if Shakespeare's words (and, presumably, those of Euripides, too) *were* "disappearing before our eyes," why should this be cause for alarm? Can't we imagine the words reappearing as quickly as they disappeared no less "before our eyes?" Isn't the evidence of lasting public interest in Shakespeare what matters here? And doesn't it explain why my assurance of Shakespeare's "singularity" remains untouched by the fact that some critics believe in the disappearance of any or all of his words "before our eyes?"

Probably most proponents of "Shakespeare is like us" talk would respond with: "This is obtuse. Obviously, the critic was speaking metaphorically about the way in which language changes. We do need modernized texts and notes to explain antiquated uses. In fact, some words in Shakespeare's lexicon *have* vanished from the language. It is reasonable to expect that losses will continue, and, given the myriad of social changes afoot, accelerate. The youth of today are raised in a nonliterary, televisual culture. Historical trends indicate that, increasingly, we will need to translate Shakespeare for English speaking readers (Taylor 378). Already, Anglophone readers have difficulty reading *The Faerie Queene*, with its quaint vocabulary and antiquated style. Is it not revealing that *The Faerie Queene* has been translated into modern English prose? *The Faerie Queene* may be, like *King Lear*, a 'singular' work, but doesn't such a translation suggest that the poem has already become, for many readers, like *Beowulf*: an English poem known to English readers only in prose translation? Can *King Lear* be far behind? Decades ago, Erwin Panofsky argued that, as soon as art is created, it is on its way to becoming a 'document' of human history" (Panofsky chap. 1).

The analogy between *Lear* and *The Faerie Queene* might work for you, although Spenser's diction was, and Shakespeare's wasn't, "obsolete" in its own day. Admittedly, something is lost with presentations that "translate" or "adapt" a literary work. But we already knew that, for most readers, Shakespeare's language is not as accessible as Neil Simon's, any more than Spenser's is. Wasn't this—the problem of Renaissance diction—the point behind the modern prose rendition of *The Faerie Queene*? To be fair, we should note that Douglas Hill offers, not a translation, but an "adaptation" of "The Illustrated *Faerie Queene.*" The accompanying illustrations by artists such as Rubens, Titian, Cranach, Dürer and Eworth of such subjects as the Three Graces, St. George and the Dragon, the Seven-Headed Beast of the Apocalypse, Elizabeth and the Three Goddesses, Lord Grey, Sir Philip Sidney, Venus, Diana and many others (86 illustrations in all) might prove helpful to someone's understanding of Spenser's poem and time. Implicitly, Douglas Hill seems to agree with Panofsky and most linguists, that language changes with the times (Hill 11). Hill wants his volume "to show modern readers the essence of *The Faerie Queene*" (11). Isn't the visual aspect something like an "essence" of Spenser's poem? Hill assumes that explicit allegory went "out of fashion" in the epochs since Spenser, and that his illustrated adaptation will serve as "an introduction and a guide" to nonspecialists. Many readers of *Beowulf* in Old English started out with Talbot Donaldson's translation. Panofsky's argument about *Weltanschauüng*, which is similar to current notions of *subjectivity*, touches both creator and interpreter. All of us need help in understanding literature of the sixteenth and seventeenth centuries; we need help even with Nahum Tate's "adaptation" of *King Lear*. Does it matter what form that help takes? The elaborate note to a line in a scholarly edition of *Lear* may be just what a scholar is looking for, but it might only perplex a student reading the play for the first time.

If all we are to infer from "Shakespeare is like us" talk

is a restatement of Panofsky's modest assertion about social change, then our skepticism regarding the assertion
that Shakespeare's words are "disappearing before our very
eyes" would seem to be misplaced, since it merely reaffirms
an unexceptional and harmless truism. But suppose the
critic wants to say that Shakespeare is not so different from
other playwrights of his time, and that he is, moreover,
"like us," his *critics*. The argument is that Shakespeare is
no less "like us" than Thomas Heywood or any of a host
of Renaissance authors who wrote for profit or patronage.
In Shakespeare's case, mere chance singled his work out,
making it appear "singular" to captives of Western culture.
Shakespeare has proved luckier than most writers in that
he wrote in English, and the drift of the time is toward
making English a language every nationality learns. This
gives Shakespeare "an insurmountable advantage . . . over
literary exports from France, Spain, Italy, Germany, Rus-
sia, Japan—not to mention ancient Athens and Rome"
(Taylor 379–80). Thus we have Russian and Japanese directors' film versions of *King Lear*, but not of Calderón's *Life
is a Dream*. This hard fact of happenstance history by no
means compels our belief in Shakespeare's "singularity."
For Shakespeare is, finally, "like us," his critics: capable of
writing something no one without extra-literary induce-
ment would read.

This view of Shakespeare is at the far pole from the bar-
dolatry of the nineteenth century. It holds that Shakespeare
is unique only in the sense that all humans are so. "Singular" only in the generic sense, Shakespeare was not
"singular" in the honorific sense accorded by critical tradition. His works are "no more immortal than the scores of
plays by the great Greek dramatists that have evaporated"
(Taylor 378). Suppose a different historical development, and
we can easily imagine a world with no Shakespeare. If radical fundamentalist Muslims take over the United Nations,
what would happen to Shakespeare? What if revolutionary
social movements sweep away the literary values that have
given Shakespeare his "advantage?" We remember the Red

Guards in China's "great leap forward," and "some brands
of Marxism might be no more friendly" to Shakespearean
values (Taylor 379). Surely we can imagine curricular
change in a less Anglophone direction. It is possible that
the advantage procured by the universality of English will
not last (Taylor 379–80). Government-sponsored art of the
future might favor less English, less aristocratic, less patriarchal, less "singular" authors than Shakespeare. Indeed,
isn't this just what advocacy critics want: an "enabling discourse for political activism?" (Howard 14) The pretense
of Shakespeare's "universality" would be dispatched, and
this would be a good thing, as, within such literary contexts, "differences of material existence—differences of
race, gender, class, history and culture—are supposedly
canceled" (Howard 4).

But why, I would ask, would anyone find the Shakespearean quality of transcending particular differences objectionable? "Because Shakespeare 'transcends . . . differences
to get at abiding truths' or 'universal truths' (Howard 4).
That is what is objectionable. The notion of Shakespeare's
'singularity' is nothing less than a disguised assertion of
his 'universality' (Howard 4), and *that* is what must be
brought into question. The problem is that criticism focusing on aesthetic features of Shakespeare's works 'essen-
tializes what is socially constructed' (Howard 5), mistaking
what is 'socially constructed' for 'natural and unchanging
truths.'[10] Through the ages this emphasis has 'socially constructed' the idea of Shakespeare standing almost alone as
the 'preeminent "major figure"' of the English literary tradition: an author whose work 'never ages and eludes all
historical implication' (Howard 6). This demeaning characterization, which derives from 'retrograde' literary values, must be replaced by a socially determined agenda,
which proceeds from the assumption that 'historically
specific factors determine the "Shakespeare" produced in
criticism, in the classroom, and on the stage'" (Howard 4).

It is not hard to see why critics of the "homiletic" or "advocacy" school are uncomfortable with terms like *essential*

and *singular*. For them, terms about "features," "origins," or "originality" disguise dubious value judgments, which always prove to be "situated" or "local," and they always involve a leap of faith into one or another version of literary jingoism. Ever since Plato's *Republic*, philosophers, critics, politicians and religious leaders have taken an interest in what the young are taught to read. "Homiletic" critics of the left, wedded to the aims of "social contrucivism,"[11] are captives, too, of a particular vocabulary. They are uncomfortable with terms like *essential* and *natural* and *universal*, but their discomfort indicates an odd belief that such words are more than words. Since these words seem to possess a talismanic power, social constructivists do not want their uses taught. Charitable characterization of this view would stress that, after all, every curriculum is established with certain goals in mind; so "advocacy critics" are no better or worse than other interest groups for advancing nonliterary goals for the study of literature. Of course, it would be foolish to argue that Renaissance critics have preoccupied themselves with the study of female or homosexual playwrights and poets. Attention to Lady Elizabeth Cary's *Miriam* and Lady Mary Wroth's *Urania* and Richard Barnfield's *Cynthia* will encourage an appreciation of a more complex range of Renaissance poetic expression. Comparison between sonnets by Barnfield and Shakespeare, in which two speakers address young men with an instruction that they apprehend their visage in a mirror, may also help develop a coherent understanding of why we pay more attention to Shakespeare's sonnets than to those of other Elizabethans.

Of course, the canon is always subject to adjustment, and probably the professor who has never changed a syllabus of a course in Renaissance literature is as fanciful an entity as Hobbes's "invulnerable bodies, iron men" and "flying horses." Questions of judgment arise in deciding when adjustment of the canon becomes overadjustment. By now it is clear that the benign motive behind establishing a more "inclusive" canon has led to unintended consequences. Some advocates of "inclusion" hold that Shakespeare's place in the literary pantheon is either an accident of history (defeat of the Spanish Armada turned the tables against Lope de Vega and in favor of Shakespeare) or, worse, a xenophobic conspiracy on the part of the dominant, largely male, largely white, largely heterosexual, largely Anglophile culture. For these critics, preoccupation with the Shakespeare canon is tantamount to social oppression (and attention to Shakespeare's *critics* would be exponentially so). By now, this argument, like "ready to wear" apparel, is familiar enough to be applied to any "major author" of any period. If Shakespeare can be "decanonized," who can't?

As I have already suggested, it is not the motives behind "canon adjustment talk," but the talk itself that leads to the dubiety of imagined "critical problems." I can think of no reasonable objection to animadversions on Shakespeare's faults. Ben Jonson admired Shakespeare, but mixed praise of his talent with blame for his lack of discipline. Likewise, more recent critics fault aspects of Shakespeare's works. Wittgenstein's impression that Shakespeare's writings were "*dashed off*" is reminiscent of Jonson's view that he would have done better had he "blotted a thousand" lines. Although Jonson rendered his opinion with the magisterial tone of one who had mastered the craft of literary criticism, Wittgenstein registers a similar estimate of Shakespeare with diffidence, as if he thinks his literary taste might be faulty:

> His pieces give me an impression as of enormous *sketches* rather than of paintings; as though they had been *dashed off* by someone who can permit himself *anything*, so to speak. And I understand how someone can admire that and call it *supreme* art, but I don't like it.—So if someone stands in front of these pieces speechless, I can understand him; but anyone who admires them as one admires, say, Beethoven, seems to me to misunderstand Shakespeare. (*CV* 86)

Like Jonson, Wittgenstein thinks that there is something haphazard about Shakespeare's method of composition. But he registers a concern, not found in Jonson, for the *reasons* given by those who idolize Shakespeare. There is something wrong with *them*, for one cannot reasonably admire Shakespeare as one does Beethoven. It seems clear that what bothers Wittgenstein is Shakespeare's "artlessness." He perceives a spontaneity in Shakespeare's work, marked by its "asymmetry," and this renders it unworthy as "*supreme* art." For Wittgenstein, "symmetry" is a *sine qua non* of the highest achievement in art. As anyone familiar with the *Investigations* and *Remarks on the Foundations of Mathematics* would expect, Wittgenstein admired a sense of inevitability and order. I infer that Wittgenstein likes Beethoven because he sounds like Mozart, but with just enough departure from a pronounced "symmetry" to allow for the thrill of novelty that we think of as typical of the move toward Romantic music. If Beethoven organized any sounds spontaneously, he had the "*supreme* art" to disguise that spontaneity.

Intelligent critics do not always share the same tastes. Nietzsche admired Shakespeare for the very quality that offended Wittgenstein. And yet, although the two critics approach Shakespeare with very different aesthetic sensibilities, they alike find him—in a strong sense of the term—*singular*. Can we infer anything from this fact beyond the obvious solipsism of "taste?" "Well," one replies, "you suggest that Wittgenstein was drawn toward music of the classical period, and, of course, Nietzsche only distanced himself from Wagner because he thought *Parsifal* too tied to the Christian past."

As I and my coauthors argue in *Nietzsche's Case*, a philosopher's style is not something ladled on after an argument or plot or fancy of whatever kind has been articulated. It is, rather, an integral part of the "philosophical" thought expressed. Subject matter, genre and point of view are among the more important choices that philosophers like Nietzsche and Wittgenstein make, and their remarks on style are important expositions of their critical outlook. As we should expect, Wittgenstein, but not Nietzsche, had reservations about Shakespeare's style:

"Shakespeare similes are, *in the ordinary sense*, bad. So if they are all the same good—and I don't know whether they are or not—they must be a law to themselves. Perhaps, e.g., their ring gives them plausibility and truth" (*CV* 49). As we can see, it is the hint of anarchy here—or, philosophically, the "problem of solipsism"—that prompts Wittgenstein's objection, however much it may be qualified by praise. Significantly, Wittgenstein justifies whatever lapses appear in Shakespeare with the suggestion that, by its own internal workings ("law to themselves") Shakespeare's plays attain the "ring" of "truth." It is this internal "plausibility" that extricates Shakespeare's works from the blind alley of solipsistic "spontaneity"; it is this element that allows him to communicate. Wittgenstein's admiration of Shakespeare, then, emerges almost with a sense of resignation, as if he concedes Shakespeare's greatness in spite of himself:

> It may be that the essential thing with Shakespeare is his ease and authority and that you just have to accept him as he is if you are going to be able to admire him properly, in the way you accept nature, a piece of scenery, for example, just as it is. (*CV* 49)

The problem is that not everyone is able to contemplate Shakespeare's plays as Wittgenstein does. It is as if Wittgenstein locates his reservations about Shakespeare's "asymmetry" in his inability to read Shakespeare's works "*easily* . . . as one views a splendid piece of scenery" (49). Typically, Wittgenstein ponders a way to articulate what looks like a problem in perception. Thus, he tries to visualize not only the essence of Shakespeare's style, but that of his own incapacity to respond to it. Shakespeare's plays are like "enormous *sketches*," like "a splendid piece of scenery," untrammelled by the artistic intervention of symmetry's restraint. They are, as Beethoven's symphonies and sonatas are not, unfinished—or perhaps incoherent would be a better word—like a dream:

> A dream is all wrong, absurd, composite, and yet at the same
> time it is completely right: put together in *this* strange way
> it makes an impression. Why? I don't know. And if Shake-
> speare is great, as he is said to be, then it must be possible
> to say of him: it's all wrong, things *aren't like that*—and
> yet at the same time it's quite right according to a law of
> its own. (*CV* 83)

When we remember the many times Wittgenstein ponders
the solipsistic possibility that one could, on a given occasion, provide a unique case of following a rule, we should
understand his unease. He cannot read Shakespeare with
pleasure; he senses "asymmetry." It is like a dream, "wrong,
absurd, composite . . . strange." Because he finds Shakespeare "completely unrealistic," Wittgenstein feels uneasy
with "the whole *corpus* of his plays"; by creating "their
own language and world," they provide Wittgenstein with
no sense of distance, no comparative mechanism, with
which he might reasonably judge the works. This is as
much as to say that Shakespeare's greatness has no purchase on Wittgenstein's notion of the real world: "It is
not as though Shakespeare portrayed human types well
and were in that respect *true to life*. He is *not* true to life"
(*CV* 84). And yet in spite of all this, Wittgenstein admits
that he stares at Shakespeare "in wonder," as at a natural phenomenon. Why? Because Shakespeare "has such a
supple hand and his *brush strokes* are so individual" that
he compels Wittgenstein's attention. Thus it is the "singularity" of the "dream rightness" of Shakespeare's plays
that overcomes their unrealistic characters and situations.
Although Wittgenstein thinks Shakespeare could say nothing of the "lot of the poet" ("Nor could he regard himself
as a prophet or as a teacher of mankind" [85]), Shakespeare
was "singular": "I do not believe that Shakespeare can be
set alongside any other poet" (84). While his similes are
all wrong and his characters not true to life, Shakespeare,
unlike all other poets, could say "of himself": "'I sing as
the birds sing'" (84).

Like the Milton whom he admired as "incorruptible" (*CV* 48), Wittgenstein thinks of Shakespeare as an untutored, undisciplined, unselfconscious genius, "Warbl[ing] his native Wood-notes wilde." He clearly denies the intellectual dimension of Shakespeare's achievement: In Shakespeare's plays, "truth" emerges almost by accident. For Wittgenstein, although Shakespeare's plays must be accepted as one accepts a landscape, he has nothing to teach; which is to say that Shakespeare's moral vision makes little impression on Wittgenstein. But these strictures are exactly the ones that separate him most markedly from his great nineteenth century predecessor. Although Nietzsche thought Shakespeare "singular," he admired him for exactly the qualities Wittgenstein imagined lacking in his works. For Nietzsche, Shakespeare *was* a poet, teacher, prophet and philosopher:[12]

> When I seek my ultimate formula for *Shakespeare*, I always find only this: he conceived of the type of Caesar. That sort of thing cannot be guessed: one either is it, or one is not. The great poet dips *only* from his own reality—up to the point where afterward he cannot endure his work any longer. (*EH* "WIASC" 4)

The implication is that from time to time the great poet-philosopher must reflect on the source of great thought, which means, for Nietzsche, pondering the "ultimate formula for *Shakespeare*." It takes a certain kind of being—like Shakespeare and Nietzsche—to undertake this task; its successful completion will never be a matter of chance. The best example of "[t]he great poet dip[ping] *only* from his own reality" is not only Shakespeare (who was really Francis Bacon), but Shakespeare creating his greatest work, which was not *The Advancement of Learning* or *The Great Instauration* or *Novum Organum*, or *Hamlet* or *Lear*, but *Julius Caesar*. Nietzsche admits that, in *Hamlet*, Shakespeare (Lord Bacon) "dips *only* from his own reality," and so masters the madness of Hamlet, which means that he both experienced and overcame it, and by so doing became "profound, an abyss, a philosopher." But Nietzsche's Shakespeare is a prototype of the "Overman" who would lead the way to overcoming mankind's "all-too-human" failings, and this quality shows itself best in "the type of Caesar" and in the glorious character of Brutus, who loved Caesar, and yet joined forces with *the conspirators* against him.

Nietzsche's view of Shakespeare had an honorable lineage when he enunciated it, and it remains common today. Beginning at least as early as Ben Jonson's famous elegy prefixed to the 1623 Folio, critical attitudes toward his works, especially in the eighteenth century, gravitated toward "idolatry": "Shakespeare criticism," writes the editor of *The Persistence of Shakespeare Idolatry*, "is an international phenomenon" (Schueller vii). And the argument for Shakespeare's greatness almost always stresses one or another aspect of his works to transcend the ordinary or historical limits of his chosen media—his (to use of term that has fallen out of favor but fits here) "universality." This is, I take it, what Jonson and Wittgenstein were talking about when they implied that Shakespeare often simply ignored the rules of successful composition. Jonson writes that no one could "praise [Shakespeare] too much," and he would lodge him by himself above Chaucer, Gower, Spenser, Kyd, Marlowe and all other English poets. In a foretaste of what was to come, Jonson ranks Shakespeare with the great Greek tragedians. But in a double edged tribute, Jonson implicitly faults Shakespeare for ignoring the hard work that authorship requires: "For a good *Poet's* made, as well as borne" (*UV* 26).[13] Similarly, Wittgenstein finds fault with Shakespeare's diction, but he is nevertheless constrained to recognize his lapses as an indication of something like a natural force: "People stare at him in wonderment, almost as at a spectacular natural phenomenon. They do not have the feeling that this brings them into contact with a great *human being*. Rather with a phenomenon" (*CV* 85).

Further investigation of Nietzsche's praise of *Julius Caesar* shows a curious and telling double edge. For,

Nietzsche believed, Shakespeare misnamed his greatest
play, a fault which historical "overcoming" in the form of
Nietzschean revision corrects:

> *In praise of Shakespeare.*—I could not say anything more
> beautiful in praise of Shakespeare *as a human being* than
> this: he believed in Brutus and did not cast one speck of
> suspicion upon this type of virtue. It was to him that he
> devoted his best tragedy—it is still called by the wrong
> name—to him and to the most awesome quintessence of a
> lofty morality. Independence of the soul!—that is at stake
> here. No sacrifice can be too great for that: one must be
> capable of sacrificing one's dearest friend for it, even if he
> should also be the most glorious human being, an ornament
> of the world, a genius without peer—if one loves freedom
> as the freedom of great souls and he threatens this kind of
> freedom. That is what Shakespeare must have felt. The
> height at which he places Caesar is the finest honor that
> he could bestow on Brutus: that is how he raises beyond
> measure Brutus's inner problem as well as the spiritual
> strength that was able to cut *this knot.* (GS 2.98)

The point is not that Nietzsche envisions a self-serving
triumph of the critic over the creative predecessor. Nietzsche does more here than merely rename Shakespeare's
play. He argues that Shakespeare himself might not have
seen how completely Brutus (like Titus, Richard II, Hamlet, Othello, Macbeth, Coriolanus and Timon) was the
protagonist and tragic hero of the play known as *Julius
Caesar.* Moreover, the reasoning behind Nietzsche's admiration of the play concerns Shakespeare's characterization
of Brutus as an agent of axiology. Shakespeare does nothing to challenge the implications of Brutus's "virtue,"
which many critics might second-guess as vice. For Nietzsche, a "lofty morality" emanates from "Independence
of soul." Such a morality could exist—and, indeed, it
would flourish—within a society in which that concept
were the norm, for it is not contingent upon anything
outside of the self. That is, for Nietzsche, Shakespeare's
Julius Caesar was great only because it *did* represent a

moral system derived by pure mentation, the axiological equivalent of epistemological solipsism, which would explain the difference between the perspectives of Nietzsche and Wittgenstein on Shakespeare.

* * * * *

It appears from current critical practice that, like the philosophical notion of *sense data*, "perception" of the "text" of a Shakespeare play is not a simple matter. Until someone skilled in a special diagnostic procedure told me, I didn't know that I am color blind. "Definitions" don't stand alone. "I said," Wittgenstein writes, "that the meaning of a word is its role in the calculus of language" (*PG* 67). Some critics perceive the "absence" of a Shakespearean "text" with greater assurance than others do print on a page. Critical differences are like textual variations: in sorting out what they mean, we may need to pay attention to the way critics talk about them. In the current conversation, textual "authority" has "transcendent" as well as "factual" application; and it is probably helpful to know this, and to keep the senses separate. We know that intelligent critics—Nietzsche and Wittgenstein, for example— may disagree in the most basic matter of the value of Shakespeare's works. But even in their disagreement, these two very different readers of Shakespeare agree that there is something "singular" about him. Someone once said somewhere that it is a mistake of many Wittgensteinians to imagine that he is "like them." They look for evidence in Wittgenstein's thought of their own reasons and inclinations. But Wittgenstein seems never to quite fit the studied mold of academic discourse, perhaps because he tried so hard to escape it. But just as we are not like Wittgenstein, Shakespeare is not "like us." One need not be an unreconstructed Kantian to acknowledge this modest "fact," which is more than a trivial condition of our life in the world. Editors, scholars, critics, historians—when they talk sense, they sometimes help others understand

Shakespeare. But what we can be sure of—certain, instilled with justified confidence, beyond doubt—is the exceptional value of Shakespeare's poetry. If someone asks, "But how can we be sure?" the answer is, We're pretty good at this. Look, it isn't a hard trick to learn. First, you go like this, and then you . . . and. . . . "Well, what?" That's it. Then we—you and I—go on, preferably, together. But it's the "going on" that fits with everything else we do:

> Giving grounds . . . justifying the evidence, comes to an end;—but the end is not certain propositions' striking us immediately as true, i.e. it is not a kind of *seeing* on our part; it is our *acting*, which lies at the bottom of the language-game. (*OC* §204)

That "*acting*," that "going on together," is the sign of our "justified assurance." It would seem odd to ourselves and others if we behaved otherwise.

4

Donne Among the Feminists

Ethics and Judgment in Criticism

> Don't take it as a matter of course,
> but as a remarkable fact, that pictures and
> fictitious narratives give us pleasure,
> occupy our minds.
>
> ("Don't take it as a matter of
> course" means: find it surprising,
> as you do some things which disturb you.
> Then the puzzling aspect of the latter
> will disappear, by your accepting
> this fact as you do the other.)
>
> ((The transition from patent
> nonsense to something which is
> disguised nonsense.))
>
> — Wittgenstein, *Philosophical Investigations*

1.

Friedrich Nietzsche once remarked on the philosopher's idiosyncratic lack "of historical sense." Sometimes, when we do critical theory, we are—although unwittingly—practicing philosophers (*TI* "Reason in Philosophy"); and now, I think, Nietzsche's observation applies to us, for as criticism moves on from theory to metatheory, Renaissance critics often become so overwhelmed by contemporary interests that self-concern replaces forthright interest in the past, and "abuse" replaces "use" of "history for life." To be fair, one should add that Nietzsche thought there were different kinds of history, and that one of these—"monumental" history—was more likely than the others to cause "abuse of history for life":

> If, therefore, the monumental mode of regarding history *rules* over the other modes—I mean over the antiquarian and critical—the past suffers *harm*: whole segments of it are forgotten, despised, and flow away in an uninterrupted colourless flood, and only individual embellished facts rise out of it like islands: the few personalities who are visible at all have something strange and unnatural about them, like the golden hip which the pupils of Pythagoras supposed they saw on their master. (*UM* 70–71)

We should be able to see how well this remark applies to Donne criticism today. As critics with newly trained lenses focus on a less "monumental" Donne, "it seems evident that virtually everywhere the shadow of a great but nonetheless partial Anglican tradition—one that stretches from Walton up through Augustus Jessop, H. J. C. Grierson, T. S. Eliot, Evelyn Simpson, R. C. Bald, Dame Helen Gardner and many others—still looms so large in Donne studies that it has inhibited our responding aright to rare voices of protest and prevented even the most respectable of modern 'revisionists' from going far enough" (Sellin *Grace* 49). Dead Donneans become obstructions as "monumental" as Donne himself.

"Tradition obstructs the flow of 'antiquarian' and 'critical' modes of thought, in the case of Donne, for instance, by distorting the ways we can think and talk about him. For decades, this pantheon of High Church Donneans held off the critique of 'modern revisionists.' Consider only Donne's early sonnet sequence, 'La Corona'":

> Those who start from crypto- or Anglo-Catholic principles will read this garland of sonnets in a way quite different from that followed by skeptics or critics under the influence of modern evangelical Protestantism, and anyone who attempts to view it through Calvinist eyes will conceive the line of action informing it very differently from Laudians or from rugged individualists bent on captaining their own fates. (Sellin *So Doth* 1)

"Nietzsche understood that to make the past our own we must overcome the 'monumentalized' version, which often cannot be distinguished from the fiction of myth-making. We must make the past, which includes Donne's literary remains, our own, by using it in answer to our own tastes and purposes. When history and the literary forms which are a part of history fail to comport with those tastes and purposes, we are justified in advancing new explanations, not just of historical works, but of their creators as well. We 'historicize' characterizations of Donne and his poems. And this process of revaluation doesn't stop at re-thinking his religious allegiance. We want to know what use we can make of his writings. In this, we do no more—and surely Nietzsche would approve—than design the past to fit our present interests and needs."

With respect to Donne criticism, I think we should distinguish between two kinds of *revisionism*. Historical critics might take issue with Paul Sellin's thorough-going Protestant interpretation of Donne's literary career and yet approve of his methodology. For that matter, while doubting certain of his conclusions, they might even agree that more traditional views of Donne require correction. Sellin urges Donneans to look at certain aspects of the poet's literary relations to the Netherlands and to the Dutch

Reformed Church. It is hard to see how investigation of
that context could harm us. Questions about Sellin's critique emerge when we consider interpretation of the evidence; but the evidence itself, say, of Donne's participation
in the Doncaster expedition, looks like the kind that critics
like Bald and Gardner would have understood and appre-
ciated. The question raised by this "interpretive revisionism" is not that of Donne's literary achievement—*that* is
assumed—but of how we are best able to articulate that
achievement. There is another sort of "revisionism,"
which holds that it is not Donne's "achievement" in the
older, "elitist" sense, but his "character," as we think of
it in a sociologically enlightened manner, that counts.
Here, history devolves into psychohistory, and what was
"monumental" is swept away by what Nietzsche called
the *"critical"* mode: "If he is to live, man must possess and
from time to time employ the strength to break up and
dissolve a part of the past: he does this by bringing it
before the tribunal, scrupulously examining it and finally
condemning it" (*UM* 75–76). It is the condemnation of
Donne that raises questions of "justification."

"And yet the postmodern critique is about precisely
such judgments. And nowhere is the tendency to 'scrupulously' examine and 'finally' condemn 'part of the past'
more evident than in recent Donne criticism, where enlightened critics argue that John Donne was a poet of the
most disagreeable sort, that there is a 'pitiless element in
Donne's nature' (Carey 95), that he was self-absorbed, adolescent, selfish and domineering." We might be able to
agree on that assertion. But it is just such normative terms
that distinguish this sort of "revisionist" talk from that of
historical critics like Sellin. And it is the normative function of that language, especially as it is often accompanied
by a pronounced emotional intensity, that interests me. I
recall, for instance, that in the same passage—indeed, in
the same sentence—Nietzsche proceeds to say that "every
past, however, is worthy to be condemned—for that is the
nature of human things: human violence and weakness

have always played a mighty role in them" (*UM* 76).

I do not want to suggest that this normative talk is strange to me. Actually, it has come to seem quite familiar. I am nevertheless unclear as to how it "enlightens." For consider, the critics just designated "enlightened" find Donne, by turns, "narcissistic," "exhibitionistic," "scopophiliac" (Easthope 58–59, Belsey 135); "unfulfilled" (Belsey 136); "homophobic" (Halley 198); "homosexual" with sex (Klawitter 100); and "homosexual" without sex (Halley 197). I worry about the coherence of this "enlightened" picture of Donne. More to the point, the same critics say that Donne had "contempt for large segments of the human race" (Carey 96, 100, 106, 107), especially women. Now, in the current political climate, this is a serious charge against Donne's reputation. But what is the proof offered? That Donne took advantage of the illiteracy of his wife, Anne, that he may have prevented her from becoming literate, and that he made Anne have too many babies. Moreover, Donne employed devices of domination and enforced "forms of oppression" for "homophobic purposes." These critics say that Donne talked and wrote too much, that he was "bulimic" (Fish "Power" 223), and that the more he talked and wrote, the more he frustrated Anne's literary aspirations. At last, Donne drove his wife into a protracted silence, which expressed itself in the absence of her voice from an array of literary genres and a variety of topics in which she might have been interested: "Amid the great torrent of words that her husband let loose, Anne Donne is silent" (Halley 188). "In fact, Donne did more than merely dominate the conversation. He monopolized it. He was a sick man, and his poetry betrays his pathology. In it, we see him as a coward, a turncoat, a careerist, a poseur, an abuser of language, and above all a terrible misogynist: 'There is in many of the *Elegies* a persistent misogyny, indeed a revulsion at the female body . . .' (Guibbory 812)."

Critics who admire Donne might be dismayed by this avalanche of accusations, and yet wish to launch a counterargumcnt. Where could they begin? It seems they must strike out in every direction. "No one would expect them to investigate all of the charges at once. But whether they begin modestly or boldly, the outcome will be the same: Donne is a misogynist, and as such a reprehensible poet." Suppose we assume for the moment that all of these characterizations of Donne are, if ungenerous, fair. Would the normative statement about the outcome (Donne's repugnance as a poet) necessarily follow? And even if it did, what are we to make of the critics who nevertheless admire even his elegies and off-color lyrics? I suspect that assumptions underlying much of this misogyny talk about Donne tend to picture the poet as a literary transgressor, and by extension to see his admirers as vicariously transgressing through him. Thus, the concept of transgression concerns the imagined enjoyment of poet and critic; that is, transgression is the *mode* of literary enjoyment. This argument seems to require that the critics making the observation place themselves in a position to judge transgressive enjoyments by refraining from them, which assumption leads to this question: Why are these Donne critics not enjoying themselves?

"Obviously, in all civilized discourse, a sense of social rectitude operates somewhere. Feminist critics of Donne are justified in saying that they do not, should not, and cannot enjoy what is patently offensive and socially retrograde." Perhaps so, but before we can justifiably talk about "justification" in general, we must be able to say something about "justification" in the particular case of critical enjoyment. I notice that gynocentric critics of Donne seem to expect only "acrid rewards" (Halley 203) from their efforts to extract from Donne's writings—from his letters as well as from his poetry—an accurate portrait of Anne Donne as the repressed victim of the poet's "masculinist ideology." Isn't this odd? If Donne fits so perfectly into the feminist's analytical scheme, why should feminists find, in his fitting there, so little personal satisfaction?

"The question itself smacks of 'masculinist ideology.'"

I want to suggest that there is something wrong with this way of talking. Critics of moral rectitude contradict themselves in their characterizations of Donne. Moreover, I suggest that it is the critical talk involved, and not Donne's poetry, that is the source of confusion. "Perhaps we should expect confusion in what could fairly be described as a thriving Donne industry during a period of rapid ideological change. Bear in mind that the hostility toward Donne that has been registered in the past decade or so in no way indicates flagging interest in his work. On the contrary, John R. Roberts has shown that, notwithstanding the obituaries for Donne's reputation published earlier in the century, articles and books on Donne run into the thousands of items (Roberts 1); and even 'traditionalists' must admit that the Donne *Variorum* now under way is one of the most successful collaborative ventures in Renaissance studies of our time. The feminist critique of Donne is only part of the innovative reconstruction of the canon. The sky isn't falling; Donne's reputation is just undergoing skeptical scrutiny by critics who have, until recently, had no voice, namely, women."

About this canard regarding Renaissance studies in general and Donne criticism in particular, it must be said that, throughout the twentieth century, women have been the most visible and admired critics. One thinks of Dame Helen Gardner, Joan Bennett, Muriel Bradbrook, Ruth Wallerstein, Helen White, Lily Bess Campbell, Marjorie Nicolson, Rosemary Freeman, Madeleine Doran, Joan Webber, Rosemond Tuve, Irene Samuels, Barbara Lewalski, Mary Ann Radzinovich, Rosalie Colie, Elizabeth Story Donno, Ann Barton, Anne Lake Prescott—and the list goes on. To attribute "silence" to this distinguished group, or to think of their work as "marginalized," is to use the terms in—if I may borrow Wittgenstein's figure—an "occult" way. And it is this sense of a critical oddity that I want to focus on, with a mind to make a modest point about Donne criticism: The dissonant note that I detect in a usually harmonic chorus of voices in Donne criticism

arises from a popular subjectivist bent in current methodology, which depreciates and even reviles the recreative
functions of Donne's more irreverent poems, especially the
elegies. Where Donne's poetry is playful and funny, these
critics impose a solemn, even severe standard of moral
judgment.

I want to point out, too, that, while attacking Donne's
recreatively irreverent poetry, this hieratic order of critics,
who sometimes call themselves *radical feminists* or *cultural materialists*, will claim that theirs is "not an *ethical* criticism" (Docherty 7). But if we give this claim close
scrutiny, do we discover how these critics can evade the
stigma of normative statements? I don't think so. For if
such assertions can fairly be described as "*ethical* criticism," their rhetorical force disappears. "Agreed. But
hence, Thomas Docherty's disclaimer. To be fair, we must
pay attention to the grammatical sequence here. And
analysis shows that, in the oppositional rhetoric of enlightened feminist discussion, the figure of 'transgressive
criminal or critical thoughts' serves to buttress the use of
'nonhypocritical' utterances, namely, those that answer to
the demands of a strict social constructivism. Our nomenclature goes hand in hand with the aims of subversive, an-
tibourgeois thought. These rhetorical aims explain why
Docherty attributes honorific status to his critique, 'the
first critical, even criminal, word on Donne'" (11).

Can you appreciate my apprehension here? Given this
honorific characterization of "transgressive" analysis, one
might ask: How, if critical remarks about Donne can be
praised for their "criminal" and "transgressive" features,
can the critic depreciate Donne's poetic achievement?
Shouldn't he be, like the critic, praised for the asocial,
"transgressive" and even "criminal" features of his poetry?
And if one critic takes pride in his "transgressive" method,
why can't others luxuriate in Donne's recreational misogyny, assuming, of course, that we can find "misogyny" in
his poetry? Why shouldn't we take pleasure in the "image
of Donne as a rakish young cad?" (62) The question seems

to me important, whether or not we justify Donne or Donne criticism on grounds of our admiration of "transgressive" and "criminal" motifs. For even if we set that issue aside, we might still claim that, in Donne's time, expressions that we find "transgressive" or "criminal" or "offensive" were looked upon as clever, socially acceptable diversions. Even today, some critics argue that many of Donne's best poems succeed, not in spite of, but *because* of their rakish, insouciant, male-to-the-marrow speakers— not in spite of, but because of, what other critics find "misogynist." Shouldn't we inquire into the propriety of characterizing Donne's poetry as "misogynist" and a cruel calumny against women *before* we decide that there is, therefore, something wrong with them? And wouldn't such a determination lead us into questions of the historicity of ethical norms? How do critics decide that, because Donne's poems are "adolescent" (Carey 269), "sick" (Fish 223), "selfish" (Carey 100), "pitiless" (Carey 95), "phallocentric" (Mueller 148), and full of "contempt for . . . women" (Gill 55), they are, *ipso facto*, unworthy subjects of criticism and/or unsuited to the classroom?

2.

"To begin with, we must not oversimplify what critics mean by Donne's misogyny. It is not merely a term that we attach to this or that poem, but rather a designation that we apply to an array of expressions and attitudes— what Wittgenstein himself refers to as a 'form of life.' We cannot simply lift the term out of the feminist critique, and pretend that we will examine isolated uses for their fairness. This is why many feminists prefer to think of themselves as cultural critics. We are trying to see Donne's poetry through the lens of social critique; and this means that we must expect less traditional, even startling, responses to Donne's poetry. Feminist criticism changes the way we see the world. For example, Stanley Fish says his distaste for arch-rhetorician Donne stems from the fact that his 'act of writing is gendered in ways that have been made familiar to us by recent feminist criticism' ("Power" 228). The point here should be clear to any well-meaning reader: We must not expect a critic so initiated to sound like Grierson or Eliot or Gardner or any other traditional Donne critic. Fish is saying that his reluctance to teach Donne derives from—is an effect of—his reading of 'feminist criticism.' That is, feminist criticism is in some way responsible for the picture Fish has of Donne, in whose works, 'The male author, like God, stands erect before the blank page of a female passivity' (228), exercising the creative power of language to manipulate audiences. Given the responses learned from 'recent feminist criticism,' the alternative to manipulative, masculine power is 'the *feminine* principle'—egoless passivity—which is the logical opposite of '*self*-assertion.' 'The *feminine* (italics mine) principle' entails passivity; one lays oneself open to be acted upon. One surrenders. In contrast, Donne never gives in. He is always domineering; he is, like God, 'a self-aggrandizing bully' (Fish 241). And more often than not he directs his aggression 'against women'" (Fish 229).

The argument seems to make sense thus far, but a problem emerges when the assumptions of the critic-as-rhetorician intrude (assumptions which impute "depth" to language).[1] Doesn't Fish think that Donne is worried about his personal identity in relation to this "*feminine* principle?" We encountered the same problem of a hidden poetic substance in our discussion of Spenser criticism, and here as there, the impression left is one of controversy. How do we gauge the relationship of a poet to "the *feminine* principle?" Do we know that such a substance existed in Donne's time, or that it survives today? If the term is used as no more than a synonym for *passivity*, does it justly apply to Donne? Is Donne never passive? Do his sermons never praise the soul's surrender to Divine Love? What about the lovers in "The Extasie," who recline "like sepulchrall statues?" One of them is probably male, and doesn't Donne depict him as passive? "Well, obviously,

Fish is talking about the gender dynamics of male versus female—about sexuality in the gendered sense of that term." He might be doing that; but the controversial nature of this characterization won't go away with recognition of that possibility, because we too easily recall that one critic finds in Donne "very tender feelings for several of his male friends" (Klawitter 86)—so tender, in fact, that it approximated "an obsession" (Klawitter 95) with Thomas Woodward and showed itself in "highly charged homoeroticism" (Klawitter 100). Clearly, the "masculine power" of Donne's voice is not at all self-evident.

"These divergent views of Donne's sexual temperament need not dismay us, and they surely do not refute the feminist argument. Donne wrote poetry at very different times in his life, so the 'same' Donne provides warrant for a composite portrait of a virtual Proteus of conflicting sexual impulses. The problem is that some critics will only play the critical game if its rules demand winners and losers. In contrast to this male-oriented rage for mastery and control, we exhibit interest in the social, cultural setting of Donne's gendered poems, and this concern alters the way in which the 'gender game' is played. As we think of it, gender is a construction of the mythology of a particular time, hence, a political phenomenon. Given this view, critical interest in Donne's 'misogynistic' poems is not misplaced. We could say: 'Donne's Ovidian elegies reflect some of the social and economic struggles of Inns-of-Court gentlemen who were involved not only in their immediate urban surroundings but in the larger society as well' (Marotti 52). Or Donne might be thinking of Queen Elizabeth as 'a threat to patriarchy': 'The *Elegies* suggest that Donne was deeply disturbed that the old hierarchical order was threatened by a blurring of gender and sex distinctions'" (Guibbory 829).

The figure of "blurring" here suggests that we might do well to admit that there is a wide range of "feminist" criticism, and perhaps we should remember that some commentators distinguish between "equity" and "gender feminists."[2] It seems fair to say that, regardless of how we categorize them, some feminist critics of Donne take the matter of attaching such labels as "misogynist" very seriously, so seriously, in fact, that they are inclined, after labeling Donne, to turn on the "(male) critics" who admire him: "Most (male) critics seem to have condoned an image of Donne as a rakish young cad" (Docherty 62). This seriousness of tone seems to me a tactical error, for the term "condone" implies more than that the critics simply overlook or excuse Donne's moral lapse. All but the most minatory feminist could attribute this to an oversight or to a lack of training. But the accusatory tone here seems more ambitious. Offending critics appear immune to disapprobation; they even enjoy Donne. The serious feminist cannot condone Donne's critics' condoning of "Donne as a rakish young cad." And in this specific case, since Docherty's disclaimer imputes a negative value to *"ethical* criticism," we are left with the clear impression of a serious condemnation of Donne's "(male) critics."

The point here is that, for "gender critics," gender is important. Thus, by placing the word "male" in parentheses, the critic draws attention to the demographics of the critical landscape. At the same time, the "(male) critic" implies that in his case the issue of gender is beside the point because he either never had the capacity to enjoy Donne's persona as a "rakish young cad," or if he ever could and did enjoy it, he rid himself of both the pleasure and the capacity to experience it before undertaking the critical task. Like Fish's registering of attitudes learned from feminist critics, Docherty's awareness of the faults of "(male) critics" results from his reading of "recent feminist criticism."

"What worries traditional critics here is the unmasking of both Donne *and* his critics. So rather than deal with the energetic critique, they would question the feminist's intellectual mettle. But in fact, the vitality of the new approach is only the manifestation of the way in which 'recent feminist criticism' has been informed by a healthy and proper skepticism. Their strength is not just a proclaimed special awareness, but a nomenclature consistent with that purported 'transgressive' style, which pits Docherty and Fish against a very real, not an imaginary, hegemonic '(male)' Donnean tradition in criticism." Be that as it may, we are left with these normative questions: What is the criterion for the application of the label, "hegemonic?" Why is enjoyment of the typical speaker of typical Donne elegies a gender issue for Docherty, Fish and other (though by no means all) feminist critics? "Perhaps not all, but surely most feminist critics of Donne would agree with Docherty and Fish. They are far from alone in their misogyny talk; I would say that the trend among the current generation of Donne critics is definitely in their direction: 'A number of Donne's poems,' Michael Schoenfeldt asserts, 'are incorrigibly implicated in the most repressive forms of Renaissance patriarchy'" ("Patriarchal" 25).

Admittedly, this sounds like "misogyny talk." But doesn't the quotation concede my point about normative statements? In the current situation, *repression* and *patriarchy* are terms of opprobrium, and Schoenfeldt claims that Donne was "implicated" in both, in fact (and this seems worse) "incorrigibly implicated." Nothing Donne could or we can do would help, for here prognosis precedes examination. But I want to ask: Why? For even if we set aside the epistemological implications regarding what proof of an "incorrigibly implicated" assertion would look like, we would still be left with the odd assumption that there is a difference between "corrigibly" and "incorrigibly implicated" proponents of patriarchal repression—an oddity within an oddity. Are there poets who, although "implicated" to some comparatively lesser degree, are *not* "incorrigibly implicated in the most repressive forms of Renaissance patriarchy?" If so, how do we teach critics to recognize the difference, or instruct those who don't perceive the difference to perceive it? But if not, what work, if any, is the concept of *incorrigibility* doing in this context?

"The direction of the argument here is not toward an account of the concept of *incorrigibility*. We must not

introduce normative judgment prematurely. Feminist critics assume that enjoyment of 'incorrigibly implicated'
texts results from 'masculinist ideology,' which means that
they address not only Donne's elegies, but the social system of which they are a part, indeed, a symptom. This is
only to say that a poetic outlook not only expresses, but
defends a way of life, a system of values: 'This sexist approach to the poetry is in some degree anticritical, even
anti-intellectual, for it refuses to discover anything which
is genuinely troublesome or problematic for the masculinist ideology within which it is written' (Docherty 62).
What we have here is not so much an analysis of Donne's
patriarchal values, but a critique of the criticism that
blinds itself the consequences of reflection on the social
operations in question: the relationship between men and
women in Donne's poetry and in Donne's time, and, given
the delight of many Donne critics today, in our time as
well. For aware men and women, which is what we mean
by the designation 'feminist,' the refusal to see what 'is
genuinely troublesome or problematic' in 'the masculinist
ideology' of these expressions is tantamount to a form of
'anti-intellectual' obscurantism. We would be left with
nothing but a self-concerned eccentric writing insular verse
for a few dandies about town. And who would care about
that? It would be better—and more honest—to take the
'genuinely troublesome or problematic' mental state implicit in 'masculinist ideology' as our standard of judgment,
which is about what Schoenfeldt does. He argues that,
in the current situation, reading the problematic Donne
poems leads to 'our aesthetic or ideological discomfort'
(Schoenfeldt). This means only that we regard the admiration of certain Donne poems as a critical lapse on the
part 'of most [Donne] critics,' who fail to experience appropriate 'discomfort.' Worse, some of them take perverse
pleasure in 'masculinist ideology,' and in this way they are
responsible for an erroneous reproduction of 'masculinist
ideology, a sense of the 'ignorance of woman' in the reading and celebration of Donne's texts today."

I think I understand the line of thought, but, frankly, its logic is hard for me to fathom. It seems to require that a sexual utopia exist prior to any legitimate enjoyment of Donne's poetry. And the idea of a "hierarchized" system of critical reactions is likewise confused, for it presupposes the availability of an alternative, nonhierarchized—or horizontal, "egalitarian"—system. Don't we justify our sense moral indignation by positing an element of choice? Unless we are talking about a fictive sexual utopia, we must assume the possibility of a comparative system of judgment in which dimorphism cannot appear. I am aware that Janel Mueller tries to justify "Donne's thematics" (Mueller 116) on the grounds that "Sapho and Philaenis" represents a "fully utopian moment of human possibility" (125), but this hyperbolic defense of Donne makes too much of a rather strained joke, and wrongly assumes that only certain kinds of political rhetoric justify critical interest in Donne: "Donne's thematics call into larger question the conventions of heterosexuality that ruled love poetry, erotic behavior and social arrangements in his day" (116). The picture we get of Donne in ideological Renaissance talk, whether it praises or maligns the poet, depends on debatable assumptions about social history—for instance, the belief that such categories as *patriarchy, masculinist, utopian*, and *ideology* designate recognizable and "defined" sets, and that these in tandem function as an agency of the fictional responses of Donne's protagonists, some of whom may behave, for instance, as if women they know are "ignorant."

But can't we imagine experience—common sense—informing them of the same thing, without the help of ideology? Just because some critics admit that "recent feminist criticism" shaped their reactions to Donne doesn't mean that we can't imagine other causes of male attitudes and of critical reactions to them in literature. Even the claim that Stanley Fish's attitudes derive from "recent feminist criticism" is, after all, just a claim that skeptical critics might consider, as they say in legal proceedings, "subject to proof." Moreover, the assumption that a critic's perception of another critic's "discomfort" forms a reliable basis for assessing what a critic says about Donne is also dubious. We can easily imagine a critic being comfortably or uncomfortably aligned with any ideology, masculinist included. And if this is so, we must allow that comfort or discomfort cannot serve as reliable criteria of judgment in criticism.

3.

One could infer from the title of this chapter that, like the critic who argued that Milton "is the first great feminist in Western culture" (Gallagher 171), I want to defend Donne against the charge of misogyny, and to some extent this is true. My strategy will be a little different. Philip Gallagher sought to make Milton look good by setting him against a background of hopeless misogyny: "Milton proceeds to confront the far more formidable burden of transubstantiating the admittedly subtle but morally dubious chauvinist etiologies of [Genesis] 2.18–25 into a thoroughly rational justification of God's ways to man—and to woman too" (33–34). Gallagher wants to separate the feminist sheep from the misogynist goats. Hence, for him, the Bible is misogynist (129), St. Paul is misogynist (113), the Old Testament is misogynist, and so is the New (102). Starting with Adam (127), ancients and moderns alike are misogynists, including St. Augustine, Thomas Aquinas, William Perkins, Sir Thomas Browne, Alastair Fowler, James Sims, Leland Ryken, Stanley Fish. Gallagher finds that even some of the women who write about Milton are misogynists, including Georgia Christopher (128), Barbara Lewalski, Diana Benet, Joan Bennett, Georgia Christopher, Cheryl Fresch, Diane McColley, Maureen Quilligan and Stella Revard (172). The problem with this broad brush approach is that it makes fine delineation difficult. For instance, the same critic who claims that the Bible is misogynist then praises Milton for relying on Scripture as the sole basis of his thought (129). Similarly, although Gallagher refuses to the very end to proclaim "sexual egalitarianism" as his standard of judgment for excluding Miltonists from the taint of misogyny, he nevertheless insists that Adam is more to blame than Eve for the Fall, and so, rather than an egalitarian reading, replaces a misogynist with a misandrous understanding of *Paradise Lost*.

My aim is to avoid these critical inconveniences by asking what work we expect the term *misogyny* to do in Donne criticism. Admittedly, that aim is twofold. I want to soften the sense of acrimony and condemnation in Donne commentary Donne; but since I admire Donne for many of the poems that other critics regard as flawed by misogyny, I hope also to elude the charge of misogyny myself. Given this dual defense, it would be pointless to deny the element of self-interest in my analysis. And yet I will argue that the very Donne texts most often cited as "misogynist"—the elegies—are not in fact misogynist, at least not misogynist in the sense that they are any more misogynist than they are misandrist. Having chosen this line of argument, I cannot proceed on the strong but counterintuitive proposition that the protagonist in, say, "The Perfume" does not treat his mistress badly. Rather, I will settle on the more modest one[3] that he treats everybody so, men and women alike—the mother of his mistress, yes, but her household's "grim eight-foot-high iron-bound serving-man" and her irksome brood of sibling-informers, too. From this point of view, self-centeredness, not contempt for women, is this lover's nature. He may hate his mistress, but only in the sense that he hates everybody and everything—even his squeaky shoes. To the question, "Why is this?" the answer comes: Because they are impediments to sexual liaison with his mistress. Hence, the tone of unrelenting harangue in the poem. Rather than "misogyny," Donne's poem exhibits only the resentment of a young man seriously beset by circumstances out of his control—wavering mistress, prying parents, nosy siblings. So why not take the initiative and, at least in the imagination, eliminate one enemy (by suggesting to his mistress that her mother has already lived too long)?

"Unfortunately, this supposedly 'modest' perspective

misleads by its tendentious choice of examples. 'The Perfume' doesn't objectify women as brazenly as some other Donne elegies. Why not look at 'To his Mistris Going to Bed' (14–16), which says a more about Donne's attitudes toward women?" Ponder these lines:

> Licence my roving hands, and let them goe,
> Behind, before, above, between, below.
> O my America, my new found lande,
> My kingdome, safeliest when with one man man'd,
> My myne of precious stones, my Empiree,
> How blest am I in this discovering thee.
> To enter in these bonds is to be free,
> Then where my hand is set my seal shall be.
>
> (25–32)

"Surely the critic is not merely 'misogyny mongering' when he protests that the woman here literally 'disappears' (Docherty 79). This isn't lovemaking, and it isn't 'metaphysics' either, but rank imperialism. Here, lovemaking becomes a 'colonial project' (Belsey 139). The woman isn't just silenced as she is in 'The Perfume,' but occupied and colonized. It is no wonder that the feminist complains that woman as a 'self-identifying subject disappears' (Docherty 80), becoming nothing more than the 'merest adjunct of Donne's own maleness' (80). Nor is it any exaggeration to say that, by its '"colonial" eradication of the Other space of the woman' (81), the egocentric speaker finally descends into 'autoeroticism, masturbation, talking to [his] isolated self' (81). In this sense we could say that '[w]hat is mapped by the text is not a body at all, not the fullness of a presence, but the unrepresented gaze as the symbol of an absence, the lack that precipitates desire'" (Belsey 137).

It seems to me that in mixing feminist metaphors, feminist critics run the risk of allowing inappropriate comparisons to slip in. The speaker in "To his Mistris Going to Bed" does allude to the woman's body as his "America," "new-found-land," his "kingdome," his "myne," his "Empiree." But surely these figures are more intensely personal

than governmental; the lover expresses the sense that
there is something in his experience that is truly his, as *if*
it could not have been otherwise. That is why he wants
his lady to let him touch her: for *his* pleasure. To think of
these figures as cumbered by the martial and bureaucratic
complications of colonization seems rather tangential to
the experience being described. The drift of the argument
toward autoeroticism seems even more strange. What does
it mean to say that "the text" doesn't "map" "a body at
all?" If it doesn't do so, should it have? Why would an
"unrepresented gaze" symbolize "an absence" rather than
a "presence" (supposing, of course, that we could discriminate between the two)? In this particular case, what is
absent? The answer is, "completeness of vision as possession." But why should we think of the speaker's vision
here as "unrepresented?" Doesn't the fact that we talk
about it suggest that we are talking about something,
namely, these lines—this expression or "representation"—
from Donne's poem? If Donne's lover sees his mistress
with an "unrepresented gaze," would a "represented gaze"
help him see better?

"The issue in question is Donne's focus, which is not on
the woman, as subject, at all. And 'The Anagram' (21–22)
is an even worse appropriation of the body of woman. This
poem literally luxuriates in 'the woman-as-inferior-sex-
object' feelings, so much so that the feminist critic justifiably complains that 'Donne strips woman of a stable
identity,' imposing, in effect, 'anonymity' on the entire species of women. This is the sense of Donne's misogyny, be
it 'aesthetic' or 'ideological,' that feminists quite properly
disparage." Any response here runs the danger of appear-
ing obtuse as well as self-serving. But suppose that Donne
had imposed "anonymity" on women, so that woman in
general becomes "stripped of stable identity, anonymous
in fact" (Docherty 65)? You seem convinced that because
the poem accomplishes this thematic purpose, it therefore
is pernicious. But surely this is a huge leap, especially for
a critic who denies that his is an "*ethical* criticism." I am

reminded of Wittgenstein's wry response to his interlocutor's insistence that one knows only one's own pain:
"In one way this is wrong, and in another nonsense" (*PI*
§246). Isn't there a gap in the argument that needs filling?
Or better still, if we proceed in another way, we might be
able to agree on a more charitable characterization of the
poem and of Donne.

To begin, can we agree that Flavia is ugly? Does it distort
the text to say that even her name sounds faintly noxious
or effluvial? If we agree thus far, then haven't we, in effect,
rescued Flavia from the threat, if it ever existed, of "anonymity?" And in so doing, haven't we opened discussion
to possibilities other than Donne's craven desire to obliterate the female subject? True, one could ask, "What's in
a name?" But the answer in this case is, "quite a lot," for
instance the grammatical function of the genitive with all
of its associated linguistic possibilities, among them being
personal history (occupation: prostitute), venereal disease,
unique distribution of body parts, and the like. In other
words, the pejorative label depends upon an interpretation
of the poem, which might just as easily have gone in a
direction that would make the term, *misogyny*, appear
harsh and inappropriate.

"Surely we must do more as critics than merely recognize the use of hyperbole in Donne's poem. Just how ugly
do you think Flavia could be? Dildoes don't care what they
touch? Don't you provide a case of the critic so numbed
to the consequences of thoughtless, cruel humor that you
cannot muster a properly indignant response to Donne's
hostile witticism? Well, proper feminist critics assert an
entirely different reaction here. Under our system of government they have that right." In discussions of value of criticism, rights and ethical imperatives get all mixed up. If I
understand *your* argument, "we must" take the inferred
consequences of rhetorical devices into our account of their
expression. I can see how such a view arises from conviction
that poems like Donne's are akin to—or even the equivalent of—physical rape. But here the picture of a comparison

takes hold and drives our reactions. Wittgenstein characterizes the situation: "A *picture* held us captive" (*PI* §115).
The "we must" locution implies, not that we are free to exercise judgment in the matter, but rather (for a reason or reasons not yet specified) that we are constrained to do so. So
in a perhaps laudable effort to flee the dangers of misogyny,
the critic rushes into the grasping arms of misandry.

Can't we, instead, proceed further with an alternative
characterization of Donne's poem? Consider: In "The Anagram," the speaker proclaims his courage in touching
Flavia, who, if she had her way, would have been more
than merely touched by so many men that only the foolhardy lover will risk infection. We might say that in making this lover the imagined exception to the male norm,
Donne advances the mischievous, misandrous suggestion
that, unlike Flavia, who cannot help being ugly, the unsophisticated lover (and all men other than the speaker)
inflict suffering on themselves. Notice how this line of
thought tends to erode the claim that "[t]he woman in the
last part of the poem does not even seem to be the same
person" described in the first. By focusing on faults of the
male, we redirect sympathies. Then, from this less contrary point of view, suppose we accept for the purposes of
further investigation that "[t]he woman in the last part of
the poem does not even seem to be the same person" de-
picted in the first. Can't we suppose a benign purpose for
this alteration? Why should our concession entail belief
that a change of Flavia's character constitutes a fault in
either her or the poem? Hamlet changes. In act 1, we do
not know him to be a theater-goer, drama critic, playwright, stage director, swordsman and aspirant to the
throne. Even if Flavia *were* to change, this would not necessarily besmirch her character, and certainly not that of
womanhood in general.

Suppose we find that our concession regarding Flavia's
change of character does not advance discussion, that we
don't "go on together." We can, still for the purposes of
investigation, say: What if, in fact, Flavia does not change.

And might note, for instance, that the text permits this interpretation; for in the opinion of the more experienced lover, other women change, Flavia doesn't. Compared to "such as shee," they are fairer, but in being so, they are subject to the vicissitudes of flesh:

> Women are all like Angels; the faire be
> Like those which fell to worse; but such as shee,
> Like to good Angels, nothing can impaire:
> 'Tis lesse griefe to be foule, then to'have beene faire.
>
> (29–32)

While "Women are all like Angels," they can be differentiated from one another on the basis of their moral qualities. Only Flavia and other ugly women are "Like to good Angels," because they do not give evidence of the Fall. Beauty fades into ugliness, but ugliness remains constant, and so, "good." Hence, Flavia's stability, which according to Docherty Donne undermines, is recaptured the moment it slips away. The claim is that the poem amuses by forcing a perspective in which "the normal opposition of fair and foul is disturbed." But now we ask: What makes anything "disturbed?" "Normal opposition" is subsumed beneath the overarching standard of frustration; beauty exacerbates, ugliness attenuates, grief.

Rhetorically oriented critics cannot overlook the venom directed toward men in "The Anagram." To whom, after all, is the speaker's exhortation to "Marry" addressed? Who is too blind to see that Flavia will make him the best wife? Who stands in need of the wisdom of the more experienced lover? Who, because of his inexperience with women, is on the verge of making the mistake most common to men? The novice is inclined to reject Flavia because of her looks; experiences teaches otherwise: The bachelor contemplating marriage would be better off if he would reverse all of his values and expectations with respect to women, and repudiate his promiscuous appetite for female beauty. He should do so because beautiful women have a promiscuous appetite to cause men woe; and they succeed in their plunder because men are haplessly drawn to feminine color and texture in certain spatial arrangements. The problem is that, although Flavia has all the feminine qualities that young men desire, she possesses them in what seems in the here and now an unpleasant configuration. But this is where the novice makes a mistake. He is too quick to judge. Time will obliterate the disappointing aspects of the auditor's expectations of beauty, and in so doing, it will reveal that Flavia's anagrammatic charms, and, in the end, reward the patient lover by removing all taint of disillusion from his relations with women. Thus, if he will but listen to and follow the speaker's advice, the novice will expect disappointment, and so, not be disappointed. Even now, if he behaves prudently in accord with his mentor's advice, the lover can spare himself the heartache of chasing after "beauties elements" with "all her parts . . . in th'usuall place": "a good face," large eyes, small mouth, white teeth, smooth skin. And what of that imperceptible virtue, chastity? Flavia needs nothing from men to guarantee her unique state of chastity. Like "beauties," Flavia is available, but unlike them (for lack of opportunity), she is, in essence if not in fact, pure. At the same time, it would be pointless for the lover to think of lending his virginity to "beauties." (What makes him think they need what none of them claims to miss?)

"Obviously, this 'take' on Donne's poem is 'possible,' but it doesn't explain the arrogant male assumption that women are made only to please men—to provide them with beauty and pleasure and, finally, even deliverance from their own self-induced jealousy. This is to 'objectify' women with a vengeance—to deny the ugly as well as the beautiful any claim anywhere to the position as determined 'subject.' To *your* auditor, it seems that something important follows from the principle, 'All love is wonder.' Through the discipline of suffering, experience teaches that the 'best land' is only that held without anxiety: love free from the torment of jealousy. But how, in a world of cruel mistresses, can the novice find and enjoy that blissful terrain? The answer is: only in the arms of Flavia. And why is this? You want to say: Because, like the misguided novice, other men are too stupid to avail themselves of Flavia's anagrammatized value. That they can't solve the puzzle of her availability. That, paradoxically, her universal availability proves Flavia possessed of a rare chastity. That her anagrammatic charms could survive the greatest threats to chastity: life in a brothel, or a visit from the lover's best friend. But analysis cannot stop here. On the contrary, only now do we begin to recognize the kind of world Donne imagines. Your 'misandrist' reading permits all men to choose to be stupid, if they wish, to chase beautiful women who will dash their benighted hopes, if they wish. But women do not choose, because they have neither intellect nor will. They may frustrate men, but they do so only as mindless beasts unintentionally annoy their masters."

This analysis seems to me unduly harsh. Why must we construe "The Anagram" as a diatribe against either Flavia or women? The speaker's aim might suggest an entirely different attitude. Perhaps men are all like this uninitiated lover: mindless sufferers of a self induced obsession to enjoy what all men desire, namely, to enjoy legions of beautiful women as if, as exceptional gentlemen, they are each and every one, as individuals, the only man for whom feminine charm was created and the only one on whom its blessings have been or could ever be legitimately bestowed. Since only Flavia has her virginity, only she can actually meet the condition that the young lover desires; but in order to have that condition met—copulation to his heart's content, and this without taint of jealousy—he must separate himself from what he shares with "th'usuall" male, namely, desire for unanagrammatized beauty. He can have what he wants if and only if he alters the spatial expectations of what he wants. The problem is that what he wants all men want; and, unfortunately for him, "things in fashion every man will weare." Here, men are the victims, not of women, but of the promiscuity of other men.

4.

Again, we should ask: What is wrong with *that*? Isn't it the social function of an idea that matters? The speaker's wisdom in Donne's poem is far from esoteric. According to one influential Frenchman, if a man "get himselfe a handsome wife; his neighbours commonly will have as much to doe with her, as himselfe" (Ferrand 227). They will do as he does—ignore Flavia—who longs to receive men as her beautiful sisters do—promiscuously, to give men what they want. Pathologically, men prefer to suffer, just as he, the untutored lover, will suffer. Doesn't the historical context support the misandrist reading. "Well, the claim is that the auditor willfully refuses to recognize that men only imagine 'beauties' to be untouched." "Beauty, and chastity," writes Jacques Ferrand, "seldome meet in one person. For beauty is as it were a kind of prey, that hath continually a thousand in chase of it" (228). The point is, to return to the "animal" figure, that men, not women, exhibit a primitive, hunting instinct. This is hardly a flattering picture of men.

"Unfortunately, I don't see how this historical context-building is supposed to help. Donne's characterization of men here may not be flattering, but it nevertheless depicts man as the eternal subject, the active agent defining the moral cosmos. Man defines the action, and woman merely responds, as if by reflex. Obviously, since all men insist on importuning 'beauties,' 'beauties' are often importuned; and for thanks, beautiful women teach men how to be jealous. Our objection is to the sense that they do so mindlessly, as if a woman's actions were no more than an involuntary twitch or tropism. Donne's poem provides no insight into why women behave as they do in this continuing fiasco. Nor is it clear how a benign characterization of the mentor's purpose can alter the overall impression of a disgustingly dehumanized attitude toward woman. The mentor exhorts the novice to elude self-inflicted pain, to enjoy the

'best land' with no worry about proprietary rights. For if
the tolerant bedstaves refuse to touch her, he need not
worry about sprouting horns. He can leave his wife in the
company of the men most likely to cuckold him, namely,
his friends. This may be a sad portrait of the state of friend-
ship among men, but it does nothing at all to vivify the
women they seek to use as sentient, rational beings."

In fact, Donne's mentor in "The Anagram" makes face-
tious use of an argument well known in feminist writing
of the Renaissance. In *The Nobilitie and excellencye of
Woman kynde* (1542), a popular work published and translated often in the sixteenth and seventeenth centuries,
Henry Agrippa argues that, since they were created by God
with "one similitude and lykenes of the sowle" (A2), man
and woman have the "same mynd . . . reason and speche"
(A2^v).[4] On the other hand, this "equall libertie of dignitie and
worthynesse" is limited to the spiritual being that the two
sexes share with angels: "But all other thynges, the which
be in man, besydes the dyvyne substance of the sowle, in
those thynges the excellente and noble womanheed in a
maner infynytely dothe excell the rude grosse kynd of
men . . ." (A2^v–A3). Men chase women more or less indis-
criminately, but certainly not because they are *superior* to
women. Agrippa admits of many differences between the
sexes, and invariably these indicate the superiority of
woman. Holy Writ bears witness to the fact that even in
their creation and name, woman, created last of all creatures—and fashioned from the part of man nearest the
heart—was named for "life" (Eva) rather than earth (Adam).
Furthermore, she is marked by signs other than name "of
the very thynges, dueties, and merites" (A5^v) declaring that
"man is the worke of nature, and womanne the worke of
God" (B2). She is in both sense and feeling more attractive,
more amiable, than man: "In al the hole heape of creatures,
there is noo thynge so wonderfull to see" (B4) as a woman.

Not only is woman more beautiful than man, as can be
seen in her serenity and pulchritude, but she is "endowed
with a certaine dignitie and worthines of honestie, whiche

is not given to man" (B7), besides which she is, as her less pronounced genitalia indicates, "gyven more [to] shamfastnes . . . than . . . man" (B7ᵛ). Woman is, as can be seen in man's weakness for her, more modest, less inclined to incontinency, and—and for Renaissance criticism this is highly significant—not culpable for man's fallen condition. Contrary to vulgar opinion, Adam, not Eve, bore responsibility for the Fall, since it was he, not Eve, who was enjoined not to eat the fruit of the Tree of the Knowledge of Good and Evil (C5ᵛ). This important distinction can be seen in the significant role the Virgin Mary plays in man's redemption. For the Virgin Mary, whose female sex and modesty—virginity was the very sign and essence of chastity—became the vessel of divinely inspired parthenogenesis through which Adam's transgression was forgiven: "The man gave us deathe, not the woman. And all we synned in Adam, not in Eva" (C5ᵛ). To many such minds, even woman's faults must be understood in an exculpatory way, for, as Edward More proclaims in *Defence of Women* (1560), "It lyth not in them [i.e., women], these sayd thyng[s] to correcte" (A4ᵛ). Written from the point of view of one who would be "a Champyan bold" (A4) of women, the *Defence of Women* protests that women cannot help being as they are formed by "Nature . . . accordyng . . . to gods wyll" (A4ᵛ). Thus Adam had "strenght sufficient" ("sufficient to have stood, though free to fall"), while Eve did (and women do) not.

The suggestion here is modest: We should consider the hortatory form of "The Anagram" from the point of view of Renaissance commentary, not because they are apposite expressions of Renaissance feminism, but because Donne artfully exploits quite opposite notions of women without surrendering their comparative disdain toward men. After all, the most important rhetorical relationship exhibited in "The Anagram" is that between the enlightened instructor and his unsophisticated auditor: "Marry, and love thy *Flavia*, for, shee, / Hath all things." The speaker's tone implies that his pupil is in no mood to change his ways. If he were in a frame of mind to marry Flavia, the experienced lover wouldn't need to argue so strenuously. So why does the young man resist? Why can't he learn that the true virtue of women cannot be seen? That it is moral and spiritual? His erroneous thinking in the matter is the subject of the poem—the novice lover's false reasons for refusing to commit himself to Flavia. He cannot accept the fact that Flavia possesses everything that he desires, which is "all things" that womanhood can offer. Hence, the title. The anagram is a puzzle which, when solved, is clear and simple. The solution comes in knowing that the parts appear to be disordered only to the senses. But this is only because the lover is blind to imaginative rearrangement. He needs to balance the usual organization of details with the "yet" of other possibilities:

> Marry, and love thy *Flavia*, for, shee
> Hath all things, whereby others beautious bee,
> For, though her eyes be small, her mouth is great,
> Though they be Ivory, yet her teeth are jeat,
> Though they be dimme, yet she is light enough,
> And though her harsh haire fall, her skinne is rough;
> What though her cheeks be yellow, 'her haire is red,
> Give her thine, and she hath a maydenhead.
>
> (1–8)

Now, we may smile perhaps because we, too, enjoy the difficulty of the rhetor's task here. Tactile enjoyment of large lips is possible, but difficult while one is distracted by a longing for small ones, and the same is true of the source of other sensations: "light"/"dimme"; soft/"harsh", "yellow"/"red." It seems that the mentor cannot quite keep a straight face (at his own series of jokes), and at the last he tells the young lover that he must part with what he does not have—except in the metaphoric sense of sexual inexperience—in order to enjoy what he really wants: the pleasure of a beautiful woman's love untrammelled by the woes that usually accompany this satisfaction. But of course the more the instructor argues, the clearer it is that more argument won't work.

"It won't work because it shouldn't work, any more than the sexist jokes with gender and racial Others always as the butt are ever 'just good fun.'" On the contrary, I think we have grounds to say here that, as Donne's poems often do, "The Anagram" has something of the "metaphysics" in it. For, notwithstanding his momentary lapse into common sense, the speaker does propound a corrective to the inexperienced lover's problem. If the novice will only entertain a different arrangement, adducing nonaesthetic but nonetheless perceptible value, he will see that all of the parts of the puzzle are already available: "These things are beauties elements, where these / Meet in one, that one must, as perfect, please" (9–10). That is, having had all of his demands of beauty met in discrete parts, the lover must not cavil about the spatial arrangement of those parts. To make his point more emphatic, the mentor shifts attention from the visual to the olfactory sense. One experiences a fine perfume's lovely fragrance, not its source, which remains a tantalizing "wonder" or mystery; and by this shift in attention he tries to widen the scope of the lover's interest. He is in a position, then, to chastise the neophyte for his incapacity to see "unusually," that is, as most men do not see—with insight, as if all the pieces of the puzzle were not only present but in place. The speaker makes the unseen "virtue" of Flavia the subject of the young man's choice, and in so doing apprehends Flavia, even if only in a joke, as the fully human subject in the contemplation of marriage.

5.

"Critics cannot decently brush aside the challenge to the misogynist description of Donne's poetry by saying that it's okay to 'objectify' women when one also 'objectifies' men. Two wrongs still don't make a right. Besides, you set out to prove that the characterization of Donne as a misogynist was wrong in the first place, but show instead that he was also a misandrist."

I have only suggested that Donne's contemporaries might not have found contempt for women in Donne's poetry. We did see that there was an inconsistency in the feminist analysis of Flavia. So we have grounds for doubting the underlying assumption that Donne's elegies are blind to women as sentient, willing creatures. Shouldn't we then be skeptical of "Donne as misogynist" talk? Look at this example:

> Feared, as their Other, by the men who were in power, ideologically and factually, women are accorded only the status of "object" of study and thought; this demonstrates that the real source of this male fear is a worry about the subjectivity of the female, as a consciousness or mode of desire or will which could challenge male authority and domination or masculinist epistemology and ideology. (Docherty 62)

Would you agree that this is a familiar line of thought? Here, the critic implies that "wholeness" and "stability" are *a priori* human values that "Donne and his society" refused to extend to women, not only to "Flavia" in "The Anagram," but to women generally. But although Docherty is at pains to deny that his is *"ethical* criticism," surely he would impose on Donne critics—without warrant—an ethical norm for the humorous treatment of a young man in such a dilemma. Why is it wrong to strip "woman" of something she might never have had and might never need, especially if, in the process, the poet tenders opportunities for "enjoyment" to many, if not all, Donne critics? That is, even if the charge that "The Anagram" is "misogynist" were fair, it would not constitute serious grounds for disparagement of Donne's poem, nor would it say anything about the propriety of his moral outlook. Stanley Fish professes outrage at this poem, claiming that it represents a repulsive expression of a repulsive attitude. Donne looks down on women. He commodifies women.

He turns them into objects. Valuing his poetry is therefore tantamount to physical oppression of women. For words are, as Donne uses them, fancied assault. I want to say: If we are not dealing with *"ethical* criticism," what is wrong with fancied assaults?

Whether they admit it or not, these critics assume that it is the job of criticism to expose licit and illicit critical enjoyments. But even if we accept that assumption, the question would still be: How do we discriminate between licit and illicit literary enjoyments? This is—Docherty's disclaimer notwithstanding—an ethical question. We should keep at least two considerations of the ethical issue in mind. First, how do we learn and teach the difference between licit and illicit literary enjoyments? Given the ordinary secular and scientific understanding of knowledge in the academy, we expect some effort to disentangle that understanding from extraneous bias. We look for agreement—"going on together"—not contention. Wittgenstein imputes such a temporal distance to therapeutic philosophy that no *"theses"* could ever be debated, "because everyone would agree to them" (*PI* §128). In our situation, he might ask: What is the nature of the disagreement here about the use of the term *ethical*?

Why should we shrink from ethical judgment? "Many feminists don't. We find brutality against women, whether in fiction or in fact, reprehensible. Shouldn't everyone? Don't we condemn, and even outlaw, expressions lacking a minimum of 'redeeming social value?' When I say this, I am mindful of the fact that Critics For a Politically Correct Curriculum might take my remarks as support for their dream of power to enforce 'speech codes' and censorship. But haven't thinkers from Plato to the present time worried about what the young read? Why do we establish a curriculum, if not for our social good? After all, what teachers teach is what passes into young minds as incontestable: the way things are, in science, in mathematics, in literary studies. So if Donne is good, why then, so are the characters in his poems. Eliot was only reiterating Plato when he noted that strong writers—D. H. Lawrence, for instance—exercised a pernicious influence on impressionable readers, especially the young. Perhaps I am only agreeing with Eliot and Trotsky, then: We can only read so many books, value so many authors. We can only allocate so much time to literature. And for every work we include, we exclude *n* number of other possibilities. Why bother, then, with such vile expressions as 'The Anagram,' when we have the less pernicious—the better—*X, Y* and *Z*?"

I follow most of the distance here. Of course, we must choose how we will spend our time and resources. We cannot do otherwise. If one is on a curriculum committee or school board, one is obliged to make choices for others, and the high intensity characterization of that task as "censorship" probably doesn't help. If the issue were only that of selection, one might say: Away with Donne, let's have a look at Emily Dickinson. But what if the choice is that of an inferior writer, Richard Barnfield, for instance? "I can think of a perfectly valid argument in favor of that change: Studying Barnfield will help students of Renaissance literature with alternative sexual orientation to come to terms with their own sexuality. This is an example of what we mean by the notion of a curriculum 'for our social good.'"

Again, the question is: How do we best accomplish agreed-upon social goals? Let me give you an example of how we might proceed with a benign motive to an unexpected and perhaps undesirable end. Suppose the general catalog of a major university had this description of the more or less standard second part of a year long survey of English literature under the quarter system: "English Literature from the Early Seventeenth Century to the Late Eighteenth Century." Admittedly, this fairly broad description allows for a good deal of variation, depending on the instructor assigned to teach the class. But now suppose the individual course description offered in fulfillment of the catalog copy announced the following:

ENGLISH 23B: THE ENGLISH LITERARY TRADITIONS—ENGLISH LITERATURE FROM THE EARLY

SEVENTEENTH CENTURY TO THE LATE EIGHT-EEN[TH] CENTURY. We'll be reading works by a diverse group of women writers in the eighteenth century, and addressing issues such as the following: the relationship of these writers to the period's "myth of passive womanhood"; women's access to modes of literary production and distribution; the impact of class as well as gender on women's political ideology; female literacy and readership; the conception of a female career; women's contribution to the development of various literary genres (drama, fiction, poetry, satire, didactic literature, autobiography, travel memoir, etc.); women's role in the growth of capitalism and colonial expansion; women and revolution. Assigned authors will include Aphra Behn, Delarivier Manley, Mary Wortley Montagu, Frances Burney, Frances Sheridan, Mary Wollstonecraft, Mary Hays and Maria Edgeworth.

Would you find such a course description puzzling? "Well, I might ask if, on that instructor's campus, course descriptions are customarily this long." And that's all? The course description doesn't strike you as odd? "The issue of the 'From the Early Seventeenth Century' phraseology might draw my attention." In what way? "Well, perhaps the seventeenth century is somewhat slighted. For instance, what about Aemylia Lanier, Anne Finch, Mary (Sidney) Herbert, Elizabeth (Tanfield) Cary, Anne Clifford, Anne Howard and Lady Mary (Sidney) Wroth? And then there is the question of overlooking minor women writers of the Caroline and Jacobean period: Rachel Speght, Ester Sowernam, Diana Primrose, Mary Fage. An uppity student might claim violation of 'truth in packaging' norms. We live in litigious times."

You imagine a lawsuit? Two days after I read this course description, a major retailer of sporting equipment published a disclaimer in the *Los Angeles Times*, stating that the designer sunglasses they had advertized were "not authentic." They withdrew the counterfeit sunglasses, and apologized for any inconvenience to the consumer. But we are talking here about the ethics of the business world; I was thinking, not of "false advertizing" in the legal or economic sense, but, less dramatically, of the ethical considerations involved in teaching literary history, about the concept of literary tradition. Wouldn't a student in a survey of English Literary Traditions expect an introduction to John Milton? How can you understand Pope and Dr. Johnson without reading Milton? "The point is: Students will 'be reading works by a diverse group of women writers in the eighteenth century,' not Pope and Johnson, so they won't need Milton. But even if the idea is to focus on women writers of the Restoration and eighteenth century, some critics would say that the unaccountably omits mention of Ann Collins, Anna Trapnel, Margaret Cavendish, Susanna Parr, Katharine Evans, Sarah Cheevers, Mary Carleton, Alice Thornton, Sarah Davy, Anne Wentworth, Hannah Allen, Joan Vokins and Bethsua Makin."

That follows, I think. On the other hand, under the rubrics outlined in the general catalog, wouldn't instructors in the later segments of the English literary tradition expect some mention of John Donne, Ben Jonson, Robert Burton, Sir Thomas Browne, George Herbert, Thomas Herrick, Richard Crashaw, Andrew Marvell, John Dryden, Abraham Cowley, Thomas Middleton, John Webster, John Ford, Samuel Pepys, John Evelyn, George Fox, John Bunyan, William Congreve, William Wycherley, Richard Sheridan, Alexander Pope, Jonathan Swift, James Thomson and Dr. Johnson? Given the importance of political developments in the period, shouldn't students at least get a taste of Thomas Hobbes and Gerard Winstanley? Students may have heard about the "rise of the novel." What about Defoe, Richardson, Fielding and Smollett? "I suppose if you can leave Donne and Milton out, you can leave them out, too."

Perhaps the question we should ask, then, is this: Why omit Donne and Milton? And the eighteenth century without Pope and Johnson—does this make sense? Supposing that it doesn't, how do we come to terms with Dr. Johnson without reading Donne and Milton? Tradition implies an integral relation among elements. Does Dr. Johnson talk about the authors in this Eighteenth Century list of "Women Writers?" "It looks like the question must be: Do they talk about Dr. Johnson? Isn't this the idea of shifting our focus, of seeing literary history as a development, not of *an* English literary tradition, but of many literary traditions? Traditionalists react with distress because the list of readings excludes male authors."

The latter proposition, which posits the mental states of "traditionalists" as the cause of curricular objections to the innovative list, might be true, but, of course, true or false, it is not a literary statement, for its truth or falsity would be established according to the ordinary protocols of inquiry in the social sciences. "But regardless of how we must inquire into them, the attitudes—the mental states— of poets and critics matter in how we conceive literary history." Here, we easily confuse two notions of valuative judgment. In the last chapter, we discussed the difference between the "trivial" or "factual" and "absolute" sense of ethical propositions. Wittgenstein suggests that there is nothing difficult in pointing out the *"right* road" when one only means *"the right road relative to a certain goal."* If the aim is just to get people to read books written by women writers, then requiring them to do so would accomplish that goal. "And this initiative will, in time, alter the way we think about women, in general." Again, social historians might show that statement to be true or false. But they would not be addressing a literary or "ethical" question. In his "Lecture on Ethics," Wittgenstein claims that he is not interested in factual or scientific judgments:

> But this is not how Ethics uses them [notions of right and wrong]. Supposing that I could play tennis and one of you saw me playing and said "Well, you play pretty badly" and suppose I answered "I know, I'm playing badly but I don't want to play any better," all the other man could say would be "Ah then that's all right." But suppose I had told one of you a preposterous lie and he came up to me and said "You're behaving like a beast" and then I were to say "I know I behave badly, but then I don't want to behave any better," could he then say "Ah, then that's all right"? Certainly not; he would say "Well, you *ought* to want to

behave better." Here you have an absolute judgment of value, whereas the first instance was one of a relative judgment. (LE 5)

When we say that, given a choice, one ought to read Milton rather than Quarles or Edgeworth, which kind of statement are we making? "This question implies that the 'nontraditional' curriculum is indicative of a 'relative' judgment, because it directs our attention to such factual concerns as the 'patriarchal' system. But surely it is no fault in our thinking that we address such 'factual' conditions as the attitudes of '(male) critics,' since it is only by addressing these inner realities that we can alter external conditions. Doesn't Wittgenstein say that 'There are no propositions which, in any absolute sense, are sublime, important, or trivial?'" (LE 6)

Wittgenstein is trying to distinguish between the world of facts and the constellation of feelings we have about it, on the one hand, and the value judgments that we might make about both. Supposing that we had all of the statements of science reduced into one book, he argues, "this book would contain nothing that we would call an *ethical* judgment or anything that would logically imply such a judgment" (LE 6). This view relates to the question I have raised about the critic's proclamation that the feminist critique is "not an *ethical* criticism," and to the insistence that the "nontraditional" curriculum for The English literary tradition represents nothing more than a strategy to contend with individual and societal attitudes toward women. This is why "states of mind" talk in criticism so often misleads:

> But what I mean is that a state of mind, so far as we mean by that a fact which we can describe, is in no ethical sense good or bad. If for instance in our world-book we read the description of a murder with all its details physical and psychological, the mere description of these facts will contain nothing which we could call an *ethical* proposition. The murder will be on exactly the same level as any other

event, for instance the falling of a stone. Certainly the reading of this description might cause us pain or rage or any
other emotion, or we might read about the pain or rage
caused by this murder in other people when they heard of
it, but there will simply be facts, facts, and facts but no
Ethics. (LE 6–7)

I do not mean to imply by my use of this quotation that
the curricular issue here doesn't concern an ethical judgment. For literary, in the sense of aesthetic, judgments
aren't, in the Wittgensteinian sense, "trivial" or "factual,"
although many of the statements used to justify them
might be so. For instance, I am interested in the reasons
why anyone would think that the "nontraditional" list of
authors, above, should replace those that we usually think
of as shaping The English Literary Tradition. And saying
why I am thus interested in no way tells us what those
reasons are. Merely saying that there are Many English
Literary Traditions would not settle questions of the historical and aesthetic judgments involved. Even "nontra-
ditionalists" might say that Aemylia Lanier, Margaret
Cavendish and Katherine Phillips should be on any list of
required readings in any survey of English literature from
the early seventeenth through the eighteenth century.
Furthermore, the casual division of criticism into "traditional" critics ignored women authors is doubtful. My
mentors would probably not mind being thought "traditional" scholars of The English Literary Tradition, but
Aphra Behn and Katherine Phillips were routinely assigned
reading in their courses. So the question must still be: Is
the list of assigned women writers made up of women
writers *because* they are women writers, or *because* these
women writers are—each and every one of them—actually
more worthy and more important to literary history than
Donne and Milton and Swift and Pope and Johnson?
It seems clear that questions of canon formation involve
ethical judgment. Again, Wittgenstein helpfully distinguishes between two kinds of normative judgments. Ethical

norms cannot be provcd or disproved by an appeal to one or another empirical study: Statistics show that critics of such and such a gender or sexual preference under or over such and such and such an age with annual salaries of plus or minus so many dollars think so and so—say, that, given the choices that must be made in any curriculum, it is better that the student learn Donne and Milton than Hays and Edgeworth. Obviously, such decisions entail value judgments. When critics choose to ignore coverage of seventeenth century authors, they must imagine that it is more important to read those of the later period. If the question involves curricula, then professional standards as well as critical values come into play: What, if any, obligation does the instructor of a course in "English Literary Traditions" have to teach figures representative of The English Literary Tradition? In the most famous of his *Devotions*, Donne wrote that "No man is an island, entire of itself." Can we say, by analogy, that none of the many "traditions" of English literature are "entire" of The Tradition?

6.

"Many would argue that the question is in and of itself coercive. You would insist that women writers be matriculated into a larger scheme, which would only mean that, aftcr a long struggle to recover them, they would recede before a wave of so-called 'stronger includences.' Determined feminists would simply consider the source and ignore the question. We are not, after all, dealing *only* with literary and social values, but with the larger scheme of social organization. Even before any question of ethics arises, what we know about Donne and his world will never be precisely known. So we can never 'go on together' with absolute assurance that we have the facts and their interpretations right. Historical knowledge is itself imprecise. The history of language doesn't yield certainty. We are not dealing with 'proof,' as they do in mathematics."

Coming to terms with Donne's language is difficult, but

the certainty of any agreement we reach in the matter is akin to consent in any empirical description, which is not so different from the confidence we have in mathematics. There seems to be something wrong in the *way* in which you think of "proof." What determines "proof" that Donne was understood in such and such a way? If, "knowing" the dates of his birth and death, I err in estimating how long he lived, is it completely unlike any mistake I might make in the other case? Toward the close of *On Certainty*, Wittgenstein deals with this sort of question:

> I cannot be making a mistake about 12 × 12 being 144. And now one cannot contrast *mathematical* certainty with the relative uncertainty of empirical propositions. For the mathematic proposition has been obtained by a series of actions that are in no way different from the actions of the rest of our lives, and are in the same degree liable to forgetfulness, oversight and illusion. (*OC* §651)

Look for the modest, nondeclamatory help here. We make mistakes in calculation no less than in our historical descriptions. But when we say we make mistakes, we affirm a means of correction. Inaccuracy only makes sense in contrast to accuracy. What we trust concerning the history of language, which includes our understanding of Donne no less than of the letter that arrived today from the mortgage lender, fits, just as does the customary means of mathematical calculation does, with everything else in our lives. Our confidence in both areas of practice isn't misplaced, is it? When a mistake is corrected in either domain of thought, the process itself exhibits the justified confidence we have in "going on together."

This is a point that deserves emphasis, because we do not ordinarily ponder the bases of our justified assurance, say, that the market will still be using the system of mathematics today that were operating yesterday. We might express doubts about our knowledge of Donne's language and culture, but we seldom ponder the usefulness of those doubts. We doubt that we understand, but we don't proceed to any resolution of our doubt. But Wittgenstein writes: "A doubt without an end is not even a doubt" (*OC* §625). Obviously, there can be both "factual" and "ethical" considerations at play in the deciding how we will characterize Donne's elegies, but insofar as pleasure and pain are involved, we remain in with Wittgenstein thinks of as the "factual" or "relative" realm. And it is here that literary history might be of some help. One asks: Why do some critics enjoy, while others disdain, Donne's poetry? And another answers: Perhaps it is a matter of not understanding the language in which the elegies were written? Or of not feeling comfortable with the norms of expression of that time?

When Wittgenstein asks, "What happens when we learn to *feel* the ending of a church mode as an ending?" (*PI* §535), he implies that our recognition, if we have it, will concern hearing in a certain way in order to know or "*feel*" a sense of closure. Past experiences come into play. Although we can say that sound impressions are heard even by the tone deaf, we must concede that they might not recognize the crucial transition to the church mode. Even perfect pitch will not do the trick. To recognize the transition one must have heard others like it—grown used to such musical developments. Wittgenstein continues:

> I say: "I can think of this face (which gives an impression of timidity) as courageous too." We do not mean by this that I can imagine someone with this face perhaps saving someone's life (that, of course, is imaginable in connexion with any face). I am speaking rather of an aspect of the face itself. Nor do I mean that I can imagine that this man's face might change so that, in the ordinary sense, it looked courageous; though I may very well mean that there is a quite definite way in which it can change into a courageous face. The reinterpretation of a facial expression can be compared to the reinterpretation of a chord in music, when we hear it as a modulation first into this, then into that key. (*PI* §536)

Let us consider this the situation with the feminist critique of Donne today. We have this picture of Donne, such that, as feminist critics claim, men in the Donne poems under consideration think women are stupid, and, in so thinking so, they betray "male fear" of women's sexuality. Now we want to know: How do we justify saying so? Suppose other well-meaning Donne critics are unable to perceive this aspect of the proposed picture of Donne? Suppose, too, that even though they try, these critics cannot perceive "male fear" of women's sexuality in a Donne elegy. Can we say that it is through some failure in the sensory apparatus that these critics are unable to perceive this thematic interest in the text? I show you a picture, and then tell the story behind the portrait of the man who appears to you as timid. The portrait was painted just prior to a momentous battle, and the subject knew at the time of the sitting that he must lead his troops into battle against superior forces. And now, although the picture has not been changed by a brushstroke, the face that had seemed timid conveys a sense of firm resolve and courage. In such a circumstance, Wittgenstein writes, "Perhaps one says: 'Yes, now I understand: the face as it were shews indifference to the outer world'" (*PI* §537).

Wittgenstein's point is that what goes before seeing and hearing will bear on seeing and hearing. So if I do not perceive the timorous aspect of the male protagonists in a particular Donne poem, and if, after hearing the narrative told by the critic who does perceive it, I am still unable to see it, what will constitute a criterion for deciding that this aspect is present in the text? "Well, somebody saw it!" So is this an answer to my question, or a statement of historical fact? Recognitions of a shift to the church mode may involve quite diverse experiences in many keys and in many different circumstances; but they will share certain features—"family resemblances"—even though we might not be able to list or articulate them. This is what Wittgenstein calls "mastery of a technique" (*PI* §150, 208); it is like learning a language. In reading Donne's poems with "rakish lovers" in them, we will want to know what notions fit. In Elizabethan and Jacobean England, are they customarily—or ever—like this? Are men in such poems afraid of women's sexuality?

Now suppose that aspect—of timorousness—were suddenly manifest. Here is solid evidence that the speaker in "The Anagram"—or someone very like him—fears Flavia's—or some other woman's—sexuality. (The evidence might appear, say, from analogous contemporary situations in which a mentor explicitly expresses such apprehension to a less sophisticated auditor.) The question now becomes: Where do we go from here? Are we then in a position to allay anybody's fear—the lover's or Donne's—of female sexuality? Or, failing that, are we doomed to watch helplessly as bounders cope with what we know to be irrational fear of female sexuality? "Well, the speaker feels that men are losing their grip on women, and that is what they fear. The charge that women are ignorant only masks the speaker's anxiety, which is, in turn, a symptom of Donne's malady, which we only choose, for convenience, to call *misogyny*. The cynical lovers in such poems as 'Communitie' and 'The Indifferent' and in certain of the elegies are afraid of women's sexuality, so they characterize women as stupid and amoral. You would like to disabuse anyone attracted to this perspective by arguing that Donne's fictive indictments of women as moral idiots is actually an attack on the uneducable men who consort with them. Hence, I will argue, at the very least, a measure of misandry accompanies whatever expression of misogyny, if any, we find in these poems."

It seems to me only fair to consider the fairness of that designation. Assuming that discussion of the propriety of attaching a name to an individual should precede its general application, what would inform such a discussion? For decades, critics disputed the sense of applying the term "Metaphysical" to Donne and others. Names and labels matter, not because there is some natural or eternal link between what we say and the world, but because what we say either helps or hinders communication. If I say that Donne, and not Quarles, is the author of *Sions Sonets*, I am making a mistake. If I say that Donne, and not

Shakespeare, is a "misogynist," am I making a mistake, and if so, is it the same *kind* of mistake? Given the linkage between Donne and his admiring critics, the question might be phrased this way: Can I be mistaken about my own name? Possibly a drug has induced me to believe that I am "L. W." and not "S. S." But suppose someone says that I am a misogynist, and I am inclined to deny the assertion. Can I be sure of my grounds in my denial? Does the same question work the other way around? Can the claim that I am or am not a misogynist be lodged on sure grounds, supported by all the available evidence? Can we "know" that Donne was or wasn't a misogynist? Well, can our doubts in the matter serve a useful purpose? Could John Donne have been a misogynist without knowing it? "Isn't it possible that others recognized Donne's incapacity to 'know himself' in this matter?" Can I be a misogynist without knowing it? Or can I have been a misogynist, say, a long time ago, and forgotten the episode?

"Now, I think you are not taking the concept of misogyny seriously, and this seems to me a mistake. The term as we use it characterizes a constellation of attitudes and practices. It isn't simply a label that we hang on poems or people we don't like. I might concede that what you call a 'misandrist' motif recurs in certain of Donne's secular poems. But there is nothing new in saying this. You cannot argue that the emphasis between misogyny and misandry is tipped against men, or even that it stands in perfect poise in these Donne poems. What about 'Communitie?' It is a mean and vicious declaration of the most reprehensible male impulse to exploit women with no thought to consequences. Feminist critics are surely on firm ground to denounce it." I can imagine a critic saying that "Communitie" is a powerful and fascinating poem, and yet acknowledge that it shocks and offends. Many critics find a scurrilous undertone of resentment in the poem, as if a jest intended for a sophisticated audience has gone awry. But the fact that critics single the poem out as a morbid example suggests that it is something of an anomaly.

"This strategy will not work. For if it worked, we would

hear of 'misandrist criticism.' Government agencies would establish task forces to examine offenses against men, and academic deans would launch national searches to fill chairs endowed for the advancement of 'Masculist Theory.'5 I can imagine no circumstances under which such a development would be feasible. It seems to me simpler and better to admit the obvious: That Donne, indeed, is a misogynist." If it will help us "go on together," I will concede the futility of arguing that the emphasis between misogyny and misandry is in perfect poise in these Donne poems. Would you, then, agree that, even when a Donne lover expresses fear of particular women—as in "Change" (Donne 19–20), for instance—he soon reveals that it is neither that woman, nor women in general, that he fears, but men? Women cannot help being women, but neither can men help being men: "If I have caught a bird, and let him flie, / Another fouler using these meanes, as I, / May catch the same bird" (7–9). Nature made women "apter to'endure then men" (14), but she also made a great multitude of men to compensate for the lack in individual stamina. "Change" in the sexual sense—or its synonym, "incontinency"—is so much a part of human nature that to rebel against it is pointless. True liberty is the product of movement and change, which means that the lover must adjust to the limitation on his endurance. Comfort comes in knowing that compensation for his insufficient sexual stamina is already available, thanks to the ceaseless efforts of competing but likewise soon-tired males. He must only learn not to fear his—or their—incontinence, which is, to the mature initiate, "the nursery / Of musicke, joy, life, and eternity" (35–36).

It doesn't seem inappropriate to ask: Where is the misogyny here? Or to say with some confidence that "Change" is a misandrist poem, in the sense that members of Donne's audience probably got the joke: In Jacobean England, "incontinence" implied a lack of moral rather than of physical stamina. A Renaissance contemporary of Donne describes "Women" as "the second English Evill" (the first being drunkenness), for from them men are led into *"Incontinencie."* Indeed, from the lips of beautiful women men will "sucke effeminate humours," and lose the capacity to take advantage of "advise from . . . freinds" (Stafford 33). Would it be unfair to use this context as a gloss on "The Anagram?" But what is the experienced lover in this and many other Donne elegies doing? Why should we think that, by advising the young lover that no man can be trusted (since they are all, like him, lured by incontinent women into incontinent ways), Donne's mature mentor is a misogynist? Isn't he, instead, unduly pessimistic about men, who seem never to learn how not to be manipulated by women? Perhaps not. My guess is that critics will continue to disagree about "The Anagram." I wonder, nevertheless, how much is gained by attaching the name of either "misandry" or "misogyny" to the poem? Or is he, in the end, being merely hyperbolically "realistic?"

* * * * *

I have suggested that, on both descriptive and normative grounds, the charge of misogyny against poems like "The Anagram" raises a problem of historical interpretation, and may confuse normative categories as well. Before we rush to judgment about the dramatic and ethical characteristics of such poems, we need to know more about how such witty expressions were construed in Donne's time. Were men and women, alike, amused by Donne's self-centered young lovers? Or were men in particular offended by seeing male proclivities exposed and ridiculed? Do we need a post-postmodern school of "Masculist Theory" that would shun poems like "The Anagram" as "a calumny against men" for its *de facto* evidence of "contempt for men?" Suppose we as Donne critics were, under pressure of such a movement, forced to choose between a masculist understanding of this picture of "The Anagram" and enjoyment of the joke at men's expense. "Well," the masculist asserts, "our theoretical position requires determination in the here and now that we position ourselves as resolute opponents of antimasculist propaganda. If we value poems like 'The Anagram,' how will we encourage young men to feel good about themselves?"

On the other hand, there is no incontrovertible reason why we should not read these poems as stunning and enlightening works of verbal art in the here and now. We may, if we are interested in talk about Donne's verbal art, wish to set aside such normative terms as *misogynist, misandrist* and *realistic*. Would such a determination tell us how we ought to read "The Anagram," or would it necessarily militate against our historical understanding of the poem? Wittgenstein's aside might not answer this question, but it does suggest that critics need not respond to every joke as if it were a serious move in a universal propaganda war: "The real discovery is the one that makes me capable of stopping doing philosophy when I want to.— The one that gives philosophy peace, so that it is no longer tormented by questions which bring *itself* in question" (*PI* §133).

5

Herbert and the Historicity of Critical Metaphor

We want to establish an order in our
knowledge of the use of language: an order
with a particular end in view; one out of many
possible orders; not *the* order. To this end we shall
constantly be giving prominence to distinctions
which our ordinary forms of language easily
make us overlook. This may make it
look as if we saw it as our task to
reform language.

Such a reform for particular practical
purposes, an improvement in our terminology
designed to prevent misunderstandings in practice,
is perfectly possible. But these are not the cases we
have to do with. The confusions which occupy
us arise when language is like an engine
idling, not when it is doing work.

— Wittgenstein, *Philosophical Investigations*

Herbert criticism began with Nicholas Ferrar's suggestion that perhaps it was presumptuous to expect patronage of *The Temple* from "any mortall man" (Herbert 3).
Ferrar's focus on Herbert's character and motives ("the condition and disposition of the Person") initiated the hagiographic tradition that was to dominate seventeenth and
eighteenth century commentary. Since then, the knowledge industry, with its exponential increase of information
and misinformation, has changed but not extinguished
critical interest in Herbert. Many Herbert critics no longer
remember the poet as a saint in the calendar of the Christian year, which fact could justly be regarded as progress
or decline of some order. For it seems reasonable to say
that the computer age has helped to create, rather than to
answer, the questions that confront criticism today about
the Herbert whose expressions Ferrar may have understood
better than we undertand them. On the other hand, perhaps Ferrar would have been puzzled by the questions that
now interest us: What did Herbert believe? Did he say
what he believed? Did he believe what he said? Did he
know what he said? *Could* he know what he said?

1.

Stanley Fish claims that Herbert is not a "postmodern,"
and that sounds right, but it is not clear what follows from
the assertion, except perhaps some general implication
about the difference between Herbert's world and our own.
It is one thing to acknowledge that the world has changed
since 1633, and quite another to articulate the areas of difference which are most likely to help our contemporaries
understand Herbert's poetry. We need to practice articulating these differences if for no other reason than that we
have inherited, not just Herbert's literary texts, but centuries of critical tradition along with them. Thus, we can trace
the demise of hagiographic Herbert criticism to at least as
early as 1853, when a decisive interest in the Herbert critic,
as distinct from Herbert, emerged in Coleridgean hyperbole.

With a proto-postmodern flourish, Coleridge extended the hagiographic picture of Herbert's texts to include the critic himself. Coleridge argued that, since Herbert was "a poet *sui generis*," the "merits" of his poetry were imperceptible to anyone lacking "sympathy with the mind and character of the man" (Coleridge 2.379). So over a century ago, Coleridge shifted the emphasis from Herbert to the "subjectivity" of his critics: "To appreciate this volume, it is not enough that the reader possesses a cultivated judgment, a classical taste, or even poetic sensibility, unless he be likewise a *Christian*, and both a zealous and an orthodox, both a devout and a *devotional*, Christian." We see here a demand much like that made by advocates of race, class and gender theory today: What critics *are* determines what critics *say*, as well as what we ought to think of what they say. In its most incandescent form, this method holds that it is not enough to know the intellectual and generic features of a Herbert poem, or even to know its tradition and to view its unique features within that tradition with judgment and taste. Before that, the critic must *be* a certain kind of person, a "*Christian*," and more than that, a particular kind of "*Christian*": zealous *and* orthodox, devout *and* devotional.

And yet, for the Coleridge of critical rectitude, not even this severe limitation will do the trick. For such sympathies in a critic would still permit too wide a range of possibilities. Coleridgean principle demands a serious thinning of the field:

> But even this will not quite suffice. He [that is, the proper Herbert critic] must be an affectionate and dutiful child of the Church, and from habit, conviction, and a constitutional predisposition to ceremoniousness, in piety as in manners, find her forms and ordinances aids of religion, not sources of formality; for religion is the element in which he lives, and the region in which he moves. (2.379)

And, we might add (for here Coleridge echoes Paul's speech to the Areopagus): "and has his being." For Coleridge perceives in Herbert, not "the Romish fopperies and even the Papistic usurpations" that others do, "but . . . more correctly, as well as more charitably . . . the *Patristic* leaven" (2.379) of nonidolatrous devotion. He reads Herbert as leaning toward both Canterbury *and* Rome. Hence, ceremony is the key to understanding Herbert. Coleridge is not always comfortable with Herbert in this regard; he thinks a line ("Holy *Macarius* and great *Anthony*") from "The Church Militant" overrates the early fathers, and he registers his objection, also, to Herbert's "Judgement": "I should not have expected from *Herbert* so open an avowal of Romanism in the article of *merit*" (2.381). This inclination to read Herbert as having a Roman inflection is nowhere more evident than when Coleridge engages the representation of the Eucharist in "Divinity": "But he doth bid us take his bloud for wine. / Bid what he please; yet I am sure, / To take and taste what he doth there designe, / Is all that saves, and not obscure" (135). Of these lines, Coleridge writes:

> "But he doth bid us take his blood for wine." Nay, the contrary, take wine to be blood, and *the* blood of a man who died 1800 years ago. This is the faith which even the Church of *England* demands; for Consubstantiation only *adds* a mystery to that of Transubstantiation, which it implies. (2.380)

Syntactically, the "it" here seems to refer to "Consubstantiation," but it might, alternatively—or also—refer back to the line in "Divinity" that Coleridge means to gloss. Either way, Coleridge indicates that Herbert's "faith"—the faith of "even the Church of *England*"—buttresses the ceremonial observance of the mystery only deepened by the the concept of "Consubstantiation," and finally depended for its impact, as does Herbert's poem, upon an understanding of "Transubstantiation."

Nowadays certain Herbert critics exhibit a renewed interest in theories, which, although inflected with current interests, attempt to characterize the genetic limits of what a critic says or believes on the basis of what Coleridge thought of as one's "constitutional predisposition." Many critics assume that, by some mechanism ("materialist" or whatever), what critics are *before* they become Herbert critics determines what they say about Herbert. Although in 1853 the editor explains away the locution that bothers Coleridge (2.381n), Coleridge seems to attribute High Church views to Herbert,[1] the same view, in fact, that would take hold almost a century later in the "Metaphysical Revival," when T. S. Eliot and the New Critics attempted something like a recuperation of values believed lost or attenuated during the neoclassical and Romantic periods. At the same time, critics unsympathetic to T. S. Eliot's magisterial outlook on literary tradition claimed that he and others like him unapologetically fawned on the esoteric High Church values of the Metaphysicals, creating a coterie criticism of coterie poetry to fit their coterie values. But, perhaps in reaction to those values, some practitioners of the current generation of Herbert critics look back to Coleridge, but for a different reason. Arguing that one's ethnic or religious being enables, defines and delimits the range and, implicitly, the validity of a critic's perspective, these critics insist that ideology (like noses, in that everybody has one) functions in such a way that Anglicans like T. S. Eliot and Dame Helen Gardner understand and appreciate a text written by an Anglican in a certain way; their groupings of texts, accompanied by prescribed attitudes (the canon) reflect no more than the sociologically determined biases of uppercrust, Oxford, High Church Tories.

The situation now is that Herbert critics disagree, and sometimes their disagreements are substantive, touching the foundations of the discipline—what we know and how we talk about what we know. Even historicists, who share many basic assumptions, exhibit irreconcilable differences, differences which Gene Veith colorfully describes as a recurrence of "the religious wars of the seventeenth century" ("Wars" 19). Veith confesses that, although himself a combatant, he nevertheless finds the critical descendants of the

Roundheads and the Cavaliers both "utterly convincing in illuminating Herbert's poetry" (18). (It is doubtful that "war" can be sustained if belligerents remain so agreeable.) I find Veith's tone commendable. I, too, admire Sir Thomas Browne's famous remark on toleration for its recognition that, as a practice, tolerance serves the interests of personal growth: "I COULD never divide my selfe from any man upon the difference of an opinion, or be angry with his judgement for not agreeing with mee in that, from which perhaps within a few days I should dissent myselfe" (Browne 1.15). But does investigation of the critical record show that there are, as Veith claims, truly no "necessarily incompatible" assertions separating Herbert critics, even historically oriented Herbert critics?

I suggest that, as long as critics propound serious theses, contention and confusion will mark the critical conversation. "But why is this?" Because theses, as distinct from questions or assertions, seem inappropriate to the task of linguistic inquiry into Herbert's language. Wittgenstein writes: "If one tried to advance *theses* in philosophy, it would never be possible to debate them, because everyone would agree to them" (*PI* §128). What he means, as applied to this discussion, is that critics will probably agree on what they "know" about Herbert's language. So unless they are going to argue from *being*, as Coleridge does—to the effect that only critics *like* Herbert in their private devotions, etc., are qualified to make statements about his poetry—they are going to have to content themselves with their disagreements. For, as Wittgenstein observes, "Philosophy simply puts everything before us, and neither explains nor deduces anything" (§126). Theses are the residue of explanation. Implicit here is the assumption that critical differences arise, not from questions of Herbert's poetry, but from critical talk about it. Explanations and characterizations introduce those differences which, arising as they do from a myriad of personalities quite unlike Herbert's, allow for the confusing sense that something in Herbert's poetry evades "the discipline" of literary criticism. Experience tells us that Herbert critics disagree, and we imagine that there is something in Herbert's poetry eludes even the most energetic and resourceful effort to describe it.

2.

The misguided critic inquires: What did Herbert believe? And the judicious response is probably evasive, because it would be better if we first asked: What did Herbert say? "Except that this question seems to presuppose that Herbert believed what he said. Isn't it possible that he and other poets in the seventeenth century simply expressed themselves in a certain conventional way? Didn't clerics then, like academics today, have to get along, as we do now, by going along with 'speech codes' and the like? Or is Herbert's usage so extraordinary as to make it, in the language of his time, unintelligible?" Well, what will serve as a criterion of judgment here? (Yes, he did. No, he didn't. The evidence [. . .] suggests [. . .], or, on the basis of the evidence [. . .] we infer that [. . .].) Suppose that the response comes: Historical interpretation is a branch of lexicography (see Stewart "Dictionary"). This would make literary analysis a subfield of the history of the language: Rosemond Tuve places Herbert's poetry in the context of liturgical uses; Louis Martz elucidates Herbert's practice in the context of contemporary meditative writings. "Historical" critics assert the relevance of a range of linguistic possibilities in Herbert's time: in Anglo-Catholic theology (Asals), in Protestant prose and poetry (Lewalski), in Luther (Strier), in Calvin (Hodgkins), in catechisms (Fish), in the Bible (Bloch), in Cambridge divines (Sherwood), and so on.

Although at times historical critics appear to be at loggerheads, they share important areas of agreement. For instance, historicists assume that correction of interpretive error is possible, because a valid criterion of accuracy enables critics to distinguish between descriptions in need and those not in need of correction. They might designate this standard in different ways: "propriety," "probability," or "in accord with the evidence," but the purpose is the same. For historical critics, this question may be: Can we *know* what Herbert said? And it is answerable, for it is understood as something like this: Can we know *his* emphasis among the myriad of historically certified possibilities? We might say that we can look at what Herbert said in the context of how such expressions were customarily used. Then, if the question ("can we *know*") means "Are we able, without recourse to preternatural means, to look and see print on the page in the various archives?" then we have Herbert's texts; and we have the descriptions of Tuve, Martz, Lewalski, Strier, Sherwood and other historical critics, just as we have the OED—as guides to places where Herbert's expressions might fit within the range of demonstrable uses in 1633. Like the textual scholar (see chapter 3), historical critics deal with the demonstrable. It would not distort matters to say that, whether they know it or not, historical critics adhere to Wittgenstein's description, with which we are already familiar, of the therapeutic philosopher's function: "Philosophy simply puts everything before us, and neither explains nor deduces anything" (*PI* §126). For historical critics present documentary materials with a mind to suggest the relevance of that evidence to an understanding of the matter at hand. Their implicit imperative—that participants in the conversation focus on the cited evidence because it is relevant to the question asked—arrests attention with the ethical claim *of* that relevance. I want to say that the "understanding" elicits articulation *about* that evidence, but the articulation may seem to be only partial, even as it "satisfies" or "explains" (think of the moment after consultation, but before we close the OED with the sense that we have found what we were looking for).

"So," our interlocutor might ask, "are we to infer, then, that the historical critics' 'explanations' are somehow different from other 'explanations' ('there is nothing to explain'), even though they provide occasion for what one critic characterizes as a war?" I would say that "war" may

be too colorful a figure. But acquaintance with the literature seems to make one thing sure: Historical criticism and
contention go together. But this doesn't mean that the past
is somehow Sphinx-like in its mystery. Presumably, it is
not "description," but "characterization" of the past, that
is in dispute. So perhaps it will help to focus our attention
on a particular example of disagreement between historical critics. ("The work of the philosopher," Wittgenstein
suggests, "consists in assembling reminders for a particular purpose" [*PI* §127].) Much has been written and said
about Herbert's "Calvinism," and indeed there are shad-
ings of the terms *Calvinism, Protestantism* and *Puritanism*
that allow for something approaching their interchange-
able use. It is no exaggeration to say that the "Protestantiz-
ing" of poets like Herbert has in the past decade boldly
turned a challenge to the "traditional reading" (Hodgkins
166) of metaphysical poetry into a growth industry. It is
as if a generation of readers came to view the writings
of Donne and Herbert through the eyes of an influential
Miltonist; and, in fact, it seems fair to say that the spate
of books on the Lutheran or Calvinist or Protestant or
Puritan Donne and Herbert indicate the persuasiveness of
the method and vocabulary of Barbara Lewalski's *Protestant Poetics and the Seventeenth-Century Religious Lyric*
(1979). Even when it looks as if skepticism might set in
(note the subtitle of Christopher Hodgkins' book on
Herbert: *Return to the Middle Way*), the prevailing wisdom
emerges that Herbert's *via media* was best articulated in
John Calvin's *Institutes of the Christian Religion*, even as
the thought of that work was popularized by that avatar
of The Middle Way, William Perkins. Hence, as a proponent of the Elizabethan "Old Conformity"—a "[v]ery,
very nearly" Calvinist "Conformity" in the first place
(Hodgkins 20)—Herbert sought a "regenerative nostalgia"
in the form of a local and internalized version of the
"Tudor humanist social vision" (Hodgkins 214).

As we might expect from historical criticism, the Calvinist hypothesis depends on evidence of affinities between
the thought of Herbert and the great Genevan theologian.

Naturally, selection of examples is important. Proponents of a Protestant Herbert—Hodgkins is a good example—focus on similarities between Herbert and his Puritan contemporaries: "like Perkins before him" (Hodgkins 102), Herbert does or says X or Y; therefore, Herbert's views on election, church government, the sacraments and vestments were to the left of Richard Hooker (166), and like those of William Perkins, Richard Bernard and Joseph Hall (106). Herbert favored a "Genevan model of church discipline" (106); no Laudian (128), Herbert thought in a "peculiarly Protestant way" (155); against the Laudian regime, his views look "Puritanical" (104). Because he in fact had "deep temperamental and doctrinal divergence from the Laudians" (64), in that Laud had replaced the "Calvinist consensus" in England (63) with a tyrannical sacerdotalism of which he disapproved—or would have disapproved, had he lived longer (Laud became Archbishop five months after Herbert died), Herbert was Protestant. In other words, the opposition that works here is between "Protestantism" and Archbishop Laud. Accordingly, Herbert belongs on the "borderline between the 'Old Conformist' and Puritan Positions" (Hodgkins 172), inclining, like Thomas Fuller, to "moderate Puritanism" (Hodgkins 211).

The repetition of quotations here deserves attention, not because incremental usage of a term might have a cumulative rhetorical effect. There would be nothing wrong with that, unless it indicates attenuation of an argument. Even this might result from a harmless linguistic "fact" of usage (part of a specialized language or jargon) within the confines of a "community of interpreters" (Fish *Artifacts* "Appendix"); terms like *Protestant* and *Calvinist* recur in Herbert criticism. But we can imagine that even within such a community mistakes might occur (for another perspective on this point, see Currie). "Consider, for instance, the concept of *critical problems*, which has its analogue in that of *philosophical problems*, which arise," Wittgenstein suggests, "when language *goes on holiday*" (*PI* §38). I suspect that something like this happens with the repetition of words like *Protestant* and *Calvinist*, when applied to poets like Herbert and Donne. Imprecise to begin with, common usage encourages the sense that the terms are doing more work than is the case. Wittgenstein does not imply that it is *a priori* dangerous for language to remain idle, but, less drastically, that taking nonfunctional for functional uses within a language can lead to misunderstanding. If we say "Calvinist" or "Protestant" over and over while considering particular Herbert poems, we might imagine that one or both terms correspond to something transcending the ordinary use of ordinary words:

> This [that is, naming—"Calvinist," "Protestant," "Catholic"] is connected with the conception of naming as, so to speak, an occult process. Naming appears as a *queer* connexion of a word with an object.—And you really get such a queer connexion when the philosopher tries to bring out *the* relation between name and thing by staring at an object in front of him and repeating a name or even the word "this" innumerable times. (*PI* §38)

With this caution in mind, I would argue that, as far as Herbert's beliefs and attitudes regarding sacerdotal functions in the Church of England are concerned, they are most convincingly represented in poems like "Lent," "The Priesthood," "The Sacrifice," and "The Agonie," poems which do not seem very "Calvinist" or "Protestant." Not only does the figurative language of these poems derive from pre-Reformation Catholic traditions, but they are in fact amenable to a number of interpretations of the nature of the Host. Similarly, Herbert's poem on the "Blest Order" assigned to impart the sacraments doesn't seem like a promising vehicle for the Protestantization of Herbert either.

It would be pointless to deny that there are "Calvinist" elements in Herbert, as there are in the Book of Common Prayer (especially in the prefatory "Of Ceremonies why some be abolished, and some reteined" [1630], which echoes Calvin's argument in the *Institutes* that different nations and different times require different liturgical

observances). Problems in criticism arise when we take
such categorical designations too seriously. To the question, "Is Herbert a Calvinist?" perhaps we should respond:
Well, since we can parse the Herbert and Calvin canons
into numerous parts, we might not be able to answer helpfully without knowing which parts to talk about with respect to whatever aspect of appositeness might be thought
to justify either an affirmative or negative response. Then,
to the question, "Can't you think of Herbert texts which
either do or do not lend credence to the assertion that
Herbert believed, with Calvin, in 'predestination'?" The
answer might be: "The Water-course" immediately comes
to mind. Here, the speaker urges an auditory subject to the
human condition of suffering not to complain, for to love
"life" is the same as to love "strife":

> But rather turn the pipe and waters course
> To serve thy sinnes, and furnish thee with store
> Of sov'raigne tears, springing from true remorse:
> That so in purenesse thou mayst him adore,
>
> Who gives to man, as he sees fit { Salvation.
>   { Damnation.
>
> (170)

"Surely no one doubts that this poem echoes the attitudes
and even the imagery of Calvin's *Institutes* (Veith *Spirituality* 91), and even an apposite Augustinian caprice"
(Strier 85). This sounds right, for here, as elsewhere in his
verse (in "The Flower," for instance), Herbert imagines
God's power as the source of "Salvation" *and* "Damna-
tion" (which is not to say that God's judgment of what is
"fit" is void of propriety with respect to human conduct).

   And yet, commenting on the same poem, Louis Martz
convincingly argues *against* "a strictly Calvinist" (Martz 65)
reading of Herbert. While not denying that certain Herbert
poems are "capable of Calvinist interpretation," Martz dis-
criminates between the tone and doctrine of such poems
as "The Water-course," "Redemption," "The Priesthood,"
and "Perseverance," showing how consistently Herbert
resists the strictures of Calvinist theology as laid out by

Archbishop Whitgift in the controversial Lambeth Articles. In resisting the "powerful tendency" to read Herbert "as a strictly Calvinist poet" (65), Martz emphasizes the many "eucharistic allusions" in the final version of *The Temple* as well as the "mood of assurance that dominates the last twelve or fifteen poems in the final version" (70). Herbert affords a place for "conscience" in man's salvation (76); he inclines "toward a middle way," and so is neither Calvinist nor anti-Calvinist.

"Obviously, Martz and Hodgkins apply the spatial figure of the *via media* in very different ways." We could characterize the difference in that way. But I would say that, in any case, when we are talking about "The Watercourse," the designation "Calvinist" may work very well. It might be just the term to articulate perception of a feature in the poem that we want to talk about. Here, it is the richness of the context that makes the word work. We might charitably say that not even the description of the poem as "obtrusively Calvinist" (Hodgkins 21) misleads. On the other hand, when the critic wants the same term to do the same work in describing Herbert's "Lent," semantic slippage is inevitable and, with it, confusion. This equivocal usage leads to the question, unanswered, I think, by Herbertian Calvinizers: Does Herbert *never* separate from Calvin in matters of doctrine and discipline? Wasn't there opposition within the British Church to certain zealously held opinions of Calvin—such as those concerning festivals and fasting, in general, and the observance of Lent? And wouldn't it be fair to describe that opposition as anti-Calvinist? "I thought we had agreed not to address such questions, but only to consider parts of the canon relevant to the particular text or topic." Quite so. More narrowly, then, and in accord with our critical protocol, on the matter of Lenten observances, Calvin wrote:

> ... I do not want to waste many words in a matter so obvious. I say only this, that both in fasts and in all other parts of discipline the papists have nothing right, nothing sincere, nothing well-ordered and arranged, to give them occasion

> to boast, as if anything remained among them deserving
> praise. (*Institutes* 2.1248)

Calvin was annoyed by the implicit assumption that, by
enduring 40 days of dietary duress, supposed Christians
practiced "an imitation of Christ" (*Harmonie* 1.126), a
claim that Calvin considered a "madde boldnesse spite at
God," in that it misconstrued the sense of Scripture:

> I woulde to God that they had onely plaide like apes with
> these follies. But it was a wicked and a detestable scorning
> of Christ, in that they attempted in theyr fained fasting to
> frame them selves after his doing. It is a moste vile super-
> stition that they perswade themselves that it is a worke
> meritorious, and to be some part of godlinesse and divine
> worship. (*Harmonie* 1.126)

Calvin insisted that Christ's 40-day sojourn in the wilderness had nothing to do with temperance, nothing in fact to
do with physical regimen. His fast was a sign and seal of
"authoritie," not of self-control. It appears, then, that these
texts distance Calvin from the practice of fasting during
Lent, and, indeed, from the observance of Lent itself.

In Elizabethan and Jacobean England, the issue of Lent
was controversial at least partly because Anglican apologists—Hooker, for instance—did not wish to separate themselves too sharply from the position laid out by Calvin
(Cressy *Bonfires* chap. 3). And yet, while conceding that
the scriptural basis of the practice was not impressive,
Hooker tactfully supported traditional activities of Lent.[2]
Thus Hooker's more or less centrist posture in matters of
doctrine and liturgical decency includes a mild disclaimer
on fasting and Lent. But what were Herbert's views? Were
they like Hooker's, or did they shade toward Calvin's, or
were they somewhere between Hooker's and Laud's?[3] We
should remember that Herbert did include a poem entitled
"Lent" in *The Temple* (86–87), and this in the appropriate sequence of the Christian calendar. Moreover, he does
so in an almost polemical manner—atypical of Herbert:
"Welcome deare feast of Lent: who loves not thee, / He

loves not Temperance, or Authoritie." Calvin argued that too often men would miss one meal only to gorge at another, thus using the Lenten season to heighten self-indulgence. The worshipper of "Lent" addresses this objection. For him, "sweet abstinence" is made sweeter in part because it is enjoined by the Church: "The Scriptures bid us *fast*; the Church sayes, *now*." That is, the Church imposes a particular temporal order upon a general biblical duty. Then, as if to meet the Calvinist charge that Lenten exercises were replete with scandal, Herbert writes:

> The humble soul compos'd of love and fear
> Begins at home, and layes the burden there,
> When doctrines disagree.
> He sayes, in things which use hath justly got,
> I am a scandall to the Church, and not
> The Church is so to me.
>
> (7–12)

It could be said that here the issue is not doctrine but motive. Where Scripture and the Church have spoken, "passion" is an improper response: "who loves not thee [that is, Lent], / He loves not Temperance, or Authoritie." Although Herbert tactfully steps around the specific doctrinal issue ("doctrines disagree"), he is quite explicit in suggesting that "love and fear" of both Scripture and Church enjoin the "true Christian" to adhere to the Christian calendar. Fasting is good; fasting during Lent is doubly so: "True Christians should be glad of an occasion / To use their temperance, seeking no evasion."

Again, for Calvin, who was incensed by the analogy of the seasonal observance and Christ's 40 days in the wilderness, Christ's fast was singular, and its protracted length was a sign of that singularity. How, then, would Calvin have responded to these lines from Herbert's poem?

> It's true, we cannot reach Christs forti'th day;
> Yet to go part of that religious way,
> Is better then to rest:

> Wc cannot reach our Saviours puritie;
> Yet we are bid, *Be holy ev'n as he.*
> 　　　In both let's do our best.
>
> 　　　　　　　　　　　　　(31–36)

Calvin held that one season was no holier than another;
nor was it conceivable that humankind could ever sustain a 40-day fast. Rather, the imposition of seasonal demands provided an extended occasion for hypocrisy and
self-indulgence. In contrast, for Herbert the Church calendar was no occasion of scandal, but rather it was the individual (false) Christian who fell short: "Neither ought
other mens abuse of Lent / Spoil the good use; lest by that
argument / We forfeit all our Creed."

It is worth noting that "Lent" is atypically argumentative
in that, unlike the speakers of, say, "The Collar" and "The
Crosse," the speaker here ponders, not recalcitrant aspects
of his own soul, but troublesome ideas disturbing the calm
of "Authoritie" within the Church. Even the prayer at the
end of the poem seems not to fit the Calvinist charge that
Lenten observances incline to insincerity, as if eating
might encourage "faults" of self-indulgence, the Christian
prays for guidance in "improving" the fast by redering it a
spiritual means to deprive "sinne" of its substance:

> Yet Lord instruct us to improve our fast
> By starving sinne and taking such repast
> 　　　As may our faults controll:
> That ev'ry man may revell at his doore,
> Not in his parlour; banquetting the poore,
> 　　　And among those his soul.
>
> 　　　　　　　　　　　　　(43–48)

These lines are no more Protestant and no more Calvinist
than Herrick's in "To keep a true Lent," in which many
of the same questions arise concerning the aims of "a true
Lent": "To fast from strife"; "to circumcise thy life"; "to
sterve thy sin" (Herrick 519). In Herbert, too, the ceremonial observance of Lent is only the outward sign of a hoped-
for inward grace, namely, the transformation of man's
sinful nature into something closer than it would other-

wise be to "an imitation of Christ." The "true Christian" prays that Lenten practices will yield both inner and outer results—yes, spiritual development ("faults controll"), but also "good works" ("banquetting the poore")—an aim of Lent of no interest to Calvin at all.

"But," one might say, "this analysis overlooks the hard fact that Herbert's 'Lent' is only a fictional part of a poetic sequence, and not necessarily an expression of Herbert's true opinions in the matter." But how do we distinguish between an author's true and untrue opinions? Are the opinions on the subject reflected in *A Priest to the Temple* and in Herbert's private correspondence likewise "untrue?" ("No.") Are we then to assume that the old barrier has been resurrected between fiction and nonfiction, with the latter as the privileged domain of truth, as if no one had ever exaggerated or even fabricated in epistolary or hortatory prose? In *The Country Parson*, Herbert claims that "fasting dayes containe a treble obligation" (242), and he urges the priest to maintain the discipline even while under the stress of a journey (251). Similarly, in a letter to Sir John Danvers (written during Lent of 1617), Herbert states:

> Now this *Lent* I am forbid utterly to eat any Fish, so that I am fain to dyet in my Chamber at mine own cost; for in our publick Halls, you know, is nothing but Fish and Whit-meats: Out of *Lent* also, twice a Week, on *Fridayes* and *Saturdayes*, I must do so, which yet sometimes I fast. (365)

Herbert's texts, then, seem to contrast with both Calvin's and Hooker's on the question of fasting and Lent. Calvin feared the ill effects of "superstition." Herbert stresses divisiveness as more dangerous to the country parish, and appears to have followed a strict Lenten regimen himself. For him, it was in the "Schoole of Religion" (240) of the home that the "secret of governing" was manifest, and the observance of "fasting dayes" (242) was only one sign among many of the Parson's self-discipline and charity.

"So, in the *Institutes* and *A Harmonie of the Three Evangelists*, Calvin exhibits disdain for Lenten observances. Everybody knows that. But Herbert's poem is, far from the articulate rejoinder suggested here, 'seriously flawed' (Hodgkins 4); besides which it registers Herbert's misgivings about the 'liturgical observance of the forty days before Easter.'" If this were so, it must follow that Herbert had misgivings about the Book of Common Prayer. Just as it is wrong to think that, for Herbert, the liturgical calendar was a theological excrescence to be dismissed in a casual · footnote.[4] For Herbert, the Christian calendar and obedience are—in the context of liturgical discipline and of Herbert's writings—related to each other in important ways:

> O let thy sacred will
> All thy delight in me fulfill!
> Let me not think an action mine own way,
> But as thy love shall sway,
> Resigning up the rudder to thy skill.
>
> (Obedience 16–20)

It is not for nothing that the speaker in "Obedience" would imitate the Christ of "Dialogue" (*"Follow my resigning"*), as he would in "Lent" in going "part of that religious way." And yet Herbert critics talk about the Puritan attack on Lent as if that attack were not also Calvin's, implying that, in his writing and in the discharge of his priestly office, Herbert shared the same hostility. But in fact Herbert's figure of going "part of that religious way" (toward 40 days of denial) fits an Anglican application of Matthew 5.48 to the questions posed by Puritans about Lent: "Be ye therefore perfect, even as your father which is in heaven is perfect." Nevertheless, in language reminiscent of Barbara Harman's figure of Herbert's "collapsing" poems, the Calvinist perspective insists that Herbert's "Lent" undoes itself in the last stanza, this because the speaker seems to call for a spiritual rather than a literal feast. This is not a convincing line of reasoning. To ask the Christian to "banquet" the hungry only in a spiritual sense would do little to meet the demands of charity, which surely have something to do with the motive represented in the last stanza of "Lent." Jacobean readers would remember Christ's rebuke: "Thou hypocrite, doth not each one of you on the sabbath loose his ox or his ass from the stall, and lead him away to watering?" (Luke 13.15).

It seems dubious to say that, for Herbert, "Lent remains as a name and little more" (Hodgkins 84). As set out in the Book of Common Prayer, Lent followed Epiphany as an important part of the Christian year. Indeed, with their emphasis on preaching, Protestantizers of Herbert should, we would think, consider the significance of the Bible readings appointed for worship during Lent. On Ash Wednesday, in the words of Joel, the priest enjoined the faithful ("with all your heart, and with fasting, and with weeping, and with mourning" [2.12]) to a holy Lent. The Gospel for the second Sunday in Lent made a similar appeal: "For God hath not called us unto uncleanness, but unto holiness" (1 Thess. 4.7). Thus fasting and the Christian calendar conjoin in a way disapproved by Calvin, but followed by Herbert as both priest and poet.

3.

"Herbert-as-Calvinist" talk tends to emphasize preaching and to diminish liturgical elements in both *The Temple* and *A Priest to the Temple*. But it is just as hard to fit Herbert's "The Priesthood" as it is "Lent" into the Genevan "Temple." To defend the "strong" version of the argument, Calvinizers focus on the Puritan theme of a godly, if unlearned clergy, in effect personalizing Herbert's conception of the priesthood almost to the point of not differentiating priesthood from priest. Here the literalness of the biographical approach proves awkward, for Herbert held fast to that very distinction, which is why he offers instruction to the novice priest in *The Countrey Parson*, and why, in his poetry, a feeling of inadequacy sometimes overwhelms the speaker (in poems like "The Windows" and "The Priesthood"). The issue here is one of personal, not institutional, doubt.

Paradoxically, following the argument of Stanley Fish's "Herbert's Hypocricy,"[5] Christopher Hodgkins directs his doubt toward the formal situation separating priest from parishioner, suggesting that Herbert inclined toward a congregational approach. At the same time, he argues that Herbert is to "some degree a manipulator and a snob" (101), and he compounds the calumny by explaining that because of "his relatively great birth," it is okay for Herbert to be so, since aristocrats are like that: "What else would we expect?" The answer is: We expect that "we [should] expect" the offspring of great families to behave charitably. Indeed, to "expect" less requires that we reify a dehumanized essence of the very aristocratic disdain that Christian teaching sought to deflect, not only in aristocrats, but in everyone. (In Puritans, "disdain" was often expressed as a snobbish impulse to "manipulate" and even punish those who enjoyed quite ordinary and innocent diversions.) Although Hodgkins allows that "it is not necessary to hear [in Herbert's remarks on homiletic technique] any note of hypocrisy at all" (101), he is conciliatory toward "Herbert-as-Hypocrite" talk, while being insufficiently suspicious of the "hermeneutics of suspicion." It is not only that one is not compelled "to hear any note of hypocrisy" in Herbert's *A Priest to the Temple*, but suspicion in this context must itself be subject to suspicion of linguistic credulity—of the sort of philosophical "holiday" for which Wittgenstein suggests therapeutic investigation.

The skeptical critic would ask: Who in Herbert's time would have read Herbert's instructions on preaching as "manipulative?" What parts of his instructions are hypocritical? How, if we do not perceive snobbishness in those parts, would perceivers of this element propose to teach us to perceive it? That is, what is the mechanism of perception employed here? Is there evidence that anyone in Herbert's time perceived it? If a perceiver answers in the affirmative, we must ask: Are there relevant seventeenth century examples of this? On the other hand, should perceivers (for reasons they are unwilling to state) be reluctant to cite Jacobean instances of such inferences, what anecdotal information—other than their own claims that they perceive it—should be considered in adjudicating their claim? Personalities might come into consideration here, and, if so, Wittgenstein's remark is relevant: "I believe that if one is to enjoy a writer one has to *like* the culture he belongs to as well. If one finds it indifferent or distasteful, one's admiration cools off" (*CV* 85). Accordingly, when critics use accusatory terms, such as *manipulation, snobbery* and *hypocrisy*, we might reasonably sense a "cooling" of admiration, a falling off of interest in, or even disbelief in the importance of, "the culture" of which (in this case) the offices of the priesthood were dispensed in seventeenth century England. If pious sentiments and exhortation to pious acts offend us, we are reluctant to accord them charitable characterization.

In discussing "The Priesthood (160–61)," the term *priest* is hard to avoid; and yet the term is somewhat controversial in Herbert criticism. Christopher Hodgkins makes a case for not mentioning *A Priest to the Temple* in his book on Herbert.[6] In practice, this view may be less important than his claim that the chapter in that work entitled "The Parson in Sacraments" supports the argument that Herbert was a Calvinist:

> Thus the term *priest* is conspicuously absent from the one chapter in *The Countrey Parson* where a Roman Catholic or Anglo-Catholic might expect it most: "The Parson in Sacraments." Instead, the chapter stresses that only an experiential knowledge of biblical doctrine and of God's grace will make the Communion efficacious. (Hodgkins 109–10)

Now, this is a strong assertion. I want to ask: Is it so? Is it true that Herbert "stresses . . . biblical doctrine" in his articulation of the two Anglican sacraments? Of the communion table, Herbert writes:

> The Countrey Parson being to administer the Sacraments, is at a stand with himself, how or what behaviour to assume

for so holy things. Especially at Communion times he is in a great confusion, as being not only to receive God, but to break, and administer him. (257)

Why should "The Countrey Parson" be "at a stand with himself," or uncertain how to conduct himself? Because he recognizes that he cannot fully apprehend "so holy things." They are a mystery. And note: Nowhere does Herbert's "Countrey Parson" look for a "scrupturalist" explanation; moreover, the fact that he doesn't look for or offer one conflicts with the insistence that Herbert is dedicated to a "scripturalist mission" (Hodgkins 107) with respect to the sacraments. For that matter, "scripturalist" is an odd characterization of Herbert's view of the "administration of the sacraments." If by a "scripturalist" administration of the Eucharist, one means a Calvinist, Puritan, Perkinsian, Presbyterian emphasis on less wit and more proof texts, then Herbert's prose doesn't fit the designation, because it is marked by an infusion of the priest's being "at a stand with himself" and confused, full of wonder and mystery rather than at a loss for a relevant scripture. Herbert doesn't advise the novice "countrey parson" to think of proof texts concerning "this great work" (258). Rather, he is awed by the priest's primary function here: "to receive God . . . to break, and administer him." That is, the priest, not the congregation, "is at a stand"—confused— because it is he who must, "[e]specially at Communion times . . . not only . . . receive God, but . . . break, and administer him." Now, it is important to recognize this personalization of the Host ("him"). The priest receives the Host, but he also breaks "him," and in so doing breaks the Body of Christ in order to "receive and . . . administer him." Herbert's characterization doesn't speak of bread and wine, or of recalling an event 1600 years past. His figure is that of breaking, and what is broken—the body of "him"—is not only "the feast, but the way to it" (257–58).

Likewise, when we look closely at Herbert's instructions about Baptism, we find that they are not particularly "scripturalist" either:

> He [the priest] willingly and cheerfully crosseth the child,
> and thinketh the Ceremony not onely innocent, but rever-
> end. He instructeth the God-fathers, and God-mothers, that
> it is no complementall or light thing to sustain that place,
> but a great honour, and no less burden, as being done both
> in the presence of God, and his Saints, and by way of under-
> taking for a Christian soul. (258)

The question is, then: What "scripturalist" or Calvinist
or Protestant warrant does Herbert cite—or what biblical warrant *could* he cite—for crossing the child at all,
much less "willingly and cheerfully?" Herbert praises the
ceremony as "not onely innocent, but reverend," because
many Calvinists, including Calvin, would not have ap-
proved. That is, he defends an Anglican practice, but not
with a biblical citation. John the Baptist didn't "sign"
Christ when he baptized him in the Jordan; rather, God
sent a sign of his approval in the form of a descending dove,
not a cross. What is "scripturalist" about this conception
of the two Anglican sacraments? What is Protestant or
Calvinist—or even especially "reformed"—about making the sign of the cross? As for the witness of the saints,
what did Calvin say about them? Remember, the priest
signs the child "in the presence of God, and his Saints."
How many Calvinist or Protestant saints *could* have witnessed this willing and joyful, if in fact not biblical, sign
of reverence?

"In spite of these objections, it is still feasible to argue
that there is such a thing as 'Herbert's language of a Protestant "priesthood,"' using evidence that Herbert rejected
the 'hierarchical privilege in English country life' admired
by Elizabethans (Hodgkins 108). This analysis accords with
the theological significance of Herbert's protracted progress
toward the priesthood, which is 'strongly Protestant' in its
implications (128). Hence, stanza 1 of 'The Priesthood'
explicitly concerns Herbert's delay in being ordained, indicating that, with Bernard and Perkins, the poet 'passes
over sacramental duties of the priest' for a more Protestant
interest in preaching" (131):

But th' holy men of God such vessels are,
As serve him up, who all the world commands:
When God vouchsafeth to become our fare,
Their hands convey him, who conveys their hands.
O what pure things, most pure must those things be,
        Who bring my God to me!

                                  (25–30)

I think I follow the argument. But, again, it is not clear what is particularly Protestant about these lines. If any poem reminds one of the compactly compressed ironies of "The Sacrifice," it is "The Priesthood," perhaps because, as Rosemond Tuve some time ago pointed out, the Good Friday Complaints were intoned by the priest:

See, they lay hold on me, not with the hands
Of faith, but furie: yet at their commands
I suffer binding, who have loos'd their bands;

                                  (45–47)

Then they condemne me all with that same breath,
Which I do give them daily, unto death;

                                  (69–70)

It is not fit he live a day, they crie,
  Who cannot live lesse then eternally;

                                  (98–99)

They buffet him, and box him as they list,
Who grasps the earth and heaven with his fist. . . .

                                (129–30)

"Despite these so-called 'liturgical echoes,' which are more syntactic than semantic, 'The Priesthood' unequivocally demonstrates Herbert's 'Protestant' sensibility. Note, for example, that Herbert distinguishes *presbyter* from *sacerdos*. This fact, in turn, supports the view that Herbert doesn't think of the Eucharist as 'mystical,' but rather in the 'Protestant' manner, as an occasion to exercise such Protestant virtues as faith and holiness."

    It is at just this juncture that proponents of the Protestant Herbert could do with a rereading of C. A. Patrides's

"A Crown of Praise: The Poetry of Herbert" (Herbert *English* 6–25). Not only does Patrides perceptively suggest that "[t]he Eucharist is the marrow of Herbert's sensibility" (17), but he reminds us, too, of how, in the contention about the manner of Christ's presence in the sacrament, Herbert— and Anglican divines generally—sought to evade a strict, theological precision:

> While Calvinists claimed that Christ is present solely through the communicant's faith, Roman Catholics asserted (as a rather crude formulation had it) that he is present "not only to fayth, but also to the mouth, to the tongue, to the lips, to the flesh, to the bowells of all Communicants". Characteristically eschewing both extremes, Anglicans proclaimed in flexible if vague fashion that "the Body and Blood of Christ are really and actually and substantially present and taken in the Eucharist, but in a way which the human mind cannot understand and much more beyond the power of man to express." (17–18)

The point here is that Herbert is "flexible if vague" on some of the very things that the Protestantizer would hammer home as "Calvinist" and "Protestant" and "Puritan." Herbert may be less "flexible if vague" in "The Priesthood" than he is in "The Agonie," where the language allows for a range of interpretation of the manner of Christ's "Real Presence" in the sacrament, including transubstantiation: "Which my God feels [present tense] as bloud; but I, as wine." This is not to say that Herbert believed in transubstantiation (he didn't), but only that the figurative language of the poem allows for a wide range of possible inferences regarding the mystery. In "The Priesthood," the figure is not one of the present tactile sensation of feeling liquid (blood and wine); nor is it "spiritual rather than physical" (Hodgkins 134). For that matter, even the efficacy of the contrast between spiritual and physical isn't clear. In any event, the figures of "service" and "Fare" designate the holy office of the Eucharist, according to the rite prescribed in the Book of Common Prayer. The figure of "ascent" on which Hodgkins rests his earlier discussion of Herbert's Calvinist interpretation of the Sacrament doesn't seem to fit here either. Rather, the "fare" to be consumed is "served," delivered by priests ("Who bring my God to me!"). Remember the dual imperatives of the Sacrament: "Take, eat . . . drink."

"The problem with the 'traditional' Herbert is that it is too simple, too literal. It overlooks the most complex aspect of Herbert's thought, namely, his attitude toward the sacraments of the Church of England: Often, 'Herbert seems inwardly at odds' with himself and with the liturgy. The argument is that Herbert's speaker advises those committed to his charge to 'obey unquestioningly.' This explains why Herbert delivered his priestly offices with a Calvinist suspicion of the sacraments, which he Protestantized—or scripturalized—in every way he could." This doesn't sound right. At the very least, in the absence of evidence of Herbert's discontent with the Book of Common Prayer, the insistence that Herbert "passes over" the sacramental aspect of the priestly office does not merit assent. In the Book of Common Prayer, the priest is instructed to be liberal toward the poor, to help the sick and dying, and to assist in such matters as writing the will. These injunctions do not conflict with advice given in *A Priest to the Temple*. The Book of Common Prayer lays out the liturgy, not only for Lent, but for private baptism and private communion for the sick, of which services Calvin, but not Herbert, disapproved. As Amy Charles points out, although Herbert is seldom argumentative in these controversial matters, he is quite firm on perhaps the most important liturgical issue of the time:

> [Herbert] is . . . specific, though far from argumentative (let alone belligerent), in urging the most important of the Laudian practices, that of drawing near the altar and kneeling for Communion rather than remaining seated at the nave, or even coming into the chancel but declining to kneel. (Charles 233)

Herbert is, of course, not only specific but succinct on the subject: "The Feast indeed requires sitting, because it is a

Feast; but man's unpreparednesse asks kneeling" (259). In the Order for the Visitation of the Sick, the Book of Common Prayer stipulated that, when parishioners were too ill to receive the sacrament, the priest could take it for them. And if a sick person should "feele his conscience troubled with any weighty matter," the priest was instructed to invite him to "make a speciall Confession," after "which confession, the Priest [was to] absolve him after this sort":

> Our Lord Jesus Christ, who hath left power to his Church to absolve all sinners which truely repent and beleeve in him, of his great mercy forgive thee thine offences: and by his authority committed to mee, I absolve thee from all thy sinnes, In the name of the Father, and of the Sonne, and of the holy Ghoste, Amen. (1630, Q2)

It is no wonder that, with such responsibilities, one entering the priesthood might experience misgivings, or that he would express occasional doubts about his own worthiness "to break, and administer" God Himself. Be that as it may, it distorts Herbert's role as a priest to suggest that he "passed over" its sacramental duties in favor of preaching. If anything got "passssed over" in administering the sacraments and on such occasions as the Visitation of the Sick, it appears that it was preaching.

It is too strong a statement to say that "strong evidence in Herbert's poetry suggests that he had deep ambivalence about the established church of his day as a secure bastion of godliness" (Hodgkins 183–84). I doubt that in "The British Church" we find even weak evidence of superficial ambivalence toward Herbert's "dear Mother" or her "perfect lineaments and hue." It is true that, in "Church-rents and Schismes," Herbert registers concern regarding "debates and fretting jealousies." But there is nothing particularly Calvinist—or "peculiarly Protestant"—about that. As an anodyne to the inconveniences of Herbert-as-Protestant or Herbert-as-Calvinist talk, suppose we think that neither these terms nor the repetition or contemplation of their orthographic forms bear any necessary relation to anything beyond particular uses within a particular grammar and lcxicon. (Here, we might recall Willard Quine's clarification of the linguist's task [Quine, chapter 3].)

4.

In linguistics, the term *idiolect* designates the individual particularities of speakers within a dialect of a language (Hill 13, 57–61; Langacker 49–50). In fact, individuals may exhibit mannerisms and inflections that are idiosyncratic, evident in spectrographic analysis—not only peculiarities of diction which arise from social setting, but even variations in expression affected by myriads of possible differences in body shapes, sinus sizes, and so on. We might say that the concept has its analogue in the reading experience, for unless a limiting device is encoded in our system of decision making, it will produce *n* "readings." As we have already noted, I. A. Richards addressed this feature of critical discussion when he referred to one function of his project with students as "a piece of field-work in comparative ideology" (Richards 6). He was talking primarily, but not only, about what he called *"mnemonic irrelevances"*— those "misleading effects of the reader's being reminded of some personal scene or adventure, erratic associations, the interference of emotional reverberations from a past which may have nothing to do with the poem" (Richards 15). The question for us is this: How do we determine which associations from whose past reverberate appropriately in accounts of Herbert's poetry? One critic, characterizing her perspective as "materialist" (Harman 34), inquires: "What does writing make visible to me in the work that I am reading?" It seems to me that this is precisely the question Richards's students were invited to answer, although they were not burdened by knowledge of the texts' authors or biographies or intellectual and social backgrounds.

Oddly, even as theory takes a predominant role in critical discourse today, the prior question of grounds for determining the propriety of responses still requires an answer. Whatever is made visible to me in my reading of a piece of writing is "the work" in particular (the subtitle of Barbara Harman's book is *Representations of the Self in George Herbert's Poetry*). Similarly, Debora Shuger claims that, when we read Herbert,

> A) *We bring to bear our own categories, formed by our own language, culture, experiences, onto the printed surface of the text and read back our selves to ourselves. (Shuger 264)*

Now the question is: What evidence would support or rebut such an assertion? We could say that by assenting to such statements we merely observe the protocols of academic civility by extending a charitable forbearance toward propositions for which no evidence one way or the other has been—or could be—adduced. But even if we hold such an act of charity to be consonant with the norms of current discourse, it isn't clear what we accomplish by doing so. Suppose we do bring the baggage of "our own categories, formed by our own language, culture, experiences, onto the printed surface of" Herbert's works. How do we then determine whether all—or any—of that baggage is relevant to what the critic might think of as "habits of thought in the English Renaissance?"

Critics are sometimes misled by taking their spatial metaphors ("onto," "surface of") literally. They may mislead themselves into assuming, for instance, that no criteria exist for discriminating "interiority" from "exteriority," or "signifiers" from "signifieds," probably because they think these spatial figures make sense and lead somewhere. Thus, Debora Shuger concludes: "The last boundary is between an author and her subject. The knower must participate the known, and so we finally can only see what we are" (264). Implicitly, "we are" blind to everything but "what we are." Confidence in such spatial metaphor owes much, I suspect, to the prevailing rhetoric of Derrida: "It is thus the idea of the sign that must be deconstructed through a meditation upon writing which would merge, as it must, with the undoing [*sollicitation*] of onto-theology, faithfully repeating it in its *totality* and *making* it *insecure* in its most assured evidences" (Derrida *Grammatology* 73). Security and insecurity have to do with states of mind in relation to the aggregate of texts and their relation to each other ("readings" and "readers"): *"The security with which the commentary considers the self-identity of the text, the confidence with which it carves out its contour, goes hand in hand with the tranquil assurance that leaps over the text toward its presumed content, in the direction of the pure signified"* (159). This rhetorical aim here relates to the difficulty some critics encounter in disentangling the past (that is, the archeological evidence on which inferences about the past might be effectively grounded) from what we say about it, for in order to do so they must make an unmakable distinction between signifier and signified, exterior and interior, past and present—that is, between Herbert's "self" and that of the reader. Thus, it is not only Herbert's poems that collapse, but the author's imagined self collapses, too, into the more accessible self of the critic.

The proposition that, when reading a text written by someone else, one encounters oneself suggests that a reader discovers the same self in every text. Why is it, then, that, "finding myself" in my reading, I so often encounter attitudes and beliefs that seem to me so unfamiliar? Wittgenstein appears to argue otherwise and more convincingly that "One can mistrust one's own senses, but not one's own belief" (*PI* 190). Perhaps one's true self contains an unknown but very large number of beliefs and attitudes of which one is not aware. But even if this were so, one's encounter with a particular self among an indefinite number of possible selves would still depend on an interpretation, so questions could arise. For instance, what does this view imply about criteria for correcting error or misunderstanding a text? Would the remedy of correction be the same as in the case when I misspeak, saying one thing but meaning another? That is, can someone else correct me? I say such and such concerning Herbert's *Temple*—that its imagery and diction resemble expressions found in the marginalia of the Little Gidding "Harmonies" (see Stewart *Herbert* chap. 3)—and you reply, "No, you mean so and so"—that it resembles typical rhetorical flourishes in William Perkins's very popular *Cases of Conscience*. In criticism, misunderstanding is the country cousin of correction. Ben Jonson writes in "To the Reader": "Pray thee, take care, that tak'st my booke in hand, / To reade it well; that is, to understand." But how, if I encounter myself in Jonson's text, is misunderstanding possible? Whom does Jonson enjoin to understand? I encounter the same myself whether I read Jonson or Herbert or Nietzsche or de Sade or C. S. Lewis. This is strange. I say to scholars around me, "I agree" or "I disagree with myself," and neither locution sounds right.

Is this proposition—that we find ourselves in various texts—a fair account of our reading experience? If so, how do we learn the opinions of others? Or are all opinions innate, like the instinct of the snake to strike out even as it emerges from its shell? Can the problem be the formulation of the sentence—which was, after all, accompanied by this odd sensation? Again, Wittgenstein observes: "Misunderstandings concerning the use of words, [may be] caused, among other things, by certain analogies between the forms of expression in different regions of the language.— Some of them can be removed by substituting one form of expression for another; this may be called an 'analysis' of our forms of expression, for the process is sometimes like one of taking a thing apart" (*PI* §90). Our investigation must be into the propriety of the analogy introduced by critical vocabulary. We analyze our critical formula as a first step toward clarification, and if, during that process, it appears that the formula does not help to clarify the question at hand, we may if we wish set the formula aside, and try a different tack.

We might observe, for instance, that notably missing from these discussions of the interiority/exteriority conundrum is attention to the spatial figure itself. Supposedly, we cannot tell whether we are inside or outside of ourselves. As we investigate this use of spatial metaphor, let us imagine that you cannot tell whether you are inside or outside of my house. It is your first visit after a long absence, and your confusion can probably be explained by the architectural designs which I have commissioned in the interim to make the house look larger by focusing attention on the landscaping of the garden. The boundary between house and garden, once a solid wall but now a single, large pane of glass, has been attenuated for a purpose. You say, moving forward with your palms extended, "I am unsure in my judgment of the boundary between interior and exterior," and this makes perfect sense.

But now suppose I say that I cannot tell whether I am inside or outside of a rectangle within which you have asked me to stand, and, further, that you answer that you can't tell either. So which way do I move to follow your instruction? We know that the rectangle of the batter's box in baseball can become blurred and, for all practical purposes, even disappear during play. Is our incapacity to distinguish interiority from exteriority in criticism like this? What rules say whether or not we are to proceed? The point in criticism may be that we have reached an impasse. What can we do, in the Wittgensteinian sense, to "go on together?" As at the outset of this discussion (see introduction), it is unclear that we *can* proceed. We could say that, without further instruction on its employment, the spatial figure appears to be unhelpful in elucidating the aspect of the literary work in question, for instance, that of distinguishing a modern from a Caroline and Jacobean usage. We are unsure where Herbert's exterior ends and our interior begins, and the more we ponder the interiority/exteriority "problem" the more daunting it becomes. We could say that sometimes a spatial metaphor might be just what is needed to clarify a point, but this doesn't seem to be one of them. When a figure befuddles or beclouds the matter at hand, we are free to—and it might be prudent and helpful to—dispense with it.

In literary theory, interpretation precedes essence. We

can say that certain parts of a work (*The Temple* or one of the poems in the collection) cohere or do not cohere, but we cannot do so without giving an account of the thematic interests lending to or detracting from the work's continuity. And, as we have seen, the explication of parts of so complex a work as *The Temple* belongs to the ebb and flow of language and the history of thought. Coleridge argued that only a certain kind of Christian was competent to understand Herbert, and yet our present institutions permit—cynics might say even require—secular interpretations, which exist side by side with nonsecular ones, like wares at a bazaar. They bear directly upon such questions as the structural integrity of *The Temple* as well as—and this seems to me more interesting—the moral and intellectual integrity of the author. Depending on one's ideological perspective, poems develop and come to a close or fail to do so. For example, claiming that her interest in "discursivity" and "textuality" represents a "materialist view" (34), Barbara Harman says of "The Flower":

> . . . in "The Flower" experience is always in the process of changing, and descriptions of it are always in the process of becoming obsolete. This speaker is a misreader *by necessity*—someone who can only say amiss because, as a creature, he has no access to that total and unchanging vision represented by God's word in stanza three and by Paradise in stanza seven. In "The Flower" creatures are *in the business* of being and saying amiss, and the recognition of that fact makes saying amiss the only real way of saying aright. (Harman 168–69)

From this viewpoint, God's "wonders" are only another instance of misprision. Similarly, understanding of the limitations of "pride" toward which the poem appears to move is also an illusion or "saying amiss." Since Harman claims to be talking, not about Herbert, but about the convergence of a particular text with her "materialist view," attention shifts from Herbert's poem to the critic's candor. Her critical assertions either are or are not a true account of that convergence, and, reliable or not, she is the only witness. It would be uncivil if, after scrutinizing a Rorschach inkblot, the viewer says, "This is what I see," and the auditor answers, "Oh, no you don't." Polygraph tests may be in the current situation unreliable, but we can imagine technological advances which would assure us if readers tendered authentic reactions to texts. And with the help of the computer we can envision an exponential increase in our capacity to log in, collate and codify "views" of Herbert texts—materialist, Feminist, Freudian, Marxist, historicist, semiologist, structuralist, poststructuralist, deconstructionist and so on, each with n permutations to reflect individual differences. How, we might ask, are we to correct any one of them? Given our democratic institutions, is it desirable—or even consonant with law and public policy—to single out particular critical utterances for praise or blame?

This question involves not only our understanding of the sense and tone of Herbert's poem, but also our appreciation of its structure. For the "materialist" in question, "The Flower" proceeds—or fails to proceed—to an unstable, nonassurance regarding the meaning of the experience. The critic perceives a species of deep irony in the poem instead. In contrast, Richard Strier says of the same poem: "It is Herbert's greatest triumph of placing immediate experience without undermining it with irony" (Strier 244). Where one finds uncertainty, tentativeness, undoing and collapse, others (Strier, Bloch [197], Vendler [53]) find "homiletical neatness" and a "law and order" ending in the text.[7] The question is not which of the two perspectives is correct, but how we are to decide the matter of correctness. Are the two perspectives equally relevant to Herbert's poem? Are they equally valid? Although they seem to contradict each other, can we accept them both? Can we teach uninformed students that both "represent" Herbert's text? Suppose we imagine a thoroughly latitudinarian response here, with an emphatic "yes" to all four questions. Can we not then ask what method of measurement was employed to distinguish equivalence from inequivalence in "relevance" and "validity?" How did we decide upon the acceptability of contradictory statements? And, without moving into the contemporary sociology of interpretations, how do we teach students that the ending of Herbert's text conjoins "homiletic neatness" with "collapsing" instability? In the current situation, do we think of "neo-Christian" and "materialist" views as equally appropriate to our understanding of the coherence or incoherence that Herbert and his contemporary audience would have perceived in such a poem?

5.

Did—*could*—Herbert know what he said? Modern thought permits, but does not compel, us to say that Herbert's poetry expresses ideas and attitudes of which Herbert and his audience were not aware. It is even possible that the meanings involved might have had no means of expression in the language of the time. Some critics say that such meanings and attitudes were "unconscious." It is even possible that our reading of *The Temple* retains and reflects vestiges of these unconscious meanings, attitudes and impulses. For instance, critics speak of our uneasiness with sexuality and eroticism in Herbert's poems. Setting aside my skepticism regarding what counts, in an age of Madonna and "rap" doggerel, as evidence of such unease, I want to address Michael Schoenfeldt's assertion that the figure of "spirit" in "My God, where is that ancient heat" represents "a common Renaissance euphemism for 'penis'" (Schoenfeldt "Sexuality" 274). My concern is that, when objects or ideas or figures or inspirations "rise" or are otherwise "erected," Schoenfeldt infers sexual interest. He draws support for this practice from other critics, one of whom perceives "onanistic" meanings in Herbert's verses, which perception prompts Schoenfeldt to point out that his predecessor could have included (but didn't) among his Herbertian examples the "remarkably onanistic" (277)

"Sinnes round," "thc . . . ophidian form" of which "completes the closed circuit of shame and desire" (277).

Now the critic further buttresses his masturbatory thesis by suggesting that Herbert may be "deploying an unstated visual pun on 'pen' and 'penis'" (278).[8] Surely the investigator would be remiss who did not ask how one perceives unstated puns, whether verbal, visual or olfactory. Are they like unstated musical motifs, which, since they are in neither the score nor the performance, harmonize perfectly with any melody? Be that as it may, *any* pun between "pen" and "penis" *might* have been difficult even to *unstate* in Herbert's time, in that the OED does not record a use of the latter word did not enter the language until 1693. The critic-as-depth-psychologist could argue, of course, that the nonappearance of the word in Herbert's poem— indeed, in the Herbert canon—amounts to its first undocumented use in the English language. And he could point out that Herbert was a fine Latinist, and so could have known the word in its original language.

The problem with this method, I think, is knowing when to quit. Supporting evidence is everywhere available, while contrary data is impossible to find. So how do we determine when an inference is justified? Schoenfeldt quotes Helen Vendler on the subject: "'We cannot miss the tentative sexuality of his "budding" and "shooting up" and later "swelling"'" (279). While it may reassure some critics that Vendler finds Herbert's texts so transparent ("We cannot miss"), what about the others? What if we do "miss" this "obvious" meaning? The hard question is: Was it there to miss? Schoenfeldt buries a possibly relevant perspective on this question in a footnote: "Vendler seems cautiously attracted by a 'Psychoanalytic interpretation' which 'might see this poem as a masochistic acquiescence in castration; to accept castration is to be reconciled with the father by no longer possessing a rival masculine member'" (299n). Now, suppose I perceive an explanation here. How do I know if it is helpful? How do we teach the propriety of such linguistic inferences to our students? All "risings" are not the same. All tumescence is not male. Waves swell, as do bosoms, breezes and abrasions. Does a term used once in such and such a way imply poetic creation? Given our loose conceptualization of metaphoric expression, we cannot deny that it could. And, then, will they—the waves, bosoms, abrasions—suggest priapic erection? Our interlocutor responds that our logic requires an affirmative, if wary, response. Are we entitled, then, in our new taxonomy of synonyms to say that (since A = B, B must also = A) images of onanism are metaphoric expressions of ocean waves, women's bosoms, country breezes and black eyes? Well, in our lexicon, tumescence (A) is associated with genitalia (B) and both are figures of creative activity (C). But does it now also follow that as a poet writes, invariably, images of A and/or of B are before his mind?

I have questions, too, about the "resistance theory"— which holds that critics (Bloch and Lull, for instance)[9] resist the drift of their own insights into the erotic aspect of "Love (III)," a poem to which Schoenfeldt directs much of his attention. According to this genetic approach, we can explain what is left out of other critics' analyses (namely, what is present in our own). Bloch and Lull do not agree with Schoenfeldt *because* they are uncomfortable with the sexual content of the poem. But this procedure presupposes: A) that a method of measuring the sexual content of the poem is available (Bloch and Lull accord some but not enough); B) that critics impart the sexual content of a poem on the basis of their measurable comfort or discomfort (because of their discomfort, Bloch and Lull don't accord enough [286–87]); and C) that there is a corollary between comfort and correctness of interpretation. But isn't it possible for one to be comfortably mistaken, or uncomfortably well-informed?

The intellectual twin of depth psychology is depth rhetoric, which holds that, beneath the surface of verbal utterance lies a depth of meaning imperceptible to the naive reader, but penetrable by practitioners of the rhetorical school of criticism. Thus Herbert's writing exhibits a superficial meaning that rhetorical analysis reveals as misdirecting less sophisticated readers who focus on the merely verbal, surface expression. I take as exemplary of this method the most celebrated practitioner of the reader-response school. Stanley Fish's view of "Herbert's Hypocrisy,"[10] affirms that, on the surface, Herbert pretends to be—performs as if he were—as traditional critics have perceived him, "a model of sincere piety." But Fish's rhetorical analysis, with its emphasis on "artifice and theatricality" in *A Priest to the Temple*, shows him to be quite another, to be, in effect, the opposite of sincere: "to be all surface, superficial, without depth, thin, to be continually composed, confected, constructed, to feign, to be continually theatrical, to be always playing a role." In this flight from anything that is his own, we "see that there is something sinister in the parson's program." Why so? Because "The Parson's Eye" borders on the omniscient. Because the parson aims at a totality of social intelligence and sanction. Because he knows all, punishes all and forgives all. At issue are such passages as this from *A Priest to the Temple*:

> The Countrey Parson upon the afternoons in the week-days, takes occasion sometimes to visit in person, now one quarter of his Parish, now another. For there he shall find his flock most naturally as they are, wallowing in the midst of their affairs: whereas on Sundays it is easie for them to compose themselves to order, which they put on as their holy-day cloathes, and come to Church in frame, but commonly the next day put off both. (247)

Here, Herbert admonishes the priest to make his parish visits unannounced, so that he will see parishioners as they are rather than as they only seem to be on Sundays and holidays. Since parishioners have no way of knowing when he will appear, the priest finds them as they usually are, not "well drest," but "wallowing in the midst of their affairs." The locution "wallowing" conveys a negative feeling about the rural folk: "the poorest Cottage" might "smell never so lothsomly." Just as he schedules his visits randomly, the priest also rebukes misconduct at unforeseen intervals, in some cases waiting until departure "to reprove" less sophisticated members of the congregation "plainly."

We could infer from this section that the wise priest must learn to fit his visits to the needs of particular families. He must, as we might nowadays say, be sensitive. He must not treat those "sensible of finesse" as he would those "of higher quality." Preparation is the key here, as it is in the more formal demands of public preaching and prayer. The priest exerts himself to achieve the proper, benign effects. But this viewpoint entails a charitable characterization of the priest's motives and functions in the world. To the contrary, Fish argues that beneath the surface of the parson's charitable offices lurks a "sinister" undercurrent of pernicious motives. Fish prosecutes his argument by analyzing the quotation above—and certain passages from "The Parson's Eye"—in the context of Michel Foucault's *Discipline and Punish: The Birth of the Prison*: "it is impossible not to think Foucauldian thoughts and to see Herbert's idealized pastor as the engineer and operator of a system of surveillance and control that answers perfectly to the account in *Discipline and Punish* of Bentham's Panopticon." One relevant passage reads:

> All that is needed, then, is to place a supervisor in a central tower and to shut up in each cell a madman, a patient, a condemned man, a worker or a schoolboy. By the effect of backlighting, one can observe from the tower, standing out precisely against the light, the small captive shadows in the cells of the periphery. They are like so many cages, so many small theatres, in which each actor is alone, perfectly individualized and constantly visible. The panoptic mechanism arranges spatial unities that make it possible to see constantly and to recognize immediately. In short, it reverses the principle of the dungeon; or rather of its three functions—to enclose, to deprive of light and to hide—it preserves only the first and eliminates the other two. Full lighting and the eye of a supervisor capture better than darkness, which ultimately protected. Visibility is a trap. (Foucault 200)

The inference is that Herbert's priest is a jailer. His function defines his motives. Using his vision as a means of imposing his presence even when he is absent, he controls parishioners, spies on them, punishes them. Parishioners cannot know when he will arrive to visit because, notwithstanding his pretended Christian charity, he designs his itinerary in order to produce embarrassment and anxiety.

In other words, Herbert's priest is a phony, an actor, and he admits as much when he describes his conduct in the pulpit: "When he preacheth, he procures attention by all possible art, both by earnestnesse of speech, it being naturall to men to think, that where is much earnestness, there is somewhat worth hearing; and by a diligent, and busy cast of his eye on his auditors, with letting them know, that he observes who marks, and who not; and with particularizing of his speech now to the younger sort, then to the elder, now to the poor, and now to the rich" (232–33). Just as when he prays the priest raises his hands and eyes in a certain manner, so when he preaches he strives to communicate with his audience—to arouse a response. In this way Herbert implies, whether he was aware of it or not, that the priest is like an actor, pretending to be "holy" in order to achieve the reverent reaction of his parishioners. He lifts his hands and raises his eyes and intones his words in such and such a way. It is a performance; therefore, it is hypocritical *in a negative sense*.[11] Beneath the priest's daily ministrations, we perceive his misgivings about and contempt for the rural folk. They must be acted upon because, left to their own devices, they would fall back to "wallow" in economic and spiritual disarray.

There are, I think, notable inconveniences in the employment of Foucault's remarks with explanatory intent. First, Foucault imagines the prisoners—that is, the prisoners, madmen, patients, capital offenders, workers and schoolboys—as actors individuated by the system. His is a Wordsworthian metaphor: "Visibility is a trap." "Shades of the prison-house begin to close / Upon the growing Boy." But why is this? In Foucault, because society imposes the functions of the prison in the architectonics of its institutions. But if this is so, then it must follow that prisons reflect the structure of society, or that, in effect, the concept of "prison" is a mistake (hence, the slippage in Foucault's formulation from prisoner to worker to schoolboy).[12] According to Foucault, to gaze upon is to control the action of the actors on the miniature stages of hypothetical individualities.

It is not my purpose here to quarrel with Romanticism in any of its manifold expressions. I will even allow that it might be interesting to ponder the comparison between the priest in Herbert's *Country Parson* and the jailers in Foucault's / Bentham's Panopticon. I could even admit that my Wittgensteinian presentiments constrain me to allow that there could be contexts in which the juxtaposition of thesé texts might coax a recalcitrant learner to a better understanding of Herbert's text. But, if so, what would that understanding consist of, and how would it be brought about? Well, not necessarily by the reader's recognition of the similarity between Foucault's jailer and Herbert's priest. (Wittgenstein: "What I am looking for is the grammatical difference" [*PI* 185].) For Fish/Foucault, "[v]isibility is a trap." Society in the shapes of jailers (prisoners), doctors (patients), supervisors (workers) and teachers (schoolboys) imposes its hegemonic demands upon all, whether its oppressors are present or absent. Alas, everybody is doomed to be observed even when not observed, so clever are the devices of the oppressors, who gaze on gazees with the "sinister" intent of entrapment.

One might question Fish's reading of *Country Parson* by pointing out that nobody in Herbert's time seems to have given it much thought, or by objecting, as David Cressy has, to the use of Michel Foucault by Renaissance historians and literary critics (Cressy "Foucault"). If critics depend on dubious sources, how much confidence can we invest in their applications? But I doubt that this strategy will discourage practitioners of such analogical thinking, because such critiques, although valuable, suffer the disadvantages of a reasoned empiricism, namely, that they do not address the underlying, figurative conception on which analogy depends, namely, that of "depth analysis." For depth analysts will simply reply that Herbert and his contemporaries were only interested in or only prepared to grasp surface significance.

The target must be the picture of depth in depth analysis itself, for depth analysis depends on the explanatory relevance of the figure of depth. Just when did this depth meaning (say, of Herbert's "sinister" motive) come into existence? Or was it always there, like a musical piece scored for violin and harpsichord, but for centuries performed only as a violin solo? Lacking the analogue of the musical score, how do we determine what accompaniment to offer? That is, since the accompaniment is to the words written by Herbert and interpreted by his contemporaries without the accompaniment, how do we determine which notes to strike in our rendition? Some critics say, "Well, it is a new rendition in which both the score and the performance are newly invented." But this sentence provides us with no more than an appropriate instance of one grammatical use of the locution "new." What is the status of the theoretical assertion that this novelty is relevant to the piece composed prior to 1633? Can we not imagine a reinscription of Monteverdi's *Vespers of 1610* in which dissonance replaces harmony, and the 12-tone scale takes the place of that familiar to Monteverdi and his audience? Suppose we imagine performing the *Vespers of 1610* with the usual score in front of us, and with all of the historically correct instruments played by properly prepared musicians, but with this proviso: When the conductor's baton descends with the audience expecting the concert to begin with a loud sound of brass, no musicians play, and, although they peer intently at the Monteverdi score and look to the conductor in appropriate ways, they continue not playing for some minutes. Have they, then, performed 4'33", regarded by some as John Cage's finest composition (Lanham 71)?

Again, did Herbert believe what he said? *Could* he believe what he said? When Stanley Fish says that Herbert is a hypocrite, he implies that he perceives Herbert's true motives, which, in turn, conflict with his purported ones. Herbert is insincere. But what is the criterion of sincerity here? Doesn't the figure of depth permit proponents of an even deeper depth analysis to assert that there lies beneath Herbert's comparatively shallow hypocrisy a deeper affirmation of compassion and sincerity? That is, given the figure of depth permissible in depth analysis, who can claim to have plumbed the Marianas Trench—that rhetorical depth beyond which no further depth can be imagined? Is the problem, then, the intractable impropriety of the figure of depth itself? In *The Blue and Brown Books*, we read:

> Now there is no doubt that, having the visual image of a string of beads being pulled out of a box through a hole in the lid, we should be inclined to say: "These beads must all have been together in the box before". But it is easy to see that this is making a hypothesis. I should have had the same image if the beads had gradually come into existence in the hole of the lid. We easily overlook the distinction between stating a conscious mental event, and making a hypothesis about what one might call the mechanism of the mind. (*BBB* 40)

Wittgenstein is talking about the ease with which the mind moves from familiar experience to theorize about experience in general. We imagine that our way of reading or our way of expressing human problems is the only way. We have been taught to think that motives underlie expressions, and yet the figure of "underlying" implies a dichotomy, which, on analysis, we might not wish to defend. Wittgenstein suggests that it wouldn't—that it doesn't—matter what is inside the box from which the beads are being pulled. (If it helps, we can imagine that the box cannot be opened.) Perhaps the depths of poetry's origin are like that. We might even infer that critical problems are like that, too—neither deep nor shallow, but just present in the here and now of discussion.

So what about sincerity? Is an actor's performance intrinsically insincere, or can there be sincere and insincere performances, say, of the role or function of a country parson? Wittgenstein writes: "We say 'The expression in his voice was *genuine*'. If it was spurious we think as it were of another one behind it.—*This* is the face he shews the world, inwardly he has another one.—But this does not mean that when his expression is *genuine* he has two the same" (*PI* §606). Again, it is the spatial figure that misleads. There is another priest behind the mask of the benign visitor, another meaning behind the priest's utterance or gesture in the pulpit. (This actor is performing the part of Lear as if he were Volpone; this priest, under the guise of returning the parishioner to his vocation is actually trying to make him a permanent ward of the parish.) The priest "acts" in order to sustain the "aristocratic" power structure (Wolberg 177).[12]

The inconvenience of such assertions is that, in searching out depth meanings, they find "sinister" motives alien to those laid out in Herbert's instructions. The purpose of the parson's unexpected visits is to provide the priest with appropriate occasions for the discharge of one of his holy offices: moral instruction. The function of his charity is *not*—I repeat *not* (because, in this context, it is an important qualifier)—to increase or extend the parishioner's dependence upon the priest, but, on the contrary, to make that dependence a step toward independence:

> When he riseth in the morning, he bethinketh himselfe what good deeds he can do that day, and presently doth them; counting that day lost, wherein he hath not exercised his Charity. He first considers his own Parish, and takes care, that there be not a begger, or idle person in his Parish, but that all bee in a competent way of getting their living. This he effects either by bounty, or perswasion, or by authority, making use of that excellent statute, which bindes all Parishes to maintaine their own. . . . But he gives no set pension to any; for this in time will lose the name and effect of Charity with the poor people, though not with God: for then they will reckon upon it, as on a debt; and

if it be taken away, though justly, they will murmur, and
repine as much, as he that is disseized of his own inheritance. (244)

The point here ought not to be lost even on postmoderns.
When a parishioner in need takes the charity of the congregation as if it were only repayment of "a debt", the act
of giving loses the name of charity, and the destitute
parishioner becomes a dependent, "idle person" rather than
one mindful of obtaining "a competent way of getting
[a] living." As for the priest's motive in giving money
to the poor, this service is like the other offices of the
Church: the Word in the world. It is like a sermon. Indeed,
Herbert says it *is* a sermon: "So is his charity in effect a
Sermon" (245). But the Word is not meant to bind the
workman to the priest, as child to father, in an unchanging dependence. Contrary to such self-righteous, self-
aggrandizement, Herbert envisages a process based in
economic anxiety. The parish church enacts no dole, no
pension. Charity aims to eliminate dependence by encouraging poor parishioners "to take more paines in their
vocation, as not knowing when they shal be rclieved"
(245). Idleness is the opposite of such constructive efforts,
and Herbert implies a causal link between the pension—
the expectation of an unearned benefit that "they will
reckon upon it, as on a debt" (244)—and the sin of sloth.
　My point is that only an uncharitable reading of "The
Parson's Charity" will lead to an account that fails to recognize the *function* of the priestly office as Herbert represents it. What is the service to accomplish? That is the
question addressed in the chapters to the novice rural
priest. The way to avoid encouraging the sin of *acedia*[13] is
to remind the idle that someone else must work hard to
provide them and their families with bed and board. The
desiderata are that the idle learn "to praise God more," of
course, but, more to the point, "to live more religiously";
and the latter entails that they "take more paines in their
vocation, as not knowing when they shal be relieved;
which otherwise they would reckon upon, and turn to

idlenesse" (245). The priest offers no set pension because such a dole too easily insinuates itself in the receiver as one's due. Then, if that is removed, the idle complain rather than return to work, in which case the priest himself would be partly to blame, having encouraged the sin of *acedia*, not to mention that of ingratitude (a species of presumption, or pride).

Without denying the possibility that the metaphor of depth in language might have useful applications in certain instances, we can say, now, that nothing could be clearer than Herbert's surface meaning. Moreover, it is only the assertion that there is another, deeper, "sinister" meaning—that Herbert is an actor, and what is more an "insincere" actor—that enables one to impute pernicious motives to his instructions. But we are not obliged to think that this depth picture of language works in every case. If we are tempted to believe we have encountered a critical problem, we should be wary. We should remain willing to adjust our metaphor to the given situation. Why assume that Herbert enunciated instructions of which he was not aware? Wittgenstein writes:

> The problems arising through a misinterpretation of our forms of language have the character of *depth*. They are deep disquietudes; their roots are as deep in us as the forms of our language and their significance is as great as the importance of our language.—Let us ask ourselves: why do we feel a grammatical joke to be *deep*? (And this is what the depth of philosophy is.) (*PI* §111)

Here, Wittgenstein insinuates, not the "end of philosophy," but the beginning of an investigation into those moments in discussion when metaphors mislead, or, as we might say in critical theory, when our metaphors derive from a different "form of life" than do the locutions which they purport to describe.

* * * * *

If I understand correctly, postmodernism recoils at closure. For postmoderns every thematic development strives toward something transcending a Wagnerian motif: The end is not yet. They seem to perceive in fictive designs with pronounced closure a trace of the ancient, discredited teleology. God is dead, so why shouldn't finality be vanquished too? Herbert's poems do not end, but rather collapse or disappear, or in one of a number of ways deny all that they seem to affirm, namely, all evidences of temporal order leading from Genesis to Revelation, beginning to end. In the place of the Word they inscribe "writing," which simply "is," because it must "be" or nobody will get tenure. Within the surface structure of Herbert's *The Temple* is its simultaneous dissolution, this accompanied by the now familiar antiteleology of Nietzsche, Heidegger and their intellectual descendants. Are we, then, proposing a retrograde motion, as if time could or should be turned back? Or are we suggesting that beneath the surface rhetoric of deconstruction we perceive a hidden rhetorical thrust toward subversion of its purported aim to complete the undermining of the Western metaphysical tradition? The answer might depend upon how seriously we take particular expressions of rhetorical theory. Is it always the case that at some level of depth, arguments, narratives and systems of thought revert to incoherence and self-abnegation? Or could it be that rhetorical theories themselves represent prior belief systems? Does Herbert's professed belief only hide his sexual embarrassment? Or his guilt? Or his resentment? Or—perhaps more to the point—his atheism? Well, does the materialist's certainty of doubt merely hide the profoundest depth of yearning for and embrace of belief? Does the ancient teleology triumph in every spasm of the materialist's resentment of those typical Herbertian endings, with their typical sense of serene closure?

Since Herbert criticism is an ongoing fact of life, in at least one sense, "closure" of the critical questions we have engaged would not seem imminent. And yet how do we explain—or need we explain—the widening interest in George Herbert, so long regarded by so many as an Anglican saint? Is that interest only the necessary condition for a debasement of his supposed character and beliefs? Our interlocutor might, in a moment of candor, say, "I don't know. Doesn't our critical system proscribe categorical responses?" Perhaps so. But a process may follow protocol without establishing systematic procedures. We can surely distinguish between categorical and valuative statements. (We need not approve of statements we regard as abusive or destructive or wrongheaded.)

When he had fallen too ill to read himself, Wittgenstein asked a friend to read Frazer's *Golden Bough* to him. His remarks are, I think, relevant to Herbert criticism—and to the larger theoretical question today of the boundary between criticism and philosophy. Wittgenstein was, to put it mildly, annoyed not so much by any specific fact or interpretation generated by Frazer, but rather by Frazer's attitude toward the subject of his study, namely, the beliefs of the people whom he regarded as savages. These remarks serve as a fitting close—or opening or collapse or disappearance, as you wish—of this investigation:

> Frazer's account of the magical and religious notions of men is unsatisfactory: it makes these notions appear as *mistakes*.
>
> Was Augustine mistaken, then, when he called on God on every page of the *Confessions*?
>
> Well—one might say—if he was not mistaken, then the Buddhist holy-man, or some other, whose religion expresses quite different notions, surely was. But *none* of them was making a mistake except where he was putting forward a theory. (*RFGB* 1)

Exasperated, Wittgenstein exclaims: "What a narrowness of spiritual life we find in Frazer!" I would add that Frazer was not alone in his incapacity to "understand a different way of life from the English one of his time!" Times change, and Frazer's England no longer exists. But the incapacity of critics to understand religious language—an apposite "narrowness of spiritual life"—persists, and we can find its traces today where Coleridge looked for it long ago: in Herbert criticism.

6

Evidence of
Renaissance Criticism

The question is: what does
imponderable evidence *accomplish*?

Suppose there were imponderable evidence
for the chemical (internal) structure of a substance,
still it would have to prove itself to be evidence by
certain consequences which *can* be weighed.

(Imponderable evidence might convince
someone that a picture was a genuine . . .
But it is *possible* for this to be proved right
by documentary evidence as well.)

— Wittgenstein, *Philosophical Investigations*

"Forty percent of the criticism published today uses
no evidence at all." This statement, made during a
personnel meeting, was in response to a question that I had

raised about a colleague's research record. Although the essay on which the case for advancement largely depended made weighty assertions about its subject, none was supported by evidence. This seemed to me, if not a serious flaw—that is, one that might affect professional advancement—at least a philosophically interesting one. It puzzled me that some of my colleagues dismissed the matter of evidence as irrelevant to the framing and evaluation of an argument that made straightforward empirical claims about literary history.

I do not propose an inquiry into the demographic evidence relevant to the claim—or accusation—that 40 percent, as distinct from 20 or 60 or n percent, of the criticism published today is unsupported by evidence of any kind. Such an investigation might concern the sociologist of knowledge, but I am interested in assertions that pass unsupported by historically relevant evidence, and in the apparent assumption that critical statements deserve consideration, and even assent, whether or not they are substantiated by such evidence. For if an assertion about literary history lacks supporting historical evidence, on what grounds would assent or dissent be justified? "Many critics would say that the question is naive, because theoretically sophisticated discussions of 'language' have 'problematized' the concepts of 'grounds' and 'justification.'" But even supposing that the habit of "problematization" has made assent and dissent seem "ungrounded" and "unjustified," how do we explain belief or doubt regarding *any* critical statement, even that asserting a cause and effect relation between "theoretically sophisticated discussions of 'language'" and our sense of "groundedness" and "justification?" Is the concept of *problematization* unprob-lematic—a "clear and distinct" idea? (How would we decide *that*?) I suspect that this and other terms in the process of *problematization* require investigation, and that analysis of representative assertions—as Wittgenstein put it, "by examples"—will clarify confusing elements in their usage that seem to induce a sense that critical statements are, as a species, "problematic." Our aim will be, by clarification, to "unproblematize" supposed problems.

1.

Why would anyone think it unobjectionable that critical statements about the Renaissance should pass unsupported by relevant, substantiating evidence? Answers to this question will vary depending on what critics make of terms like *critical statements* and *Renaissance* and *relevant* and *substantiating evidence*. We need not look far to find critics who consider "the text itself" the plenary source of evidence relevant to assertions made about it. The assumption is that, if the text is of a Renaissance work, then remarks about that text must be *about* the Renaissance, too. Whether called *analysis* or *close reading* or *deconstruction* of a text, this method depends on "close examination of the kind now often discounted"—and perhaps even disparaged by its own practitioners—"as part of a bad New Critical heritage" (Crewe 15). When *close reading* provides the sole means of explicating a text, *reading, interpretation*, and *critical act* become for all practical purposes coterminous self assertions. Nietzsche writes: "The will to power *interprets* . . . In fact, interpretation is itself a means of becoming master of something" (*WP* 324).

With Nietzsche's remark in mind, let us consider a claim about a topic popular in criticism today, namely, incest:

> A) [I]ncest between [Sir Thomas] More and his daughter can neither be assumed nor ruled out. (Crewe 95)

On its face, Proposition *A* appears to be a modest disclaimer about the danger of unwarranted assumptions. We must not leap to a conclusion here, as there might be room for "reasonable doubt." But there is an indirect statement of fact here, too—an implication that an "incestuous relationship" ("carnal soiling") existed between More and his daughter. This is why the critic cites passages from William Roper's biography of his father-in-law as evidence.

That is, the thrust of the argument is not about the tenuous value of unwarranted assumptions, but about the
"incestuous relationship" between More and his daughter.
Thus, as if to deny the implication of his disclaimer the
full status of a statement, Crewe qualifies the insinuation
with Proposition *A*. But investigation raises the question
of what, if anything, this concession concedes. "Well, the
critic is only saying that we can't be sure one way or the
other." But shouldn't evidence of misconduct precede suspicion to be "ruled out?" Even as Crewe insinuates the
charge of incest, he claims that "these incestuous suppositions are reinforced when, towards the end of [Roper's]
book," Margaret kisses her father "'divers times together
most lovingly'" (96). The effect is to draw attention to these
many loving kisses as evidence. But of what? Of normal,
filial affection or of "incest?" Although the indictment
("incestuous suppositions") might be unclear, the insinuation is clearer because it is "reinforced."

The thesis here concerns incest, as Crewe finds further
support for "incestuous suppositions," namely, "penetration of her [Margaret's] body" (179). Oddly, Crewe claims
to mention this offense only in order to rescue More's
"'character'" from the "blackmailer's grip" (98), but he
does not identify the "blackmailer." He does admit that
incest, which customarily entails sexual contact, would
require "penetration of her [Margaret's] body." And it is
here that a subtle form of equivocation occurs, for the "evidence" cited is this: As Margaret lay near death, More suggested to her doctors that "she be given an enema." Given
the fact that Crewe characterizes the incestuous relation
between More and his daughter as a "dirty secret," this is
strange. If suggesting this remedy is the "evidence" of
"penetration," why didn't More secretly apply the "clys-
ter" himself, rather than delegate the sole hard "evidence"
of incestuous "penetration" to non-family members?

"Well, since Roper's text constitutes the body of evidence that Crewe cites as relevant, 'textual analysis' is the
only method available. Since that text provides 'the only

evidence,' it seems fair to say that Crewe is entitled to draw 'incestuous' inferences about More. Such inferences amount to what we mean by 'reading.' That is *his* 'reading,' and it is an interesting one, too." The problem with this approach is that critics can, with or without warrant, draw any inference they wish. Suppose the task in criticism is to limit inferences to the requirements of reasoned judgment about the evidence at hand. So, based on the evidence of *"interested"* Roper's text, we can legitimately infer— well, what? One could say, if not evidence "beyond a reasonable doubt," at least of "reasonable suspicion" of an "incestuous relationship." But then another might respond: Why is that? Unfortunately, an inconvenience of this particular "close reading" line of thought emerges here, in that subscribers must infer from the existence of Roper's text that "transgression" (95) occurred, and that More, whom Roper describes as "more pure, and white then snowe" (*4), was guilty of an incestuous "patriarchal construction of power" (98). But we can just as reasonably think of Roper's biography as one of many "things indifferent" in Tudor England, neither morally uplifting nor pernicious.

"You are overlooking insight. Crewe's thesis concerns 'tabooed passion' (97)." It is true that Crewe claims that something like an insight or epiphany ("we are enabled to see") accompanies his "close reading" of Roper's text:

> Through the agency of what we might now call Roper's *interested* spectatorship, we are enabled to see that the hairshirt functions as an incestuous bond . . .; as a mark of endless symbolic transgression and self-punishment; and as the emblem of a carnal soiling that is repeatedly washed away by the only one who has the power of ablution/absolution, namely the daughter who is the object of More's passion. (Crewe 95)

But now reasons for objecting to Proposition *A* become clear. For even if we dismiss the notion of Margaret as the sole agency of absolution of More's sin as an insoluble theological mystery, it is not clear what evidence we would need to agree or disagree with the nontheological remainder of Crewe's assertion. Whether we choose to believe or disbelieve his interpretation of the evidence, we cannot evade the inconvenience of our choice: Why the one rather than the other? We can protest that Crewe's inference is based on "textual evidence," and insist that this is the usual and reasonable way of doing things in criticism. But the prior question is: Can we rely on the utility and rationality of the practice that led to this inference? Specifically, do these criteria—"currency of practice" and "reasonableness"—properly met, mean that other "close readers" will draw apposite inferences from the same evidence?

This question is not easy to answer, and yet it suggests why attention to Proposition *A* would matter in literary studies. For it is, presumably, by the same method that the same critic's "close reading" of Shakespeare's "The Rape of Lucrece" affirms that overlooked or forgotten evidence in the text, that Tarquin is only "the problematic scapegoat-rapist of the poem" (143), and that Patroclus is "implied in the figure of Lucrece" (160). Accordingly, "The Rape of Lucrece" is really about a homosexual rape. The problem is not insubstantial, for, once fading memories have been jogged by this method of "close reading," things that have escaped other "close readers" fall into place. For instance, Crewe perceives a "Shake-spearean signature" (158) in an allusion to Achilles ("big prick" [157]), and Shakespeare himself is "the biggest prick known to history" (159). As we can see, then, the spatial figures employed in this kind of "close reading" provide no bulwark against critical peril, especially when it is compounded with theoretical excursions. I do not mean to suggest that it would be easy to counter the impressionistic assertions here; indeed, Crewe's "effort at representing the Renaissance" (1) purports to overcome the limited range of commentary provided by the vocabulary of received criticism. Hence, Proposition *A* must be seen as part of an effort to extend the boundaries of historical commentary, with "close reading" as the presumed device of that extension.

I do not wish to rebut Proposition *A* so much as to raise the issue of what might reasonably regulate assent and dissent. What grounds do we have for "belief" in the interpretation of literary texts? We could say that the history of criticism is nothing more than a record of personal impressions, in which case we might have some sympathy for the recent tendency of some critics to recount stories of their life history, education, tastes and the like. But, as we saw in chapter 3, the inconveniences of that approach are many and substantial. We cannot justify "choice" by merely rendering a rationalized account of how it came about. "So then Crewe's impressions aren't reasoned judgments. So what?" Obviously, I haven't made myself clear. The question is, What counts as an "impression" of a Renaissance biography? What serves as a criterion of judgment in deciding what individual impressions are *about*? Let me try to clarify this point: Imagine that "reading as" were the literary analogue of "seeing as" (in the Wittgensteinian sense). Then, we might ask: What criteria, if any, would be appropriate in limiting the range of such impressions? Are they historical statements?

What kind of evidence, for instance, would we be looking for to support this statement about Shakespeare's *Twelfth Night*?

> B) *Viola and Sebastian can be read as types of the incarnate Christ. (Hamilton 107)*

Suppose that the critic, Donna Hamilton, proceeds to "read" Viola and Sebastian as "types of the incarnate Christ," and, further, that we have doubts about her "can be read as" assertion. How do we justify or even explain them? Clearly, our doubts must concern something other than the veracity of the statement (for, obviously, *if* a text *is* read as *X* it *can* be read as *X*). If we imagine an example that wouldn't fit here (Viola and Sebastian cannot be read as *X*), don't we simultaneously imagine it fitting in some way, loosely or preposterously? We question the propriety of *B* because neither agreement nor disagreement would affect our understanding of whether or not in the early seventeenth century Viola and Sebastian were in fact "read as types of the incarnate Christ." Nor would we overcome our difficulty by presentation of an instance in which an Elizabethan actually "read" these or apposite figures in this way. For even if such a construction occurred, we might still doubt that this construction among the *n* possible constructions fits in Shakespeare's play. At the very least, we could say that Proposition *A* could be cast, in less elliptical form, in the manner of Proposition *B*. Critics *can* say whatever they *do* say about More and Shakespeare's "Rape of Lucrece." Indeed, without some additional perspective on *A* and *B*, correction—and criticism, for that matter— would be gratuitous and ungrounded.

On the other hand, we have already agreed that, in practice, limitation of the range of critical inferences takes place every time we choose one rather than another "reading as"—in framing a lecture on Shakespeare or in writing or evaluating a scholarly essay. While there may be something personal or subjective about the process, investigation of criticism of a particular poet, Shakespeare, for instance, may show how easy it is to drift from "reading as" to broad claims about the reading process and the underlying ground of perception: "It is certainly possible," Wittgenstein writes, "to be convinced by evidence that someone is in such-and-such a state of mind, that, for instance, he is not pretending" (*PI* 228)—by such evidence as "subtleties of glance, of gesture, of tone." In everyday life, we aren't called upon to explain why we think certain expressions genuine and others not, and, if asked, we might not even be able to articulate satisfying reasons. This incapacity would not, of course, diminish the importance of our acting on those judgments in business, and so on. But what happens when we encounter the question of "genuineness" in criticism? Can we dismiss the matter of candor by assuming that critics—as a class—do not dissemble?

2.

"We have discussed candor before, but I am not sure that we agreed how it would apply in cases like Proposition *A*. Would you deny that by means of his 'close reading' Crewe says something significant about Margaret's 'daughterly seduction' (Crewe 98), and something specific about 'incest' with the 'penetration' of Margaret's body by the enema? If you cannot deny that, then Roper's text *is* the evidence of an incestuous relationship between Margaret and her father." I would say, first, that this is an odd way of talking about "Margaret's body" and "incest." As for "close reading," what other kind do critics admit to? And how do we discriminate between "close reading" and "myopic"—or, as Crewe prefers to say, "microscopic"—*misreading*? Then I would ask what we can *do* to affirm or deny the claim that Crewe's statements about Roper's biography say "something significant" about More's "incestuous" relationship with his daughter. Isn't this exactly what is in question? It seems to me that this way of talking about literary perception presents a problem in our "going on together."

"Not only do you now imply the hoary standard of 'truth,' but you contradict yourself as well. You cannot say that this particular way of talking presents a critical problem, since, if that talk were to persist as a problem, it must contradict your hypothesis that such problems are illusory. I would say, to the contrary, that the problem here is not only critical, but social. How are we to distinguish between propriety and excess in the application of this spatial metaphor of 'closeness?' Social dissonance is a danger of metacriticism. It is no wonder that critics register dismay when questions are raised about their perceptions. They 'believe in' those perceptions, or they wouldn't shepherd them into print." Certainly we need some way of discriminating between an "aspect" and "perception of an aspect" of a literary work. But, in any event, this last remark about "belief" carries with it a huge and dubious assumption. As

has already been suggested (in chapters 1 and 3), I doubt
that literary criticism, as an institution, is set up for—or
would consent to—polygraph testing and narcosynthesis in
order to assure the field of assurance regarding a critic's
sincerity. But even if "veracity" could be established by
medical intervention, we would still have no basis for
discriminating between a "close" and a "myopic" reading.
Indeed, we might have clinical evidence that we cannot
"go on together," for we would have evidence, not only of
the candor of a critic's account of a "perception," but also
of the level of abreaction involved in any challenge to it.
Constructing critical assertions as no more than "states of
mind" seems to lead us into a blind alley. We are led into,
but not out of, a solipsistic *interest*. Who cares what a
critic thinks or feels, unless there is some bearing of the
thoughts and feelings of that critic on the system of language exterior to the particular critic's state of mind?

This is only to say that it is no good justifying a "close
reading" by pointing to "the text" read, for that act is both
recursive and self serving. Conceivably, we could have as
many "states of mind" about a text as we have "close readers" in *n* "close reading" situations. The question is: How
are we to "go on together?" And the answer here could be
social or historical or linguistic or literary or philosophical
or any combination of these and other categories. If it is
only social, the emphasis will probably be on "self esteem."
Criticism would aim at encouraging every reader to feel
good about the "state of mind" stimulated by the text. Our
reason for this response would be social: Literary texts are
useful as a means to encourage readers to feel good about
themselves. Most obviously, other means, especially phar-
macological ones, have preempted this field, by producing
"emotional stability" and "self-esteem" more swiftly and
consistently. But as we have already agreed, literary criticism as a discipline seems—largely but not entirely—dis-
inclined to accept antinomianism as its credo. We suspect
that feeling good about ourselves may not answer all—or
any—of the questions we might ask about a literary work.

And this is *a fortiori* the case if the text is, for instance, *Beowulf*, and the critic knows no Old English.

"Surely you aren't suggesting that linguistics and philology are the cure-all for criticism. Problems of understanding poetry often only begin when one *knows* the language in which a poem is written. What about the term *ðyle Hroðgares* in *Beowulf*. Only acquaintance with Old English produces understanding of the problem of interpretation involved with this locution. The more we know about Old English, the more we are thrown back on our creative understanding. We guess. We create. We imagine. And, rather than a weakness, this is our only strength, as it is our *raison d'etre*."

I doubt that it will help to scaffold a system on an anomaly in the language. Since we have no evidence of other uses of the noun, *ðyle*, we are limited in what we can say about it. We have no other uses with which to compare *this* one use. (Wittgenstein asks if it makes sense to talk about a unique case of someone "obeying a rule.") But we have reason to believe that the word is a noun, and the genitive form of Hrothgar fits with Unferth's conduct in the poem. Our "guess" isn't just a projection of one critic's "close reading." It fits with much other material with which many of us are familiar.

"Nor does it make sense to retreat to some notion of a communal 'close reading': how a term functions in 'the work as a whole.' How would a critic, much less a 'community of critics,' hold the 'whole' of *Beowulf* or *The Faerie Queene* or *King Lear* or *The Temple* in mind?" I doubt that one could, or that it would help if one could. In any case, my aim here is less ambitious. It is unlikely that criticism will abandon "close reading" anytime soon. Structural analysts stress continuity, poststructuralists discontinuity, but "close reading" is the mode of a "closed circuit" of reading. As for the "whole" of *The Faerie Queene*, that concept, whether of a physical representation or a phonemic structure, is "unfinished"—a "part"—which we read and remember in parts. Even though our memory proscribes holding the "whole," we are free to consider any part we wish, including that part called "thematic interest," which is the "part" critics usually refer to as the "whole" to which the various parts (diction, plot, character development, imagery, tone) are integrally related or radically detached.

When we are puzzled by a word or phrase, and seek help from, say, the OED, we are not looking only for other uses of the same words in other parts of *The Faerie Queene*. Such uses may be listed in the OED, but they might not, and yet we often "find" what we are looking for; and this is not because we find the line that sent us to the dictionary reproduced in that lexicon: "A gentle knight was pricking on the plain." We look for apposite, not identical uses, and this search leads out from the work in question to a world of contemporaneous uses. We can imagine slicing all and only those uses in the OED from, say, 1590 to 1596, and then adding to that lexicon uses from the same epoch not canvassed by the makers of the OED. This would produce a lexicon relevant to an understanding of *The Faerie Queene*. Now relevance is meant in a descriptive, not a normative sense. The poem resides within a context of certain active, functioning lexical and syntactic possibilities. This is what Wittgenstein means by a "form of life." The tendency in criticism is to employ a shorthand description for convenience; but then sometimes the convenient description is left in place as a reductionist explanation of the totality. Oversimplification might leave out the most important element. Wittgenstein writes:

> What am I believing in when I believe that men have souls? What am I believing in, when I believe that this substance contains two carbon rings? In both cases there is a picture in the foreground, but the sense lies far in the background; that is, the application of the picture is not easy to survey. (*PI* §422)

He proceeds to examine the tendency to address inner responses and expressions and the *"correctness"* of the picture, but the "sense" is in the "application" or "function" of the picture we have in mind. In the background is the understanding of the function of that picture within a system of things, a "form of life," which is very complicated, and "not easy to survey." It might help to reach for another figure. The picture that we have in mind is like an expression:

> For us, of course, these forms of expression are like pontificals which we may put on, but cannot do much with, since we lack the effective power that would give these vestments meaning and purpose.
>
> In the actual use of expressions we make detours, we go by side-roads. We see the straight highway before us, but of course we cannot use it, because it is permanently closed. (*PI* §426)

The suggestion is that our understanding depends on the simplification, but what the simplification leaves out is the function or meaning or significance. The way our expressions—the "vestments"—are ordered by a pontifical with significance—or application—"deep in the background." We need the picture in the foreground, but the understanding, which is not articulated, is what drives the need for simplification: the application, or "sense," or "significance."

"If what is important is in the background, and the background is what neither the poet nor the critic can articulate, on what ground does a critique of Proposition *A* withstand a charge of incoherence? Don't we brush this question aside as unanswerable with something like: All critics do is write poems about poems?" Some critics do that. But John Hollander offers a more helpful figure of the critic, not as a meta-poet, but as a poem's "friend."[1] Poems may relate to other poems (the overlapping concepts of *allusion, intertextuality, belatedness* and *the burden of the past*). Implicitly, the attentive critic recognizes what is *in* the poem, but not necessarily, in Wittgenstein's figure, "easy to survey." Hollander didn't seem to depend on the antonymous relation of "friend" to "enemy," but the contrast between the two figures did loom there "in the background." Rather, Hollander pointed to the way friends sometimes "see" something in us that we don't see," or "want to see," ourselves. "It's a Wittgensteinian joke," he said. The "intention" or "meaning" of a text is not a "mental act":

> "When I teach someone the formation of the series. . . .
> I surely mean him to write. . . . at the hundredth place."—
> Quite right; you mean it. And evidently without necessarily even thinking of it. This shews you how different the grammar of the verb "to mean" is from that of "to think".
> And nothing is more wrong-headed than calling meaning a mental activity! Unless, that is, one is setting out to produce confusion. (It would also be possible to speak of an activity of butter when it rises in price, and if no problems are produced by this it is harmless.) (*PI* §693)

As we recognized in chapter 2, the background of a painting isn't less "in the expression" by virtue of its being subtle, or, to some viewers, even inaccessible.

3.

"Perhaps it is hard to see what all this has to do with 'Evidence of Renaissance Criticism.'" The figure of the background's not being "easy to survey" might help here. I am not arguing that "Renaissance" talk is always transparent. Notwithstanding human limitations on critical observations about the past, we do look for reasons why we can move on from our questions about the foreground *or* the background of a part of a poem to understanding of, and talking reasonably about, a literary work, an author, a time, and so on. "But the danger is that you are 'going on' by yourself, as if we understand this 'form of life' that you call the Renaissance (and others refer to as the Early Modern Period)." I do this because that is the thing to do: ". . . at the hundredth place." For me, it is not a mysterious or

unusual way of proceeding. It might seem impolitic or
unworldly to say that it seems to me "natural"; but then
I could point out that, in the past epoch, I have probably
spent more time reading material written before than that
written after 1700. In one sense ("deep in the background"),
it might be more of a stretch to take anything I say about
literature of the "present time" seriously than to trust my
judgment about Elizabethan and Jacobean literature.

It should come as no surprise that I agree with Wittgenstein when he says: "I believe that if one is to enjoy a
writer one has to *like* the culture he belongs to as well. If
one finds it indifferent or distasteful, one's admiration
cools off" (*CV* 85). This may not be much of a test, but
Proposition *A* doesn't seem to me to reflect a charitable
attitude toward its subject, Sir Thomas More. A learned
and gentle humanist loves his daughter, who is dying of a
fever. Instead of suing her doctors at law on the grounds
that she has hovered too long between life and death, he
suggests a remedy, unsophisticated perhaps today (unless
one is a New Ager), and for this he is accused of a "physical penetration" tantamount to incest. And it seems to me
that this figure of an enema as "incestuous penetration"
is gross as well as calumnious, for it suggests that More
didn't know *how* to "father" the daughter he is accused of
debauching, in which case the charge of incest doesn't
make sense, and More looks like a cuckold. In other words,
since the idea of this offense came to me only from reading Crewe and certainly not from reading More or Roper,
I have reason to suspect that Proposition *A* and the prose
that supports it exhibit a paucity of affection for More and
the "form of life" of which his writings and his life choices
were a part. I suspect that Crewe finds the "form of life"
"distasteful." Wittgenstein continues:

> If someone who believes in God looks round and asks
> "Where does everything I see come from?", "Where does
> all this come from?", he is *not* craving for a (causal) ex-
> planation; and his question gets its point from being the

> expression of a certain craving. He is, namely, expressing
> an attitude to all explanations.—But how is this manifested
> in his life?
>
> The attitude that's in question is that of taking a certain
> matter seriously and then, beyond a certain point, no longer
> regarding it as serious, but maintaining that something else
> is even more important. (*CV* 85)

Whether one sees More as a felon or "A Man For All Seasons" seems to me to involve much more than a defense of, or attack upon, "close reading" as the sole crutch of an interpretive system. Ben Jonson and Wittgenstein were much more attuned to the complexities of the analytic demands of judgment in these matters. The emphasis on attitude in the Wittgenstein quote has an almost Heideggerean ring to it. For Wittgenstein, beliefs don't just reflect attitudes; an attitude isn't an epiphenomenon floating outside of actions and words. Wittgenstein suggests that the significance of what we say lies "deep in the background" of what is said. We cannot remove *what* we value from *how* we value. Literary critics may rely on tricks with the language, but literary criticism is not *only* verbal legerdemain. Jonson thought that to be a good critic one must first be "a good man."

"How, in the early postmodern period, can one insist on the old Arnoldian view that would make literary criticism a branch of axiology?" We need not, and should not, think of literary criticism as a branch of anything else. Nor should we—with the Marxists, Christian humanists, and ethnic and gender gendarmes—make criticism the servant of extraliterary imperatives. On the other hand, I would not exclude, but rather insist upon including, ethical considerations as an integral aspect of literary appreciation. This does not require an Arnoldian effort to replace religion with a cult of literary aesthetes, led by a priesthood of literary critics beholden to nonliterary interest groups: labor, management, men, women, government, taxpayers, blacks, whites, Latinos, homosexuals, heterosexuals and (". . . at the hundredth place"). As in the Wittgenstein quotation, religion can provide useful figures for literary discussion, but that is not the same as replacing all possible literary functions. No less than architecture, music, painting and sculpture, verbal art—such as the sermon— might have a useful place in religious practices. But even though, as in the case of John Donne, such expressions have great literary merit, this doesn't mean that literary genres (the sermon, the epic, the limerick) can ever, even in tandem, *replace* religious functions. I find it odd to think that the approach of "ordinary language analysis" pursued in these investigation aims in this direction. Indeed, it was the moralistic bent of the poet-as-misogynist talk (in chapter 4) that seemed to me, not only misguided in fact, but inappropriate in aim as well.

"You are objecting to postmodern interests and concerns. But how do we *know* when statements purporting to be *about* Renaissance poetry are about *that* poetry and not some other thing, such as late modern interests, anxieties, and so forth? The problem with historical analysis, as you seem to think of it, is that it sets aside the self-reflexivity of our critical practices. You merely assume that we recognize themes and attitudes as markedly different from our own (chapter 5), so different that there is never a blurring of the line between the two." When my attention is given to Renaissance expressions, or to a Renaissance "form of life," I usually do that, because it helps, I think, to expect differences; but if that expectation proves a hindrance, it can, of course, be set aside.

Chapter 5 was given over to discussion of historical interpretation. Obviously, it is not easy to articulate the point I am trying to make. I doubt that it will help to nail some mentalistic notion of *objectivity* to the mast, for then discussion will devolve upon the "sense" and "feasibility" of "objectivity" talk in criticism. When we talk in this way, we should be aware of the ruts we feel beneath our feet here: "A philosophical problem," Wittgenstein writes, "has the form: 'I don't know my way about'" (*PI* §123). Sometimes we are just out of our ken with the terrain of "Renaissance" talk. But we can feel unsure of our footing, too, when we sense that the path has been traced, to no purpose, by others before us—or even if we know that we have passed this way ourselves. It might help to talk about "objectivity," but if "objectivity talk" becomes an obstacle to "going on together" about Spenser, Shakespeare, Donne and Herbert, then we should not take "objectivity talk" seriously. But then, appropriately, we must set "subjectivity talk" aside, too, and for the same reason. We just say that, in the present circumstance, the distinction doesn't seem to help. And yet it makes no sense to proscribe the expressions in other cases, when they might be of use, that is, when the intellectual context makes the contrast between *subjectivity* and *objectivity* talk useful.

4.

This investigation began with a question about "clarification" in Renaissance criticism. It seems to me clear that "objectivity/subjectivity" talk concerns the use of evidence, which is, according to some practitioners, ignored by "forty [or *n*] percent of the criticism published today." "Surely that remark was made in jest, and, in any case, there is no 'fixed meaning' of the term, *evidence*, in any case. The OED lists a large number of English uses of the term: 'The quality or condition of being evident: clearness; actually present; manifestation, display; an appearance from which inferences may be drawn; an indication, mark, sign, token, trace; ground for belief; testimony or facts tending to prove or disprove any conclusion; something serving as a proof.' And then there are legal uses: 'information, whether in the form of personal testimony, the language of documents, or the production of material objects, that is given in a legal investigation. All of these uses develop from the Latin *videre*, to see.' In the OED, what is evident is 'Distinctly visible; conspicuous ... Obvious to the sight; recognizable at a glance ... Clear to the understanding or the judgement; obvious, plain.'"

"With such an emphasis on 'sight,' criticism would appear to be a radical phenomenology of relations within a historically defined boundary of linguistic possibilities. One thinks of Willard Quine's assertion that the lexicographer only gathers, sorts and catalogs historical examples. If literary criticism works in the same way, it must move ever closer to an abyss of positivism. Prospects for an account of critical judgment in that context would be pretty dismal. Somebody once said that economics is the 'dismal science,' but it has to be upbeat compared to the enumerative procedures of lexicography, which, nowadays, computers can accomplish without the help of 'the literary experience.'"

We can avoid dismay by adjusting our expectations. We use lexicography for lexicographical purposes only. Linguistic understanding is a necessary, but not a sufficient, condition of literary understanding. One could look up every word in *The Faerie Queene* (from a concordance, say) in the OED without even reading, much less understanding, the poem. Having established that the poem does exist as an expression of a "form of life" with which one may or may not be sufficiently familiar to read with understanding, we want to be able to address the foreground *and* the background whenever we wish. John Hollander's remark that the critic is a "friend of the poem" is like Wittgenstein's claim that one must like the culture in which a poem "lives and breathes and has its being." The effective critic is the "friend" of "a form of life" of which *The Faerie Queene* or *King Lear* or "The Anagram" or *The Temple* is a part.

"You sound now like the retrograde historicist who argues that we must reconstruct the poem in its historical context, which we know to be impossible." This assertion may be familiar, but it is also odd. Surely it is, in any case, no support for Proposition *A* or *B*. It seems to me that, if we don't "know" the past, it doesn't much matter what we say about it. But we do find our way to work and home every day, and if we didn't, it would be a very different world that we live in, with entirely different laws, institutions and mores. Individual and institutional memory make the past answerable to present needs and interests, in criticism and in our other endeavors. We make judgments about the past all the time. I go to Los Angeles International Airport to pick up my brother. He is about 5'8" tall, heavy set, with blond hair. But the airport is full of people who fit that description, and I haven't seen my brother for many years. Why don't we think of such rendezvous as random occurrences? How does my family *know* that I brought the right man home for the family reunion?

"The argument *is*, then, that we recognize a proper reading of a poem the same way we recognize family members? And you hold *my* characterization of your view as Arnoldian to be odd!" If the airport example doesn't help, don't depend on it. We can always go at a problem in a different way. We could dismiss Propositions *A* and *B* by observing that they do not purport to say anything about More or Shakespeare or the Renaissance—*in any strictly documentary, historical sense*. But this leaves unaddressed what we are to do when critics claim to describe historical elements other than their mental states. Most critics will concede that under certain conditions talk about the past makes sense, but they are less sure what those certain conditions are. Consider the following assertions:

> C) *Between 1530 and 1580 there were remarkably over fifty noblemen's troupes on record for performances in England, some no doubt playing only on an occasional basis, many others consisting of touring professionals. (White 12)*

> D) *Elizabethan children were the human equivalent to Kula gift trinkets . . . They were little, peripheral, detached, and—though initially unformed or even ugly— ornamental. (Fumerton 36)*

We will probably think of very different ways to challenge or affirm these statements than came to mind with *A* and *B*; both *C* and *D purport* to be historically "significant." With *C*, we might overcome doubt by inquiry into the

critic's numerical claim: Over 50? The documentary record
will or will not show the count justified, and here it is the
sense of "showing" that counts: So many and no fewer
households of "noble" standing staged theatrical performances; "touring professionals" were among those who
participated, and so on—the kind of statement referred to
in the opening paragraph of this chapter as "straightforward
empirical claims." Such claims might or might not fit the
available evidence, but we probably know what evidence
to look for in deciding the matter.

In contrast, Proposition D asserts an equivalence between humans and "Kula gift trinkets," this, presumably,
on the basis of relative size. Trinkets and children are
"little," "detached," "ornamental," and so on. If a doubt
arises regarding the propriety of the implied equation
("children" are/were [=] "Kula . . . ."), we might not be able
to refer to the documentary record as we have with C. We
could peruse the household accounts of Tudor noblemen,
examine manuscript collections at Lambeth, the British
Library and the Public Records Office, and yet not be able
to say what evidence we were looking for, or how would
we know if we had found it. For what is in question here
is not the historical reliability of the account, but rather
the ethical propriety of attributing equivalence to physically inequivalent objects. Common sense tells us that
children are larger than the necklaces or bracelets they
wear, so the critic appeals beyond the ordinary sense of
equivalence to something ethically if not measurably so.
When we recognize that in this context "equivalent"
means "inequivalent," we are on our way to understanding the critic's argument.

We must remember, though, that we can understand an
argument without assenting to it. In the case of D, the
critic depends on the reader's inference of comparability
in the examples. Indeed, we might be misled if we take
differences regarding what counts as evidence of that comparability—or even as what counts as "little" or "ornamental"—as critically insignificant, for such discriminations

might figure in our understanding of what constitutes effective commentary on the past. Critics who dwell on "trivial" or "small" incidents or artifacts tend to depreciate interpretive ventures emphasizing broader thematic approaches of "traditional" studies: "We could, for instance, place it [the Renaissance] upon the stage of intellectual history as it evolved from Enlightenment historiography through post-Hegelian *Geistesgeschichte* (the vision of the world as activated by collective Self, Spirit, or Mind) all the way to Lovejoy's Chain of Being or Tillyard's World Picture" (Fumerton 26). The implication is that "historiography" is developed in such a way as to render error in the interpretive system inevitable.

As in this example, often assumptions regarding what constitutes evidence relevant to talk about the past incline toward a critique of predecessor critics. For Patricia Fumerton, "traditional" intellectual historians mistakenly thought of the Renaissance as "whole" or "unified" rather than "fragmented." They oversimplified interpretation of the past by failing to recognize the shaping influences of "economics, politics and other cultural phenomena" (Fumerton 28). Similarly, Richard Helgerson writes:

> E. M. W. Tillyard's *Elizabethan World Picture*, which first drew special attention to this passage [from Hooker's *Lawes*], and the *Norton Anthology of English Literature*, which gave it great currency, both present Hooker's views as representative of what virtually all Elizabethans thought and feared, and both print as confirming evidence closely similar passages from Shakespeare and from the official *Book of Homilies*. (Helgerson 270)

Here, the critic does not object to the predecessor's inclusion of the cited passages, but to the exclusivity of that inclusion.[2] The predecessor overlooks so much evidence that a skewed vision of the past is the only one possible. Although Helgerson quotes the same passage at the same length as the misguided predecessor, he implies that the historian of ideas overemphasized the importance of the selected passage to the exclusion of expressions by such dissenters as Cartwright, Barrow and Greenwood: "And their view was no less central to the Elizabethan world picture than his" (Helgerson 270). The implication is that greater inclusion would prompt a more faithful picture of the time than that advanced by the predecessor critic.

On its face, this line of thought seems reasonable. But again, often spatial figures carry an unrecognized load of unargued assumptions: "central" suggests dominant or important as opposed to marginal or trivial. Since critics cannot conveniently point to "everything" as evidence supporting their Renaissance theses, they limit the claims that they will seriously entertain by invoking notions of "precision," arguing, for instance, that "our own age of postmodernity" does not so much dismiss history as it forms "precisely a representation or interpretation of history" (Fumerton 2). The problem is that in talking like this critics introduce expectations about measurement, suggesting that we can discriminate precise from imprecise representations. What makes a characterization of "trivial" evidence "precise?" Is it the same thing that makes a characterization "thick?" When a critic says that evidence of trivia is not trivial because she sees it through a "lens," which she calls a "paradigm," why, rather than assent, should we not register doubt and perhaps even a sense that nothing has been described or explained? Reasonable skepticism could derive from "thick description" of such events as the execution of Charles I simply because it is "thick"—which, if I understand correctly, means that, in the manner of "'interpretive anthropology'" (Honigman 318), critics imagine "webs of significance" (Nanda 56) in events which they subject to "close reading," this with a mind to evoke a Heideggerian sense of "being there" (Geertz *Lives* chap. 1). For instance, the "interpretive anthropologist" might infer "deep play" in a Balinese cockfight, which may then be construed as circulating "aggressive energies" much like the Elizabethan tilt (McCoy 24).[3] Posing "thick" against "unconditioned description"

(Geertz *Interpretation* chap. 1), critics of culture-as-literary-artifact focus on minuscule, often overlooked details ("trinkets of power" [Geertz *Negara* 126])—the spiced orange that Charles carried to the scaffold (Fumerton 16)—rather than on broad movements (the vestiarian controversy) or "major works" (Marvell's "Horatian Ode").

Why should critics find "thick description" talk an improvement over Lovejoyan "positivistic history of ideas" (Fumerton 12)? One reason might be that, for such critics, trifles aren't *really* trifles, but signs marking ideological anxieties and motivations. For them, trivia is evidence of English aristocratic, expansionist, imperialist plots; such critics might claim that King James was a "foreign peddler of trifles" (Knapp 174), or say that *The Faerie Queene* insists on retrograde literary conventions, "revisiting not just pastoral but England's old foolish love of trifles in general," for instance, legends and hobgoblins (Knapp 125). It is fair to infer from such diction a belief in "trifling" as an oppressive social institution. Thus settlers of the New World practiced "trifling with the Indians" (Knapp 3), and it follows from such talk that the locution, "England's colonial trifling" (4), designates a meaningful category. Theoretically considered in this way, bric-a-brac, poetry, children, indigenous people and other "trifles" are evidence previously ignored by historians looking for "mainstreams and currents of development" (Fumerton 1). Accordingly, trivial objects mark significant, if fragmentary, signs of such things as the "trivial selfhood of the aristocracy" (Fumerton 1). States of being, then, emerge from "an analytic of the fragmentary," which permits perception of a "radical disconnection" at what the critic might imagine as the "intersection between the historical and the aesthetic" (2).

Like small objects, small events or smaller fragments of small events become the foci of historical analyses. From this point of view, frequently an anecdote serves in lieu of an accumulation of documentary evidence to support historical statements. An often overlooked detail within an unfolding sequence of wide-ranging events can provide the basis for a conceptually "better" dissection of culture: "The intricate cultural fabric of Renaissance England can best be analyzed, not by trying to find a sample swatch, but by starting to pull at a thread" (Dobin 17). The assumption driving these "synchronic" analyses is that an anecdote (in this case an account of Queen Elizabeth's visit to John Dee in 1575) reveals the social structures and practices of the period; the anecdote is a "poststructuralist model of culture" because "all cultural phenomena are textualized" (Dobin 11).

One notable inconvenience of this "fragmentary" or "anecdotal" method appears when its practitioners fail to clarify or unmix their metaphors, forgetting, for instance, how, without temporal expansion, "disconnection" is able to coincide with "intersection," or how and why pulling at one thread will make a fabric's fabric more apparent than scrutiny of a swatch of a fabric. (Can't we examine a swatch and pull at a thread as well?) Then too, the spatial figure of "centrality" (i.e., relevance or propriety) is often puzzling. The claim that "synchronic analysis" holds the intersection between historical and cultural consciousness to be a random convergence of the documentary evidence with the critic's autobiography gives rise to idiosyncratic accounts: "I began my teaching career in West Africa just a few years after the countries of that region gained their independence from England and France. As I have studied the Elizabethan writing of England, I have often been reminded of postcolonial Africa" (Helgerson 17). Although such reminiscences can be fascinating in themselves, and might even provide useful data for the sociologist of knowledge, it is not clear how we determine their relevance to claims made about Tudor and Stuart England.

Of course, synchronic critics could say that an answer to this question must derive from observation of particulars, and, as observers of those particulars, we are part of the observation. But this protestation, which supposedly justifies "an analytic of the fragmentary," only pushes the problem off another step, for we might ask: How does an "analytic of the fragmentary" differ from one of the

nonfragmentary? The answer—that there is "a radical disconnection implicit in the analytic of the fragmentary"—
is likewise uninformative, for we must perceive something
larger than the fragment to know that a fragment is a fragment. And we can only say that something is disconnected
if we have, at least in the imagination, seen it as connected
to something else.

6.

"I have the uncomfortable feeling that you are aligning
yourself with the forces of reaction against the use of the
anecdote as a recoverable 'trace' of cultural practices in an
otherwise unrecoverable past. Surely attention to subject
matter marginalized in traditional critical accounts can
only enrich our understanding. Even bizarre comparisons
between Kula trinkets and youngsters in Elizabethan families might assist somebody's understanding of a Shakespeare play. Remember that we are only talking about
interpretation here, and nobody seems sure of the grounds
for deciding between competing assertions in this area.
Traditionalists complain about 'hyperbole' in 'synchronic'
analysis of such incidents as Dee's visit to Queen Elizabeth, but their reactionary's appeal to 'primary sources'
begs the question, which is 'How should we talk about
what we think of as primary sources?' Critics simply disagree on such basic matters as what 'primary sources' say.
Stephen Greenblatt says one thing, John Lee another, about
the priest's hat in the library at Christ Church. And we
ignore the matter, or choose between them."

Can't we also check the hat before we decide? If I understand correctly, Lee faults Greenblatt for his "rather loose
use of history" (Lee 285), which implies that some standard of judgment is in play: "Although history cannot be
truth, it can be more or less true, and the truer version is
to be preferred" (286).

"Well, the hat is *there* in the library at Christ Church.
Lee and Greenblatt agree about *that*. So looking at it—
even for a long time—probably won't help. Does it make

a significant difference whether the hat was sold in the nineteenth century for £63, as Greenblatt writes, or for £21 in 1842, as Lee says? It seems to me pointless to nit-pick about whether the hat is '[i]n a small glass case in the library of Christ Church' (*Learning* 161), as Greenblatt says it is, or as Lee, insisting that 'there is no small glass case at Christ Church,' claims, 'in a solid wooden case, shaped rather like a wine glass, and about four foot high' (293). I say it's what we *do* with documents that counts. And this choice can't be reduced to a matter of mere 'fact.' Indeed, we should find the controversy about Wolsey's hat—whether or not we believe it *is* Wolsey's hat in the library at Christ Church—instructive. The controversy surrounding this 'artifact' clearly indicates that the concept of a 'primary source' is hopelessly vague. Here we see that perception of an 'artifact,' such as the clerical hat, or a 'document,' such as a printed text, is perspectival. One critic sees one thing, another something else. Thomas Hariot's *Brief and true report of the new found land of Virginia* (1588) is a telling case in point. Greenblatt supports a new historicist perspective on the 'fact' that the work includes the 'beginnings of an Algonquian English dictionary' (Greenblatt *Curse* 45); advancing a more traditional outlook, Tom McAlindon argues that the glossary described by Greenblatt doesn't exist" (McAlindon "Testing" 418).

Isn't the issue point at issue how we are to understand the "primary sources" in question, Machiavelli and Hariot? Whether, for instance, in the *Discourses*, Machiavelli expresses antireligious sentiments, and whether Hariot articulates "the Machiavellian hypothesis," namely, a "radically subversive hypothesis . . . about the origin and function of religion" (McAlindon 415)? Greenblatt seems to think that,

> E) [*The Brief and true report*] *culminates for Harriot in a glossary, the beginnings of an Algonquian-English dictionary, designed to facilitate further acts of recording and hence to consolidate English power in Virginia. (Greenblatt Negotiations 45)*

In contrast, McAlindon says:

> *F) This information [i.e., Proposition E] is incorrect.*
> *(McAlindon 418–19)*

I am puzzled by your suggestion that our choice in the matter makes no difference. Are you saying that we have no reasonable grounds for deciding between *E* and *F*? If so, I disagree. Some basis for decision appears in Greenblatt's emphasis on the importance of the Algonquian words for *"fire, food,* [and] *shelter"* (Greenblatt 49), which, again, he finds to be evidence of Hariot's subversive rhetoric, while McAlindon finds no evidence of a glossary in Hariot's *Brief and true report*, and so, understandably, implicit grounds to challenge the cultural materialist "interpretive strategy" (419).[4]

"This talk about 'evidence' and 'choice' oversimplifies what is, finally, 'undecided' and 'undecidable.'"

"To say 'The height of Mont Blanc depends on how one climbs it' would be queer" (*PI* §225).

"What?"

Objection to the ligature between "evidence" and "choice" reminds me of Wittgenstein's rejoinder to his interlocutor, who thought that we could answer any questions that might arise about the length of a rod by acquiring ever more sophisticated methods of measurement. The idea was that something was being left out of the account. Here, I would be inclined to inquire how we come to know that "talk about 'evidence'" is "'undecided' and 'undecidable.'"

"Aren't you now assuming that the three words (*fire, food, shelter*), in fact, do not appear in Hariot's work? We don't exhaust ourselves trying to prove negative propositions, such as, 'the following words do not appear in such and such a lengthy volume—say, Hariot's *Brief and true report*—of Elizabethan prose. One reader easily passes over what another notes with care; and don't forget the myriad discrepancies that textual scholars have logged in between various printings of the 'same' Elizabethan work. Not only do perspectives differ, but the objects of perspectival perceptions differ too. Surely, it is not the business of criticism to look for a 'final solution' of the *fire, food, shelter*-question of Hariot's *Brief report."*

The finality in this statement of final irresolution worries me. What makes the choice between *E* and *F* undecidable? Don't we have reasonable grounds for proceeding here? Suppose I tell you that the word "cybernetics" doesn't appear in Shakespeare's *Venus and Adonis*. Would you not "decide" at once that I was either in jest or in error? Would you even bother to check Spivak's *Concordance*?

"Well, *that* would be an obvious anachronism."

Agreed. But don't we judge the obvious and the less obvious—and even the case where we lack sufficient evidence to make such a judgment—in more or less the same way?

"Cultural materialists are determined to talk about history in a self-conscious way. As a means to *avoid* anachronism, they take account of the biases of observers, past as well as present. Frankly, this practice seems pretty well established. Interpretive practices change, and with them, the understanding of a 'form of life.' We have good reason to believe that eighteenth century actors, with their declamatory style, didn't perform Shakespeare plays in anything like the manner of an Olivier or a Jacoby, besides which, in Elizabethan times, the parts of women weren't even played by women. Like social roles, interpretive practices are, in the anthropological sense, 'local' and 'isolated.'"

A response here should match the ambitiousness of the claim. If the point is modest, that is, if it suggests only that we remember what everyone else knows about the Elizabethan and Augustan stage practices, then we can be grateful for the reminder, even though it is in most practical circumstances supererogatory. If, on the other hand, something like a principle of "undecidability" is at stake, the inconvenience of assent comes to the fore: How, if we cannot decide what is knowable about the shift from Elizabethan to Augustan to late modern interpretive practices, do we decide that these practices were, in fact, different?

"Because the evidence supports our strong suspicion in the matter. We have engravings, ledgers, logs, diary entries, set designs, and the like."

But can't we elect not to decide what such evidence amounts to? Can't we in fact reserve judgment on any interpretive account of interpretive practices? Unless we decide on a criterion of judgment, how *can* we decide even to say or not say that decision in the matter is decidable or undecidable? If I take a drug that renders decisiveness in everything difficult for me for a certain length of time, for instance, would my abstention from deciding be "decided," or would my not deciding merely amount to a randomly-arrived-at critical position of "indecisiveness?" Can indecisiveness or decisiveness be characteristics of critics' personalities, like shyness or self-confidence? Isn't indecision, like decision, a choice? I vote "yea" or "nay" or "abstain" or "present" or I am absent ("not present"); and there may be other options as well. But whatever I do, whether I decide or decide not to decide, what would be a criterion for a choice that is not a choice, but "undecidable?" If I find that I cannot decide such and such an interpretive matter, does this mean that the matter is therefore undecidable? What would serve as evidence for or against the proposition, "*X* is undecidable?"

* * * * *

These investigations have focused on different kinds of assertions about Renaissance texts, and the different expectations about evidence that they might entail. Confusion enters when critical assertions purport to be about Renaissance literature and culture, but in fact devolve upon evidence regarding the critic's state of mind or the metaphysical structure of historical processes. When objections to the declarative mode of subjectivism are met by a cavalier dismissal of "objectivity, verification, impartiality, the weighing of evidence, and the rest" (Eagleton 122–23), this modest question requires an answer: If not evidence, then what? Although in many situations intuition and unreasoned gut reactions have their uses—in everyday life they are indispensable—as guides to evaluation of critical statements about the Renaissance they serve as dubious replacements for documentary evidence. Recognizing that we might not in every circumstance be able to say what gesture or facial expression prompts our conviction that we understand a person or situation, Wittgenstein asks, "what does imponderable evidence *accomplish*?" He adds: "Suppose there were imponderable evidence for the chemical (internal) structure of a substance, still it would have to prove itself to be evidence by certain consequences which *can* be weighed" (*PI* 228).

In criticism, too, publicly shared evidence can help to clarify, correct and refine our public conversation. (Think of this statement as a "reminder" rather than a "principle.") We need not deny that our personal travails figure somewhere in our understanding of the past, if for no other reason than that they are a part of the "we" who take an interest in history. "Philosophy," Wittgenstein writes, "simply puts everything before us, and neither explains nor deduces anything.—Since everything lies open to view there is nothing to explain. For what is hidden, for example, is of no interest to us" (*PI* §126). Presentation of evidence is akin to philosophy's putting "everything before us" so that "everything lies open to view." This is not to say that nothing is hidden from us, or that nothing hidden from us can be of any importance, but only that "what is hidden . . . is of no interest to us" as we go about the critical task at hand: to generate or judge statements about times and voices other than our own.

Notes

Notes to Introduction

1. Larry Wright is the founder and convener of the Wittgenstein Reading Group at the University of California, Riverside (see Acknowledgments); I have elaborated somewhat on the scenario of his "centipede effect" (*Reasoning* 297).

2. See my "Recent Studies in the English Renaissance," *SEL* 31 (1991): 179–229, an omnibus review of 110 books published on nondramatic English literature of the Renaissance in one year.

3. The subtitle of Jonathan Goldberg's book is "Postmodernism and English Renaissance texts."

Notes to Chapter 1

1. Ray Monk, *Ludwig Wittgenstein: The Duty of Genius* (New York: The Free Press, 1990). I am deeply indebted to this excellent book.

2. For a more extensive discussion of Milton's revision of this work, see Stewart "Milton."

3. Maureen Quilligan, *Milton's Spenser: The Politics of Reading* (Ithaca: Cornell UP, 1983).

Notes to Chapter 2

1. Upton makes the remark in his edition of Spenser (1,xx): "[the] poem seems to have been hitherto little understood" (*Var* 1.320).

2. There are dozens of recent critical statements which take account of Spenser's interest in sexuality, but see especially

Krier, Hendrix and Berry, who make the focus central to an understanding of Spenser.

3. For a discussion of this idea in Wittgenstein, see Kripke (47–48).

4. For a discussion of the "discovery" of Ben Jonson's annotations to the 1617 Folio of Spenser, see James A. Riddell and Stanley Stewart, *Jonson's Spenser: Evidence and Historical Criticism* (Pittsburgh: Duquesne Univ. Press, 1995), esp. chap. 3.

5. And in the *Investigations*: "Justification by experience comes to an end. If it did not it would not be justification" (§485).

6. From an anonymous reader's response to the present argument.

7. For a reliable perspective on this matter, see Williams, chap. 5.

8. I am aware that some critics regard this obsession with politics as no more than an obsession with intramural politics in the academy; but for an alternative analysis, see Gross and Levitt.

9. Marx was, of course, referring to Spenser's argument in *A View of the Present State of Ireland* that England should pursue, in winter as well as in summer, a relentless military strategy. See Marx 30–35, 324, 351. For a discussion of Marx's attitude toward Spenser and "the lousy" Sir John Davies, see Prower 362.

10. I am aware that Marx's favorite motto was "*De omnibus dubitandum*" ("Doubt everything") (Marx and Engels 145); here, I express doubt that all Marxist critics doubt the "reality" or "usefulness" of the Marxist categories that are under discussion.

11. I am aware that some critics hold nonideological formulations to be "illusory"; but this is only to say that Proposition *H* has supporters. Alternatives to *H* cannot be dismissed on the ground that such dismissal is entailed by *H*.

12. For a corrective analysis of Stone's controversial work, see also Wrightson, chap. 3, esp. 70–88.

Notes to Chapter 3

1. For recent skeptical responses to Stanley Fish, see Terry Eagleton, "The Death of Self-Criticism," *TLS*, 24 Nov. 1995: 6–7, and Scott Crider, "Just What Kind of Sophist is Fish?" *BJJ* 2 (1996): 253–61.

2. For a discussion of this matter, see *BBB* 15–25.

3. Although the Supplement to the OED lists the more common term, "masculinist," "masculist" seems less skewed in

English usage (note the item "hominist"). We don't nominalize the adjective by saying "femin*i*nist." Nor would we use the adjective "hominine" to characterize a person or behavior as "masculine." It seems to me that, just as "masculine" works as the antonym of "feminine," "masculist" is the most convenient antonym of "feminist."

4. For a detailed examination of Ben Jonson's annotations to his copy of the 1617 Folio of Spenser's *The Faerie Queen: The Shepheards Calendar: Together With the Other Works of England's Arch-Poët, Edm[und] Spenser*, see James A. Riddell and Stanley Stewart, *Jonson's Spenser: Evidence and Historical Criticism* (Pittsburgh: Duquesne Univ. Press, 1995); for Digby's probable use of Jonson's annotations, see chap. 4.

5. For an extensive discussion of the differences between the Quarto and Folio versions of *Lear*, see esp. Ioppolo, and Taylor and Warren. Although these learned discussions are essential to any decision one might make in the matter, the present analysis does not depend on that decision, but rather addresses the question of what is entailed in making it.

6. For a discussion of this point, see Stewart *Garden* 8–9. Of course, in the period, "sonnets" were "little songs," and the narrowing, generic definition ("Petrarchan," "Shakespearean"), with its focus on fourteen lines and a specified rhyme scheme, comes later, and, although Donne wrote "Petrarchan sonnets," there are no "Petrarchan" or "Shakespearean sonnets" in Donne's *Songs and Sonnets*.

7. Sir Francis Galton (1822–1911) began his scientific endeavors as a traveller and meteorologist, establishing himself as an ethnographer. He was very important in developing studies in heredity and genetics, and a strong believer in the work of his cousin, Charles Darwin, and in "pangenesis." He was interested in "eugenics," and in such anthropometric approaches as fingerprinting. His work on heredity and disease occupied much of his most productive life and concerns the area of thought that interested Wittgenstein: "Composite Portraiture."

8. Besides "*mnemonic irrelavances,*" Richards identifies nine other hindrances to literary understanding: "*difficulty of making out the plain sense* of poetry," "difficulties of *sensuous apprehension,*" of "*imagery,*" "*Stock Responses,*" "*Sentimentality,*" "*Inhibition,*" "*Doctrinal Adhesions,*" "*technical presuppositions,*" and "*general critical preconceptions . . .* conscious or unconscious" (13–17).

9. The portrait itself is in the Michael Nedo Institute in Cambridge. I am indebted to Michael Nedo for his most generous

sharing of information about this Galtonian portrait (see Acknowledgments), which was taken by the family photographer, Moritz Nähr, a protegé of Wittgenstein's favorite aunt, Clara. I am grateful, also, to Mrs. Joan Bevan, with whom Wittgenstein spent the last months of his life, for allowing me to go over papers in her possession, and for introducing me to Michael Nedo.

10. For a lucid discussion of this article of faith of "Cultural Materialism," see McAlindon "Cultural."

11. For an extensive discussion of this point, see Paul R. Gross and Norman Levitt, *Higher Superstition: The Academic Left and its Quarrel with Science* (1994); and Richard Bernstein, *Dictatorship of Virtue: Multiculturalism and the Battle for America's Future* (1994).

12. For an extensive discussion of this feature of Nietzsche's works, see Magnus, Stewart and Mileur, esp. chap. 2.

13. In *Discoveries*, Jonson is even more explicit in his critique of Shakespeare's habits of composition, which, as he sees it, led to occasional lapses in decorum, the quoted one being in *Julius Caesar*, the printed text of which reads otherwise.

Notes to Chapter 4

1. For a discussion of Stanley Fish's theory of rhetorical depth analysis, see chap. 5, §5.

2. For a discussion of the useful distinction between "equity" and "gender feminists," see Sommers, esp. 134–35; see also Bernstein, 119–22. For a learned discussion of the notion that there is such a thing as a "feminist standpoint," see Gross and Levitt, 135–36.

3. For the more detailed analysis of Donne's "The Perfume" one which my remarks are largely based, see Miner, 215–31.

4. According to the British Museum Catalogue, Agrippa's *Nobilitie* was published separately no less than seven times prior to 1700; two English translations appeared in 1652, alone.

5. I realize that the term *masculinist* is commonly used, but since we don't refer to "Femin*in*ist Theory," I employ the shorter word for parallelism.

Notes to Chapter 5

1. This was not a view that Coleridge himself would have shared, as he seems to have tended, first, toward Unitarianism, and, later, to a species of Pantheistic Universalism. In effect, Coleridge's remarks on Herbert seem to imply that he, not being

"a zealous and an orthodox, [nor] a devout and a *devotional,*
Christian," would not be the proper critic "[t]o appreciate"
Herbert's poetry.

2. It seems clear that Hooker addresses the motive behind the
practice: "For so we are to interpret the meaning of those wordes
wherein the restitution of the primitive Church discipline is
greatly wished for touching the manner of publique penance in
time of Lent." Both extremes overstate the case by pretending
that the Bible either authorizes or proscribes the practice. "They
have long pretended that the whole Scripture is plaine for them.
If now the Communion booke make for them too (I well thinke
the one doth as much as the other) it may be hoped that being
found such a welwiller unto their cause, they will more favour
it then they have done. Having therefore hitherto spoken both
of festivall daies and so much of solemne fasts as may reasonably
serve to show the ground thereof in the law of nature, the prac-
tise partly appointed and partly allowed of God in the Jewish
Church, the like continued in the Church of Christ, together
with the sinister oppositions either of Heretiques, erroniously
abusing the same, or of others thereat quarelling without cause,
wee will onely collect the chiefest pointes as wel of resemblance
as of difference betweene them, and so end" (*Lawes* 5.211–12,
212, respectively).

3. Laud and Laudians sought to return the nation to the traditional ecclesiastical calendar. Cressy points out: "The king's
Book of Sports, promulgated but only lethargically promoted by
James I, was reissued by Charles I in 1633 as part of a national
programme. Archbishop Laud ordered its distribution to every
parish" (Cressy *Bonfires* 35).

4. Hodgkins 151n; it is significant, in this connection, that
Herbert's "Obedience" is mentioned nowhere in Hodgkins's
book.

5. I am grateful to Professor Fish for providing me a copy of
"Herbert's Hypocrisy," a paper read to the English Colloquium
at the University of California, Riverside.

6. It is no oversight that the Index to Hodgkins's book makes
no mention of *A Priest to The Temple*. As Hodgkins sees it,
Herbert "retains the title of 'priest,' yet he redefines *priesthood*
primarily as the ministry of the word" (107). Further, Hodgkins
finds that the term "priest" is somewhat of a problem, in that
it implies Catholic or Anglo-Catholic overtones; and, since he
would rather see these omitted, he uses the subtitle of Herbert's
work, *The Countrey Parson*. Perhaps we should not object to
this, although it somewhat dulls the point of the way in which
Crashaw's *Steps to The Temple* echoes the title of Herbert's prose

work as well as that of the more famous volume of devotional poems. Hodgkins provides a note on what some readers may regard as an omission: "Barnabas Oley's 1671 edition of *The Countrey Parson* seems to have added *The Priest to the Temple* to Herbert's original title; therefore, I have chosen to refer throughout to the work as Herbert did" (1n). Now, it isn't clear why Oley's edition "seems" this way to Hodgkins, but even if we were to assume that Oley added the title, the question would be: Why did he do that? In 1652, was this a judicious—or even a safe—thing to do? Was Oley a Roman Catholic, or an Anglo-Catholic, or any kind of Catholic, or even a notable supporter of Archbishop Laud? Then, too, wouldn't Oley's revision of Herbert's title give strong indication of how he read Herbert, and wouldn't that serve to aid us in finding out how others in the early 1650s may have understood *A Priest To the Temple, Or, The Countrey Parson His Character And Rule of Holy Life*? By eliding all reference to the title of Herbert's work, Hodgkins, by his own admission, omits a term that he regards as suspicious: "more suspect in Geneva: *prelate, bishop, curate, vicar,* and most questionable of all to Protestants, *priest*" (108–09). So would this choice of a single title call Herbert's "strong Protestantism into doubt" (109)?

7. Vendler finds the ending of the poem a "fault," Chana Bloch doesn't, but on the content and tone of the conclusion they agree.

8. Schoenfeldt is talking about imagery, not diction, as the word "pen" does not appear in the text of the sonnet in question. In a possible indication of the beginnings of a critique of the assumptions behind the critical formulation itself, Schoenfeldt omits the term "visual" from his assertion about the unstated pun in *Prayer and Power* (243).

9. Recently, Chana Bloch informed me that she and her husband, Ariel, will soon publish a new translation of the Song of Songs. This translation in modern verse, to be published with an introduction by Robert Alter (Random House, promised for 1994), represents the lovemaking of a young, unmarried couple, and may be considered a challenge to the resistance theory, or, perhaps, further evidence of the lengths to which people will go to cover up their true motives.

10. I am grateful to Professor Fish for providing me with a copy of this paper.

11. In its Greek etymology, the term *hypocrite* referred both to a "dissembler" and to an "actor on stage" (OED). Of course, Herbert's audience would have remembered Christ's

characterization of the scribes and Pharisees (Matt. 23; Luke 11) as "hypocrites." Likewise, in namecalling today, the term often functions as an insult.

12. The incoherence of this argument appears when we consider Foucault's tone. His disapproval of prisons is hard to miss. Or, to put the thought another way, he "otherizes" the empowered "otherizers," which is okay, I suppose. But his implied advocacy of utopian liberation from all "system" must, by his own analysis (unless he seeks to offer himself as an exception to the metaphysical rule he has established), be no more than yet another expression of an inescapable prison system of gazer and gazee: We have met the Commissar, and he is us. Lest it be thought that I am registering disapproval here, I would add (sincerely) that, when it does no harm, the game of "visibility is a trap" ("Paranoia?") might be considered harmless.

13. Wolberg's theme is similar to Fish's, in that she argues for a self-interested function in the priestly office as Herbert would direct it: "Herbert's goal is to win his people 'to praise God more.' And in 'making a hook of his Charity,' Herbert retains the aristocratic purpose of liberality which is causing 'them to still depend on him.' His 'double aime' is similar to that of all liberal gentlemen, that is, to give, both for the good of the people and the good of one's own position" (p. 177).

14. For a learned analysis of this misunderstood and underappreciated sin, see Wenzel.

Notes to Chapter 6

1. John Hollander made this point in response to Eleanor Cook's illuminating remarks on his poem "The Owl," at the First National Convention of the Association of Literary Scholars and Critics (ALSC) held in Minneapolis, 24 September 1995.

2. Graham Bradshaw argues that, although "'Tillyardian' is now a pejorative term" (2), skeptical criticism of Tillyard's thesis "began in the 1940s, years and even decades before the materialists materialized and presented their *ideological* critiques" (3).

3. But for a skeptical response, see Crapanzano (esp. 72–73).

4. For a similar analysis of *cultural materialism* and the interpretation of More, Castiglione, Montaigne, Bacon and Hobbes, see McAlindon "Cultural."

Works Cited

Agrippa, Henry Cornelius. *The Nobilitie and excellencye of Woman kynde.* 1542.

Althusser, Louis. *Lenin and Philosophy and Other Essays.* London: NLB, 1971.

Belsey, Catherine. *Desire: Love Stories in Western Culture.* Oxford: Blackwell, 1994.

Bernard, John D. *Ceremonies of Innocence: Pastoralism in the Poetry of Edmund Spenser.* Cambridge: Cambridge University Press, 1989.

Bernstein, Richard. *Dictatorship of Virtue: Multiculturalism and the Battle for America's Future.* New York: Alfred A. Knopf, 1994.

Berry, Philippa. *Of Chastity and Power: Elizabethan Literature and the Unmarried Queen.* London: Routledge, 1989.

Black, James, ed. "Introduction." Nahum Tate. *The History of King Lear.* Lincoln: University of Nebraska Press, 1975.

Bloch, Chana. *Spelling the Word: George Herbert and the Bible.* University of California Press, 1985.

The Book of Common Prayer. 1630. STC 16378.

Bradshaw, Graham. *Misrepresentations: Shakespeare and the Materialists.* Ithaca: Cornell University Press, 1993.

Browne, Thomas, Sir. *The Works of Sir Thomas Browne.* Ed. Geoffrey Keynes. 4 vols. London: Faber and Faber, 1963.

Calvin, John. *A Harmonie upon the Three Evangelists.* Trans. E. P. 1584.

———. *Institutes of the Christian Religion.* Ed. John T. McNeill. Trans. Ford Lewis Battles. 2 vols. Philadelphia: Westminster Press, 1960.

Carey, John. *John Donne: Life, Mind and Art.* New York: Oxford University Press, 1981.

Charles, Amy M. *A Life of George Herbert.* Ithaca: Cornell University Press, 1977.

Coleridge, Samuel Taylor. "Notes on the Temple and Synagogue." *The Works of George Herbert in Prose and Verse.* 2 vols. London, 1853.

Coughlan, Patricia, ed. *Spenser and Ireland: An Interdisciplinary Perspective.* Cork: Cork University Press, 1989.

Crapanzano, Vincent. *Hermes' Dilemma and Hamlet's Desire: On the Epistemology of Interpretation.* Cambridge: Harvard University Press, 1992.

Cressy, David. *Bonfires and Bells: National Memory and the Protestant Calendar in Elizabethan and Stuart England.* Berkeley: University of California Press, 1989.

———. "Foucault, Stone, Shakespeare and Social History." *ELR* 21.2 (Spring 1991): 121–33.

Crewe, Jonathan. *Trials of Authorship: Anterior Forms and Poetic Reconstruction from Wyatt to Shakespeare.* Berkeley: University of California Press, 1990.

Crider, Scott. "Just What Kind of Sophist is Fish?" Review of *There's No Such Thing As Free Speech and It's a Good Thing, Too* by Stanley Fish. *Ben Jonson Journal* 2 (1996): 253–61.

Curry, Gregory. "Text Without Context: Some Errors of Stanley Fish." *Philosophy and Literature* 15 (1991): 212–28.

Derrida, Jacques. *Of Grammatology.* Trans. Gayatri Chakravorty Spivak. Baltimore: Johns Hopkins University Press, 1980.

———. "Spectre of Marx: The State of the Debt, the Work of Mourning and the new International." A paper delivered in two parts to the conference, "Whither Marxism? Global Crises in International Perspective." University of California, Riverside, 22–23 April 1993.

Dixon, John. *The first commentary of the Fairie Queene, being an analysis of the annotations in Lord Bessborough's copy of the first edition of the Faerie queene.* Ed. Graham Hough. Foreword Earl of Bessborough. Folcraft, Pa.: Folcroft Press, 1969.

Dobin, Howard. *Merlin's Disciples: Prophecy, Poetry, and Power in Renaissance England.* Stanford: Stanford University Press, 1990.

Docherty, Thomas. *John Donne, Undone.* London: Methuen, 1986.

Donne, John. *The Elegies and The Songs and Sonnets.* Ed. with intro. Helen Gardner. Oxford: Clarendon, 1965.

Dubrow, Heather. "Friction and Faction: New Directions for New Historicism." *Monatshefte* 84.2 (Summer 1992): 212–19.

Dunseath, T. K. *Spenser's Allegory of Justice in Book V of the Faerie Queene.* Princeton: Princeton University Press, 1968.

Eagleton, Terry. "The Death of Self-Criticism." Review of *Professional Correctness: Literary Studies and Political Change* by Stanley Fish. *Times Literary Supplement* 24 Nov. 1995: 6–7.

———. "Ideology and Scholarship." In *Historical Studies and Literary Criticism.* Ed. Jerome J. McGann. Madison: Wisconsin University Press, 1985.

Easthope, Anthony. *Poetry and Phantasy.* Cambridge: Cambridge University Press, 1989.

Ferrand, Jacques. *A Treatise Discoursing of the Essence, Causes, Symptomes, Prognosticks, and Cure of Love, Or Erotique Melancholy.* Oxford, 1640.

Fish, Stanley. "Herbert's Hypocrisy." A paper delivered to the English Colloquium at the University of California, Riverside. May 10, 1989.

———. *The Living Temple: George Herbert and Catechizing.* Berkeley: University of California Press, 1978.

———. "Masculine Persuasive Force: Donne and Verbal Power." In *Soliciting Interpretation: Literary Theory and Seventeenth-Century Poetry.* Ed. Elizabeth D. Harvey and Katharine Eisaman Maus. Chicago: University of Chicago Press, 1990.

———. *Self-Consuming Artifacts: The Experience of Seventeenth-Century Literature.* Berkeley: University of California Press, 1972.

Fogarty, Anne. "The Colonization of Language: Narrative Strategies in *A View of the Present State of Ireland* and *The Faerie Queene*, Book VI." In *Spenser and Ireland: An Interdisciplinary Perspective.* Cork: Cork University Press, 1990.

Foucault, Michel. *Discipline and Punish: the Birth of the Prison.* Trans. Alan Sheridan. New York: Random House, 1979.

Frankfurt, Harry. "On Bullshit." *Raritan* 6.2 (Fall 1986): 81–100.

Frantz, David O. *Festum Voluptatis: A Study of Renaissance Erotica.* Columbus: Ohio State University Press, 1989.

Fumerton, Patricia. *Cultural Aesthetics: Renaissance Literature and the Practice of Social Ornament.* Chicago: University of Chicago Press, 1991.

Gallagher, Philip. *Milton, the Bible, and Misogyny.* Ed. Eugene R. Cunnar and Gail L. Mortimer. Columbus: University of Missouri Press, 1990.

Galton, Francis, Sir. *Generic Images . . . With Autotype Illustrations.* London, 1879.

———. *Inquiries into Human Faculty and its Development.* London: Macmillan, 1883.

———. *Natural Inheritance.* London: Macmillan, 1889.

Geertz, Clifford. *The Interpretation of Cultures: Selected Essays.* U.S.: Basic Books, 1973.

———. *Negara: The Theatre State in Nineteenth-Century Bali.* Princeton: Princeton University Press, 1980.

———. *Works and Lives: The Anthropologist as Author.* Stanford: Stanford University Press, 1988.

Gill, Roma. "*Musae Iocosa Mea*: Thoughts on the Elegies." In *John Donne: Essays in Celebration.* Ed. A. J. Smith. London: Methuen, 1972.

Goldberg, Jonathan. "Dating Milton." In *Soliciting Interpretation: Literary Theory and Seventeenth-Century Poetry.* Ed. Elizabeth D. Harvey and Katharine Eisaman Maus. Chicago: University of Chicago Press, 1990.

———. "Textual Properties." *Shakespeare Quarterly* 37.2 (Summer 1986): 213–17.

———. *Voice Terminal Echo: Postmodernism and English Renaissance texts.* New York: Methuen, 1986.

Greenblatt, Stephen. *Learning to Curse: Essays in Early Modern Culture*. New York: Routledge, 1990.

———. *Renaissance Self-Fashioning: From More to Shakespeare*. Chicago: University of Chicago Press, 1980.

———. *Shakespearean Negotiations: The Circulation of Social Energy in Renaissance England*. Berkeley: University of California Press, 1988.

Gross, Paul R. and Norman Levitt. *Higher Superstition: The Academic Left and its Quarrels With Science*. Baltimore: Johns Hopkins University Press, 1994.

Guibbory, Achsah. "'Oh, Let Mee Not Serve So.'" *English Literary History* 57 (1990): 811–33.

Halley, Janet E. "Textual Intercourse: Anne Donne, John Donne, and the Sexual Politics of Sexual Exchange." In *Seeking the Woman in Late Medieval and Renaissance Writing*. Ed. Sheila Fisher and Janet E. Halley. Knoxville: University of Tennessee Press, 1989.

Hamilton, Donna B. *Shakespeare and the Politics of Protestant England*. New York: Harvester Wheatsheaf, 1992.

Harvey, Elizabeth D. and Katharine Eisaman Maus. *Soliciting Interpretation: Literary Theory and Seventeenth-Century English Poetry*. Chicago: University of Chicago Press, 1990.

Harman, Barbara Leah. *Costly Monuments: Representations of the Self in George Herbert's Poetry*. Cambridge, Mass.: Harvard University Press, 1982.

Heidegger, Martin and Eugen Fink. *Heraclitus Seminar 1966/67*. Trans. Charles H. Seibert. University, AL: University of Alabama Press, 1979.

Helgerson, Richard. *Forms of Nationhood: The Elizabethan Writing of England*. Chicago: University of Chicago Press, 1992.

Hendrix, Laurel L. "'Mother of laughter, and welspring of blisse': Spenser's Venus and the Poetics of Mirth." *English Literary Renaissance* 23.1 (Winter 1993): 113–33.

Herbert, George. *The English Poems of George Herbert*. Ed. C. A. Patrides. London: Dent, 1974.

———. *The Works of George Herbert*. Ed. F. E. Hutchinson. Oxford: Clarendon Press, 1953. 1st pub. 1941.

Herrick, Robert. *The Complete Poetry of Robert Herrick*. Ed. with Intro. J. Max Patrick. New York: Doubleday, 1963.

Hill, Archibald A. *Introduction to Linguistic Structures: From Sound to Sentence in English*. New York: Harcourt Brace, 1958.

Hill, Douglas. *Edmund Spenser: The Illustrated* Faerie Queene: *A Modern Prose Translation*. New York: Newsweek Books, 1980.

Hodgkins, Christopher. *Authority, Church, and Society in George Herbert: Return to the Middle Way*. Columbia: University of Missouri Press, 1993.

Hollander, John. Response to Eleanor Cook's Analysis of "Owl." "First National Convention of the Association of Literary Scholars and Critics." University of Minnesota, 24 September 1995.

Honingmann, John J. *The Development of Anthropological Ideas*. Homewood, Il.: Dorsey Press, 1976.

Hooker, Richard. *Of the Lawes of Ecclesiasticall Politie*. 1597.

Howard, Jean E., and Marion F. O'Connor. "Introduction." *Shakespeare Reproduced: The Text in History and Ideology*. New York: Methuen, 1987.

Ioppolo, Grace. *Revising Shakespeare*. Cambridge: Harvard University Press, 1991.

Klawitter, George. "Verse Letters to T. W. from John Donne: 'By You My Love Is Sent.'" In *Homosexuality in Renaissance and Enlightenment England: Literary Representations in Historical Context*. Ed. Claude J. Summers. New York: Hawarth Press, 1992.

Knapp, Jeffrey. *An Empire Nowhere: England, America, and Literature from* Utopia *to* The Tempest. Berkeley: University of California Press, 1992.

Koeb, Edelbert. *Wittgenstein: Biographie. Philosophie. Praxis*. Vienna: Weiner Secession, 1989.

Krier, Theresa M. *Gazing on Secret Sights: Spenser, Classical Imitation, and the Decorums of Vision*. Ithaca: Cornell University Press, 1990.

Kripke, Saul A. *Wittgenstein on Rules and Private Language: An Elementary Exposition*. Cambridge, Mass.: Harvard University Press, 1982.

Langacker, Ronald W. *Language and its Structure: Some Fundamental Linguistic Concepts.* New York: Harcourt Brace, 1968.

Lanham, Richard. *Literacy and the Survival of Humanism.* New Haven: Yale University Press, 1983.

Lee, John. "The Man who Mistook his Hat: Stephen Greenblatt and the Anecdote." *Essays in Criticism* 45.4 (1995): 285–300.

Lewalski, Barbara. *Protestant Poetics and the Seventeenth-Century Lyric.* Princeton: Princeton University Press, 1979.

Lewis, C. S. *The Allegory of Love: A Study in Medieval Tradition.* New York: Oxford University Press, 1958. 1st pub. 1936.

Luborsky, Ruth Samson. "The Illustrations to *The Shepheardes Calender.*" In *Spenser Studies: A Renaissance Poetry Annual* 2 (1981): 3–53. Ed. Patrick Cullen and Thomas P. Roche, Jr. Pittsburgh: University of Pittsburgh Press.

Lull, Janis. "George Herbert's Revisions in 'The Church' and the Carnality of 'Love (III).'" *George Herbert Journal* 9.1 (1985): 1–16.

Magnus, Bernd, Stanley Stewart and Jean-Pierre Mileur. *Nietzsche's Case: Philosophy as/and Literature.* New York: Routledge, 1993.

Marotti, Arthur F. *John Donne: Coterie Poet.* Madison: University of Wisconsin Press, 1986.

Martz, Louis L. *From Renaissance to Baroque: Essays on Literature and Art.* Columbia: University of Missouri Press, 1991.

Marx, Karl. *The Ethnological Notebooks of Karl Marx.* Ed. L. Krader. Assen, 1972.

Matus, Irvin. *Shakespeare, In Fact.* New York: Continuum, 1994.

McAlindon, Tom. "Cultural Materialism and the Ethics of Reading: Or the Radicalizing of Jacobean Tragedy." *Modern Language Review* 90.4 (1995): 830–46.

———. "Testing the New Historicism: 'Invisible Bullets' Reconsidered." *Studies in Philology* 92.4 (1995): 411–38.

McCoy, Richard C. *The Rites of Knighthood: The Literature and Politics of Elizabethan Chivalry.* Berkeley: University of California Press, 1989.

Miner, Earl. *The Metaphysical Mode from Donne to Cowley.* Princeton: Princeton University Press, 1969.

Monk, Ray. *Ludwig Wittgenstein: The Duty of Genius*. New York: Free Press, 1990.

Montrose, Louis. "The Elizabethan Subject and the Spenserian Text." In *Literary Theory/Renaissance Texts*. Ed. Patricia Parker and David Quint. Baltimore: Johns Hopkins University Press, 1986.

———. "Introductory Essay." Harry Berger, Jr. In *Revisionary Play: Studies in the Spenserian Dynamics*. Berkeley: University of California Press, 1988.

More, Edward. *A Lytle and bryefe treatyse, called the defence of women*. 1560.

Mueller, Janel. "Lesbian Erotics: The Utopian Trope of Donne's 'Sapho to Philaenis.'" In *Homosexuality in Renaissance and Enlightenment England: Literary Representations in Historical Context*. Ed. Claude J. Summers. New York: Hawarth Press, 1992. Appendix: John Shawcross text of "Sapho to Philaenis."

Nanda, Serena. *Cultural Anthropology*. 5th ed. Belmont, California: Wadsworth, 1994.

Nietzsche, Friedrich. *Basic Writings of Nietzsche*. Ed. and trans. Walter Kaufmann. New York: Random House, 1968.

———. *Twilight of the Idols*. *The Portable Nietzsche*. Ed. and trans. Walter Kaufmann. New York: Viking, 1983.

———. *Untimely Meditations*. Trans. R. J. Hollingdalc. Intro. J. P. Stern. Cambridge: Cambridge University Press, 1989. 1st pub. 1983.

———. *The Will to Power*. Trans. Walter Kaufmann and R. J. Hollingdale. New York: Random House, 1968.

Paglia, Camille. *Sexual Personae: Art and Decadence from Nefertiti to Emily Dickinson*. New Haven: Yale University Press, 1990.

Panofsky, Erwin. *Meaning in the Visual Arts: Papers in and on Art History*. Garden City: Doubleday, 1955.

Patterson, Annabel. *Reading between the Lines*. Madison: University of Wisconsin Press, 1993.

Pearson, Karl. *The Life, Letters and Labours of Francis Galton*. 3 vols. Cambridge: Cambridge University Press, 1914–1930.

Prower, S. S. *Karl Marx and World Literature*. Oxford: Clarendon Press, 1976.

Quilligan, Maureen. *Milton's Spenser: The Politics of Reading.* Ithaca: Cornell University Press, 1983.

Quine, Willard. *From a Logical Point of View.* Cambridge, Mass.: Harvard University Press, 1953.

Richards, I. A. *Practical Criticism: A Study of Literary Judgment.* London: Kegan Paul, Trench, Trubner & Co., 1930.

Riddell, James A. and Stanley Stewart. *Jonson's Spenser: Evidence and Historical Criticism.* Pittsburgh: Duquesne University Press, 1995.

Roberts, John R. *John Donne: An Annotated Bibliography of Modern Criticism, 1968–1978.* Columbus: University of Missouri Press, 1982.

Roche, Thomas Jr. *The Kindly Flame: A Study of the third and Fourth Books of Spenser's Faerie Queene.* Princeton: Princeton University Press, 1964.

Roper, William. *The Mirrour of Vertue in Worldly Greatnes. Or The Life of Syr Thomas More.* Paris, 1626.

Schoenfeldt, Michael. "Patriarchal Assumptions and Egalitarian Designs." *John Donne Journal* 9.1 (1990): 23–26.

———. *Prayer and Power: George Herbert and Renaissance Courtship.* Chicago: University of Chicago Press, 1991.

———. "Sexuality and Spirituality in *The Temple.*" In *Soliciting Interpretation: Literary Theory and Seventeenth-Century English Poetry.* Ed. Elizabeth D. Harvey and Katharine Eisaman Maus. Chicago: University of Chicago Press, 1990.

Schueller, Herbert M., ed. *The Persistence of Shakespeare Idolatry: Essays in Honor of Robert W. Babcock.* Detroit: Wayne State University Press, 1964.

Sellin, Paul R. *John Donne and "Calvinist" Views of Grace.* Amsterdam: VU Boekhandel/Uitgeverij, 1983.

———. *So Doth, So Is Religion: John Donne and Diplomatic Contexts in the Reformed Netherlands, 1619–1620.* Columbia: University of Missouri Press, 1988.

Shakespeare, William. *The Complete King Lear 1608–1623: Texts and Parallel Texts in Photographic Facsimile.* Prep. Michael Warren. Berkeley. University of California Press, 1989.

———. *The Complete Works: Original Spelling Edition.* Ed. Stanley Wells and Gary Taylor. Oxford: Clarendon Press, 1986.

————. *The First Quarto of King Lear.* Ed. Jay L. Halio. Cambridge: Cambridge University Press, 1994.

[————.] *The History of King Lear Acted at the Queen's Theatre. Revised with Alterations.* 1681. See Tate, N[ahum].

————. *The Riverside Shakespeare.* Ed. G. Blakemore Evans, et al. Boston: Houghton Mifflin, 1972.

————. *Shakespeare's Comedies, Histories, and Tragedies.* 1623.

————. *True Chronicle History of the Life and Death of King Lear.* 1608.

————. *True Chronicle History of the Life and Death of King Lear.* 1608 [1619].

Sherwood, Terry C. *Herbert's Prayerful Art.* Toronto: University of Toronto Press, 1989.

Shuger, Debora Kuller. *Habits of Thought in the English Renaissance: Religion, Politics, and the Dominant Culture.* Berkeley: University of California Press, 1990.

Sommers, Christina Hoff. *Who Stole Feminism: How Women Have Betrayed Women.* New York: Simon & Schuster, 1994.

Spenser, Edmund. *The Works of Edmund Spenser: A Variorum Edition.* Ed. Edwin Greenlaw et al. 8 vols. and Index. Baltimore: Johns Hopkins University Press, 1932–57.

Spivak, Gayatri Chakravorty. "The Politics of Interpretation." In *The Politics of Interpretation.* Ed. W. J. T. Mitchell. Chicago: University of Chicago Press, 1983.

Stafford, Anthony. *The Guide of Honour, Or the Ballance wherin she may weigh her Actions.* 1634.

Stewart, Stanley. *The Enclosed Garden: The Tradition and Image in Seventeenth-Century Poetry.* Madison: University of Wisconsin Press, 1966.

————. *George Herbert.* TEAS 428. Boston: G. K. Hall, 1986.

————. "Milton Revises *The Readie and Easie Way.*" In *Milton Studies* 20 (1984): 205–24. Ed. James D. Simmons. Pittsburgh: University of Pittsburgh Press.

————. "Recent Studies in the English Renaissance." *Studies in English Literature* 31 (1991): 179–229.

————. "Thomas Wilson's *Christian Dictionary* and the 'Idea' of Marvell's 'Garden.'" In *New Aspects of Lexicography: Literary*

Criticism, Intellectual History, and Social Change. Ed. Howard Weinbrot. Carbondale: Southern Illinois University Press, 1972.

Strier, Richard. *Love Known: Theology and Experience in George Herbert's Poetry*. Chicago: University of Chicago Press, 1983.

Tanselle, G. Thomas. *Studies in Bibliography*. Bibliographical Society of University of Virginia 43. Ed. Fredson Bowers. Charlottesville: University of Virginia Press, 1990. 1–33.

Tate, N[ahum]. *The History of King Lear Acted at the Queen's Theatre. Revived with Alterations*. 1681.

Taylor, Gary. *Reinventing Shakespeare: A Cultural History, From the Restoration to the Present*. New York: Weidenfeld & Nicholson, 1989.

Trousdale, Marion. "A Trip Through The Divided Kingdoms." *Shakespeare Quarterly* 37.2 (Summer 1986): 218–23.

Veith, Gene Edward, Jr. *Reformation Spirituality: The Religion of George Herbert*. Lewisburg: Bucknell University Press, 1985.

———. "The Religious Wars in George Herbert Criticism: Reinterpreting Seventeenth-Century Anglicanism." *George Herbert Journal* 11.2 (Spring 1988): 19–35.

Vendler, Helen. *The Poetry of George Herbert*. Cambridge: Harvard University Press, 1985.

Vickers, Brian. *Appropriating Shakespeare: Contemporary Critical Quarrels*. New Haven: Yale University Press, 1993.

Wenzel, Siegfried. *The Sin of Sloth: Accedia in Medieval Thought and Literature*. Chapel Hill: University of North Carolina Press, 1967.

White, Paul Whitfield. *Theatre and Reformation: Protestantism, Patronage, and Playing in Tudor England*. Cambridge: Cambridge University Press, 1993.

Wittgenstein, Ludwig. *On Certainty*. Ed. G. E. M. Anscombe and G. H. von Wright. Trans. Denis Paul and G. E. M. Anscombe. Oxford: Basil Blackwell, 1969.

———. *Philosophical Investigations*. Trans. G. E. M. Anscombe. Oxford: Basil Blackwell, 1958.

———. *Philosophical Grammar*. Ed. Rush Rhees. Trans. Anthony Kenny. Berkeley: University of California Press, 1978.

————. *Preliminary Studies for the* "Philosophical Investigations": *Generally known as The Blue and Brown Books.* Oxford: Basil Blackwell, 1958.

————. *Remarks on Colour.* Ed. G. E. M. Anscombe. Trans. Linda L. McAlister and Margaret Schättle. Berkeley: University of California Press, 1977.

————. *Remarks on the Foundations of Mathematics.* Ed. G. H. von Wright, R. Rhees, G. E. M. Anscombe. Trans. G. E. M. Anscombe. Cambridge: MIT Press, 1991. 1st pub. 1978.

————. *Remarks on Frazer's* Golden Bough. Ed. Rush Rhees. Trans. A. C. Miles. Doncaster: Brynmill Press, 1979.

————. *Tractatus Logico-Philosophicus.* Trans. D. F. Pears and B. F. McGuinness. Intro. Bertrand Russell. London: Routledge, 1988. 1st pub. 1961. 1st German ed., 1921.

————. "Wittgenstein's Lecture on Ethics." Transcribed Friedrich Waismann. *Philosophical Review* 74 (Jan. 1965): 3–26.

Wofford, Susanne Lingren. *The Choice of Achilles: The Ideology of Figure in the Epic.* Stanford: Stanford University Press, 1992.

Wolberg, Kristine. "All Possible Art: George Herbert's *The Country Parson* and Courtesy." *John Donne Journal* 8.1–2 (1989): 167–89.

Wright, Larry. "Argument and Deliberation: A Plea for Understanding." *The Journal of Philosophy* 92.11 (1995): 565–85.

————. *Practical Reasoning.* San Diego: Harcourt Brace Jovanovich, 1989.

Wrightson, Keith. *English Society: 1580–1680.* New Brunswick: Rutgers University Press, 1982.

INDEX